Y0-CQJ-376

Table of Contents

Preface i

Acknowledgements iii

Introduction: Why Focus On Economic Development? .. 1

Business Competitiveness and the American Workforce................ 2

Needed: A State Economic Development Response 5

Defining The Issues And Creating A Policy
Framework 11

Poverty 11
Describing the Issue 11
Analyzing the Issue 13
Impact of work, earnings, and family 14
Impact of public policy 18

Income Inequality 21
Describing the Issue 21
Income inequality among family types 21
Asset inequality 22
Analyzing the Issue 24
Causes of inequality by family type 25
A broader look at income inequality 26

Welfare Dependency 28
Describing the Issue 28
Size of welfare programs 28
Characteristics of welfare recipients 30
Length of stay on welfare 32
Analyzing the Issue 33

The Urban Underclass and Ghetto Poverty 36
Describing the Issue 36
Analyzing the Issue 41
Spatial mismatch 41
Skills mismatch 45
Impact of crime 47

Urban-Rural Differences **48**

A Policy Context **50**

Economic Opportunity And State Economic Development Activities 53

Supply-side Activities **53**

Developing the Labor Force 53

Vocational education and customized job training......55

JTPA..59

Welfare to work: what worked? 61

JOBS 64

The education-skills training-job placement-earnings link...69

On-the-job training: a closing comment 72

Accessing Company Employment 73

Hiring agreements 74

Tax incentives and wage subsidies 75

Assistance to Targeted Areas..77

Targeted financial assistance 77

Enterprise zones 79

Generating Employment and Ownership Opportunities — Demand-side Activities **84**

A Focus on Startups and Small Businesses 84

Importance of small businesses......................................85

Disadvantages of small businesses.................................88

Concluding observations on small and mid-size businesses...94

Providing Credit Assistance 94

Minority business development 96

Entrepreneurial and micro-business development ...101

Business Support Assistance...107

Entrepreneurial training..108

Incubators..111

Management and operating assistance 114

Market development 119

Business networking..121

Economic Opportunity through Supply and
Demand: A Summary 124

Delivering State Economic Opportunity Resources 127

Resource Linkage 129

Buckshot Federalism 130
Linkage Barriers and Incentives 132
    Fragmentation and turf 132
    Programmatic constraints 134
    Incentives 136
Creating Resource Collaboration 138
    Creating the environment for collaboration 140
    Structuring collaboration 141
    Nurturing collaboration 144

Local Delivery System 145

Leadership Training 145
Creating Organizational Capacity 148
    Building local government capacity 149
    Building the capacity of community organizations ...150
    Intermediary organizations 155

Examples of Resource Collaboration 156

Ohio's Demonstration Employment Opportunity
Program 156
    RFP content 157
    Local projects 159
    Interim results 160
New York's Neighborhood Based Initiatives 160
    RFA Content 161
    Evaluation 163
Maryland's Industrial Jobs Opportunity Program 163
    Performance 164
    Principles and guidelines 165
    Programming 166
Pennsylvania's Ben Franklin Partnership Program 166
    Operation 168
    Principles 169

Comments on State Collaboration..169

A State Economic Opportunity Strategy...................... 171

State Antipoverty Policy Framework....................................171

Antipoverty Policies 171
Antipoverty Themes......................................171
Targets...174
Delivery systems...177
Current antipoverty approaches.....................178
Designing a State Antipoverty Strategy 180
Region 180
Family...183
Competitive delivery system 184

Components of a State Economic Opportunity Strategy 185

Laying the Foundation: Linking Place of Work and Place of Residence..187
Letting the market respond.............................188
Housing discrimination...................................194
Structuring housing opportunity.....................195
Structuring Economic Opportunity...........................199
Minority business development 201
Tying credit assistance to employment of poor people 203
Tying credit assistance and business support services 205
Tying credit assistance with workplace education 207
Delivering Resources 211
Implementation...212
Collaboration 216
Targeting...218
Economic Opportunity and the Very Poor 221

A Brief Reprise.. 225

References... 231

PREFACE

The purpose of this report is to encourage states to expand and improve the use of their economic development resources to assist disadvantaged persons. Two premises underlie this purpose. One, providing economic opportunity to disadvantaged persons can strengthen the economic competitiveness of American business. Two, state economic development resources can help ameliorate poverty. Demographic and economic conditions and trends link these two premises: minorities, women, and people with marginal skills increasingly will make-up the workforce of American business. Most of the workforce of the future is of working age today. Unless this workforce can contribute efficiently and productively, America may have little chance of retaining, much less improving, its competitive position in the world economy. Both states and the business community need to move in new directions. They must go beyond making only marginal adjustments or doing what they now do, but better. If states and the business community do not make appropriate responses and make them now, the United States economy will give way to international competitors even more than it has in the past decade, and our society will give way to an even bleaker poverty and inequality.

The link between competitiveness and poverty has been more touted than acted on. Although the "Workforce 2000" issue has received much publicity during the past four years, few American businesses have taken the issue to heart or mobilized to deal with it. At the same time, the focus of most state-based economic development programs remains on increasing or sustaining employment and business activity at a statewide level. Neither the workforce 2000 issue nor welfare reform nor heightened concern about poverty or the "urban underclass" has influenced states substantially to rethink their economic development strategies. There are exceptions, of course, and this report will use some of them to illustrate what states can do.

The events of the past year make it more difficult to address the intertwined problems of competitiveness and poverty. The 1991 economy started in a recession: the immediate economic conditions are likely to make poverty worse. A strong national economy is critical for fighting poverty and unemployment, but a strong economy alone is not sufficient. Simultaneously, 1991 began with many states facing severe fiscal problems. Reducing expenditures and eliminating programs initially produces an atmosphere inhospitable to innovation and new ventures. Bureaucrats and organizations batten down the hatches and hold on tight during budget cuts. Also, a dulled economy and increasing unemployment make retaining existing jobs and businesses almost an economic development imperative. Solving difficult economic problems and dealing with complex economic development issues give way to preventing things from becoming worse.

At least at the state levels recessions and budget shortfalls do not last forever. Because inattention will only worsen the problems of competitiveness and poverty, it is urgent to begin or strengthen initiatives now. Several circumstances will help counter the effects of the recession and the states' fiscal crises. First, Congress recently enacted major laws that provide a better context for state initiatives directed at competitiveness and poverty. These include the Family Support Act, revisions to the Job Training Partnership Act, and the Carl Perkins Vocational Education Act, and new housing legislation, HOME, that for the first time provides a major role for states.

Second, 19 new governors began their terms in 1991. Although many of these new governors face immediate crises, both new leadership and the challenges of very difficult fiscal situations may produce an environment that fosters dramatic, new directions. As columnist Neal Peirce said: "...in this era of weakened federal government, the collective national performance of every issue from human resource development to the future of cities depends so centrally on what the individual states do, and don't do. And while legislative consent is critical, gubernatorial leadership is where most new agendas must originate." (COSCDA Economic Opportunity Seminar, Philadelphia, June 20, 1989)

ACKNOWLEDGEMENTS

This report was made possible by the support of the Ford Foundation. It is one of several activities funded by the Ford Foundation as part of a program to assist states in using their economic development resources to help disadvantaged people. The report builds on several of these earlier activities, including a national conference, three regional seminars, and six technical reports.

The author also wishes to acknowledge the assistance and insight provided to the program by Brian Bosworth, Scott Fosler, Roberta Garber, David Osborne, Neal Pierce, Marion Pines, and Michael Tierney. Although they were not involved in the preparation of this report, their ideas and comments on poverty and state economic development throughout the program were insightful and stimulating.

Roberta Garber, Ellen Hagey, Don Krupp, Steve Schmitz, and Ellen Bowyer Thompson provided helpful comments on portions of early drafts. Gail Webster prepared the manuscript, and was assisted by Nina Johnson. Julie Clifford provided editorial advice.

The content of the report is the responsibility solely of the author. The opinions expressed in the report do not necessarily reflect those of the Ford Foundation or the members of the Council of State Community Development Agencies.

1

Introduction: Why Focus On Economic Development?

State policymakers, especially those responsible for designing or implementing economic development policies or programs, are this report's primary audience for several reasons. First, much current attention to the issue of poverty has an economic, or self-sufficiency, orientation. Whether labeled "empowerment," "self-sufficiency," or "economic opportunity," one goal is now providing poor people with the means and the opportunity to become part of the economic mainstream, to earn a satisfactory living, and to reduce or eliminate dependency. Of course, economic opportunity is not the only answer; persons inherently unable to become self-sufficient will always hold down the center of poverty. Nonetheless, employment and earned income now are seen as a keystone for bridging the chasm of poverty.

Second, in the past decade, state governments became major players in economic development by assuming responsibility for microeconomic development policy. Clearly, the federal government dominates this stage from a macro perspective. Its monetary, fiscal, trade, and regulatory policies substantially affect business behavior and the economy. But state governments now deal with the business community in a fashion that is more direct, personal, and continuous than the federal government's. State officials and the business community interact regularly through international trade, foreign investment, tourism, credit assistance, infrastructure, taxation, regulations (from environmental regulations to workers compensation), support services, employment training, and education. This interaction scales the gamut from major multinational corporations, to high-tech firms, to micro-businesses, to minority business, and cuts across the manufacturing, service, mining, and agricultural sectors.

Third, state economic development initiatives frequently are part of a broader development perspective. Often local governments, educational institutions, nonprofit organizations, and community-based organizations, form an integral part of state economic development policy and programs. These state partners broaden the scope of state economic development actions and expand the resources available to states for economic development.

Finally, and most important, state leaders and economic development officials are the primary audience because their constituency is the business community, and the issue of competitiveness directly concerns American business. Our living standards and our societal benefits in the coming decades may depend on the ability of business to remain competitive in the global economy. The competitiveness issue is largely a workforce issue, and the workforce issue is intertwined with the issue of poverty.

We now have a window of opportunity to integrate economic growth and equity by providing economic advancement to poor people and minorities. This opportunity is provided by the slowing growth of the labor force and the increasing importance in the labor force of tomorrow of minorities and those who are now unemployed or poorly paid. We will miss this opportunity if these workers continue to be unskilled and poorly educated. Will employers invest in today's labor force, or will they disdain such investment? Will public policy facilitate this investment, or will good intentions die? Will the gap between the rich and the poor narrow, or will it widen?

Business Competitiveness and the American Workforce

The workforce issue is both a current and a future business competitiveness problem, explicitly related to poverty and inequality. Over 80 percent of the workforce for the year 2000 has already left school, yet before the recession much of the employment demand of business was not being met. The chairman of the board of Bellsouth Corporation estimated that in 1987 fewer than 30 percent of the company's job candidates met its skill and ability requirements for sales, service, and technical jobs, and almost 50 percent of those tested were not qualified for jobs requiring even light typing. Fewer than one in 10 applicants met all the company's qualification standards. (Fiske) In 1987, 84 percent of job applicants from New York City failed the New York Telephone Company's entrance exam. Metal Fab Corporation estimates that it could save $1.2 million annually if its employees were better prepared in math and science. (FCB Associates) Both MCI Communications Corporation and John Hancock Mutual Life Insurance Company had job vacancies in 1989 because not enough qualified applicants were available. (Fiske) In 1990, the chief executive officer of Helene Curtis reported that his firm had to review 8,000 applications to fill 140 jobs. (Orfield)

These anecdotal examples reflect a widespread reality. The U.S. Department of Labor estimated the language proficiency level of the 105 million nonmilitary jobs existing in 1984 was 3.0 (on a 1- to 6-point scale), typical of retail sales people or skilled construction workers. The reading level of the average young adult (aged 21 to 25) was estimated at 2.6, indicating a mismatch between workers' skills and job requirements. (Fiske) Although 20 percent of these young adults could not read at the eighth-grade level, most job manuals and related work documents presume 10th to 12th grade levels. (Stone) A recent study of 3,600 persons aged 21 to 25 by the National Assessment of Educational Progress found that 40 percent of whites, 60 percent of Hispanics, and 75 percent of blacks could not locate information in a news article or almanac; 66 percent of whites, 80 percent of Hispanics, and 92 percent of blacks could not calculate the change for a two-item restaurant bill; and 75 percent of whites, 93 percent of Hispanics, and 97 percent of blacks could not interpret a bus schedule. (*Economic Developments*) The U.S. Office of Technology Assessment suggests that 20 to 30 percent of workers are so deficient in basic work skills that they cannot work effectively in their current jobs and cannot implement new technology. (Stone)

As bad as things are now, without intervention they will get worse. First, the mismatch between job requirements and worker skills levels likely will increase. In 1987 about 55 percent of employed workers had a high school degree or less, but by the year 2000 jobs that require this level of education will be available for only 47 percent of the workforce. The Hudson Institute estimates that 87 percent of the jobs created between 1987 and 2000 will require reading skills at the 3 and 4 levels (an average of 3.6 for all new jobs), while now 97 percent of young adults have skills at level 3 or below. (Fiske) By the year 2000, more than one-half of the new jobs will require at least one year of college education, but now 20 percent of American adults are functionally illiterate, and one out of five students does not graduate from high school. (NAB and SRI) Of the fastest growing job categories all but one, service occupations, require more than the median level of education; of those growing more slowly than average, not one requires more than the median education. Only 27 percent of all new jobs fall into the two lowest math-language-reasoning skills levels, compared to 40 percent of current jobs; 40 percent of the new jobs will be in the highest skills group, compared to 24 percent of current jobs. (*Labor Area Summaries*) Fifty percent of the jobs now being performed will change in structure in the next 15 years and work and learning may become inseparable. It is estimated that about 25 million workers will need to improve their skills an average of 38 percent. (*Economic Developments*) The well-educated worker is more likely to get a job and more likely to receive further training from employers. Those without appropriate skills will fall further behind.

Second, in the next 10 years the population and workforce will grow more slowly than it has since the 1930s. The U.S. Bureau of Labor Statistics estimates that the number of new jobs created between 1987 and 1995 will exceed new labor force entrants by about 300,000. Only 16 percent of the workforce in 1995 will be between the ages of 16 and 24, while entry-level service jobs are expected to increase by 33 percent. The slow growth rate could slow down economic expansion, shift the economy toward luxury goods and convenience services, and constrict labor markets, perhaps causing employers to use more capital and less labor. Companies that have grown by adding many flexible, lower-paid young workers will find these workers in short supply. As a response, employers may increase wages of white labor force entrants, seek to substitute capital for labor in many service areas, or move job sites to places with more youthful labor.

Integrating minorities into the workforce is critical. Immigrants and minorities will make up 42 percent of new workforce entrants; women will make up nearly two-thirds of new labor force entrants, and single female heads of household will increase as a proportion of workforce entrants. (NAB and SRI) The Carnegie Corporation estimates that minorities will comprise 30 percent of the workforce by 2000. In contrast to their rising shares of new entrants into the labor force, black men will hold a declining share of all jobs if they simply retain existing shares of each occupation. Black women will comprise the largest share of the increase in the non-white labor force and by the year 2000 will outnumber black men in the workforce. From 1970 to 1984, the proportion of black men in the labor force dropped from 79 to 74 percent, while the proportion of black families headed by women rose from 28 to 43 percent. Middle-aged workers and women will not see job increases concomitant to their workforce increase. (*Labor Area Summaries*)

David T. Kearns, former chairman of the Xerox Corporation, makes the point that America cannot have a world class economy without a world class workforce. Without an improved workforce, American companies can off-shore skilled positions, substantially increase automation to accommodate a low-skills workforce, or accept low productivity and low skills. These options may cause high unemployment or underemployment and low standards of living. (Fiske) Unfortunately, the division of the county into employment have and have-nots is increasingly polarizing along racial lines. Half of minority children are growing up poor, one-fourth drop out of school, and another one-fourth do not come close to having the skills necessary to be employed.

The mismatch between jobs and labor skills is part of a larger change in American business caused by international competition and the global economy. While these broader changes are not as quantifiable or certain as changing skill demands, American business appears to be changing in ways that only reinforce the problems related to the jobs-skills mismatch. Many management and business consultants expect businesses to be flatter and leaner, with fewer opportunities for advancement. More employment opportunities in the future will come from new, small entrepreneurial firms. There will be extraordinary pressure for maximum performance and for team cooperation and production. Flexibility, creativity, and breadth of knowledge will be much more important, because mass production of standard commodity goods — the core of American prosperity for decades — is outdated. A much greater premium will be placed on processing, analyzing, and rapidly responding to information and data. Increasingly, wages and salaries will not be based on base salaries and across the board pay increases, but on bonuses, incentive pay, and performance pay. Employees will need more self-control and be ready and willing to undergo continuous training and learning. (Boyett and Conn) Yet, even here American business is slow to change because of "ingrained beliefs, attitudes, and practices." (Dertouzos et al., p. 167)

Needed: A State Economic Development Response

State economic policy currently does not hold center stage in addressing the linkage between competitiveness and poverty. There are several reasons why state economic development policy is not at center stage. The business community itself has responded only partially or superficially to the Workforce 2000 issue and its connection to poverty. A recent article in the *Wall Street Journal* cites a "lack of "leading-edge" recruitment and training strategies, as well as a scarcity of progressive "support structures" for women and minority workers," and further notes that "although 39 percent of the surveyed companies are boosting starting salaries, fewer than one quarter are rehiring retirees or recruiting the elderly, disabled and other "nontraditional" workers." (Fuchsberg)

Many businesses do not recognize or accept the challenges presented by long-term economic trends and the condition and demographics of the workforce. Most businesses are still concerned primarily with good a work ethic and appropriate social behavior. According to the Commission on the Skills of the American Workforce, less than 30 percent of the firms it sampled were concerned "that women and minorities will make up the vast majority of new entrants to the workforce in the 1990s and jobs requiring higher skills will grow faster than low skill jobs. Few of these firms are worried about skills. Their focus is on providing day care for workers' children or English as a Second Language classes....only 5 percent of employers are concerned about growing educational skill needs." (Commission on the Skills of the American Workforce, pp. 24-25)

Although business leaders often begin or support initiatives to restructure and significantly improve primary and secondary education, they usually pay little attention to their current workforce. As one business journalist said, their chronology is off because over 80 percent of the workers who will be in the workforce at the start of the 21st century are in the workforce today. The education that business leaders find unacceptable in primary and secondary schools is the education possessed by their current workers. "If today's workers can do today's jobs — and tomorrow's — their companies will thrive. If they can do yesterday's jobs, sooner or later their companies will fail. Most of the U.S. workforce is prepared for yesterday's work." (Stone, p. 47)

A vice president of Motorola describes the new reality: "Ten years ago, we hired people to perform set tasks and didn't ask them to do a lot of thinking....Ten years ago most workers and some managers learned their jobs by observation, experience, and trial and error. When we did train people, we simply taught them new techniques on top of the basic math and communications skills we supposed they brought with them from schools or college.

"Then all the rules of manufacturing and competition changed...we found we had to rewrite the rules of corporate training and education. We learned that line workers had to actually understand their work and equipment...that change had to be continuous and participative, and that education — not just instruction — was the only way to make all this occur.

"Finally...we discovered to our utter astonishment that much of our workforce was illiterate. They couldn't read. They couldn't do simple arithmetic like percentages and fractions." (Wiggenhorn, p. 71)

How can a workforce lead American business into global competition with new technology when 60 percent have trouble with simple arithmetic? The old values of being willing to work and showing up for work are no longer sufficient. But simply upgrading standards and selection criteria may be pointless — if only one applicant in 47 meets the higher criteria, the supply of potential hires will soon be exhausted.[1]

Yet, modernizing plant equipment and processes, opening up export markets, obtaining protection from imports, providing financial subsidies and infrastructure support, and even improving early childhood and primary education take most of the attention of the business community and the state leaders that work with them. One reason for this is the momentum of past practice. Although states have moved beyond "smoke-stack chasing" in most of their economic development policies and prac-tices, they and the business community they work with still focus on traditional economic or business activities, such as markets and financing. Education and training have always been primarily the responsibility of other parts of state government. Business often responds to poverty through community relations and social investment practices, usually at the margins of corporate operations. Two-way education and communica-tion between and among the business community and state leaders must occur so that the linkage between competitiveness and poverty can be better and more widely understood. Then, business and state lenders can begin to understand the role state economic development policy can play in dealing with both competitiveness and poverty.

The relative absence of the business community and state economic development policy in dealing with the workforce 2000, competitiveness, and poverty issues does not mean that state policies have not addressed this issue. Welfare reform, and to a lesser extent state participation in the Job Training Partnership Act, have directly bolstered state involvement in poverty issues, and more indirectly in competitiveness and workforce 2000 issues. Yet, notwithstanding the economic opportunity rhetoric of welfare reform and job training, state economic development policies and par-ticipants have been largely uninvolved. Thus, the poverty-welfare issue, even though it is framed in an economic context, is becoming owned largely by the state welfare and job training institutions. For example, a recent article proudly discusses how well a particular state is coordinating its JOBS program by stating that the department of human services has "non-financial agreements with JTPA service delivery areas; Job Corps

---

[1]In 1985, only 40 percent of Motorola's workforce at one of its plants passed a test with questions like "Ten is what percent of 100?" When Motorola implemented a hiring standard of ninth grade reading and also required that applicants pass a drug test, only one in 47 met the criteria. (Wiggenhorn)

centers; eastern state educational opportunity center; department of employment service; state Indian Tribes; Head Start; state university technical branch; other state colleges, universities, and community colleges; and a financial agreement with the department of education." (Burroughs, p. 7)

The dominance of job training and welfare policies and personnel in economic opportunity can be explained partly by organizational and institutional turf. If the clients of a program are people on welfare, then the organization that traditionally works with these clients nearly automatically claims dominance in dealing with these clients. If poverty and economic opportunity issues focus on welfare reform or welfare participants, then welfare agencies tend to play the key role regardless of whether the goal is to make welfare recipients participants in the economic mainstream.

A similar bias occurs when the focus is on a set of activities, such as short-term occupational training. If this training is seen as the key way to help poor people become employed or better employed, then the organizations and institutions that have historically been involved in occupational training claim key policy and program roles. When the focus is on both a specific activity, such as occupational training, and specific clientele, such as persons on welfare, then turf conflict can easily arise. This occurs sometimes with the JOBS portion of the Family Support Act. These biases and potential turf conflicts are part and parcel of policy and must be explicitly addressed, as this report does later.

As long as the business community pays more attention to modernization, markets, and financing, than to Workforce 2000 or poverty issues, state economic development policies and personnel are unlikely to risk estrangement from the business community by pursuing activities the business community does not support. Unless the business community takes some initiatives in the Workforce 2000 and poverty issues, state policy leaders must take risks to move economic development policy in new directions. The risk is worth taking, and sustained communication and exploration between state leaders and the business community on Workforce 2000 and poverty issues may eliminate the risk as common interests and future needs become better identified.

The lack of involvement of state economic development policy and leaders in welfare reform and job training generates several weaknesses, neither of which denigrates the importance or resourcefulness of welfare and training programs or personnel. First, the portion of state government that has the best access to and is most familiar with the business community often does not or cannot offer its resources to welfare reform and job training. Second, welfare reform and job training initiatives easily can become supply driven. Pre-vocational training, general education, job search, and vocational training may become primary activities, while job development and placement become secondary. Also, training and skills development and job placement activities may not be relevant to the immediate employment market and long-term job development.

The dominance of state welfare and training policies and personnel in poverty and economic opportunity issues can be further explained by geographical characteristics. Welfare, income maintenance, social insurance policies, and short-term occupational training policies are primarily national in scope. Social Security, food stamps, Aid to Families with Dependent Children (AFDC), Supplemental Security Income (SSI), unemployment compensation, Medicare, Medicaid, and short-term employment training policies are based on federal laws, and the federal government pays most of the costs. Although states play administrative and policy roles in welfare and job training programs, these policies and programs operate under a national framework of laws and regulations.

Economic development is largely the province of the states, and most state economic development activity is state-based and state-funded. Although the federal government's macro policies on taxation, budget, regulations, and trade are critical to the economy and the business community, federal economic and community development policies and programs, whether based in the Economic Development Administration, the Department of Housing and Urban Development (HUD), the Farmers Home Administration, or the Small Business Administration, are relatively unimportant in the aggregate to state economic development policies and programs. States play either no role or a very minor role in them, with the exception of HUD's small cities Community Development Block Grant program.

This difference in policy and program scope and funding is important. Poverty and economic opportunity policies become concrete and specific events at the local level. Because states play key policy and administrative roles in welfare and occupational training programs, they must set up systematic and comprehensive policy oversight, organizational, or administrative arrangements to implement these programs across the entire state, and often with local governments. In the welfare system, most states do this through regional or county-based state welfare offices or through contracts with local, usually county, governments. In occupational training, it is done by state-based policy or coordinating councils, through discretionary funding, and through monitoring and evaluation practices. There is no similar state organizational or management framework for economic or community development.

Thus, while states through their welfare, and less directly through their employment training, policy delivery systems are involved in local poverty issues or with poor people, their economic development involvement, especially in urban areas, is much more superficial. States may work directly with businesses that are located in urban poverty areas or that employ poor people or people with low skill levels, but this involvement is more anecdotal than systematic. Likewise, state economic development personnel may work with local governments and the business community in poverty areas or on poverty issues, but again this is usually more anecdotal than systematic. The differences in geographical characteristics between welfare and employment training policies and economic development policies form additional barriers to the involvement of state economic development policy and personnel in poverty and economic opportunity issues, and help explain the dominance of state welfare and employment training policies in these issues.

This report is based on the belief that state economic development policy, resources, and personnel, with their knowledge of and access to the business community, can contribute to the intertwined issues of competitiveness and poverty. However, state economic development practice must overcome its relative aloofness in Workforce 2000 and poverty issues, must recognize the contribution state welfare and employment training resource can make to economic opportunity, and must participate in welfare, employment training, and education activities that now dominate economic opportunity. Further, and more important, state economic development practice must begin to respond fully to several vitally important characteristics of the economy — especially the location of job growth and the types of businesses that are now the net producers of jobs.

2

Defining The Issues And Creating
A Policy Framework

The worst, most corrupting lies are problems poorly stated, said French theologian Georges Bernanos. In thinking about how state economic development policy should approach or relate to competitiveness and poverty issues, it is important to frame the issues. Too often policy responses to problems are based more on how current programs can be used to address apparent problems than on examining the nature of the problems to determine the most appropriate policies. Thus, this report presents data on the nature and extent of poverty and related problems.

This portion of the report examines four related issues: poverty, income equality, welfare dependency, and the urban underclass. After defining the issue an attempt will be made to provide a policy context by analyzing the issue (e.g., why is the poverty population increasing, how do people get off of welfare) or by summarizing policy approaches to the issue. Urban and rural poverty are compared briefly before concluding the chapter.

Poverty

Describing the Issue

The official poverty level for a family of four in 1990 was $13,359.[2] The official poverty rate in 1990 was 13.5 percent, but the rate varies considerably among various groups of people. In 1989, blacks and individuals in female-headed households had the highest poverty rate, 30.7 and 35.9 percent, respectively. Hispanics had the next highest poverty rate, 26.2 percent, followed by children, 19.6 percent. The groups with the lowest poverty rate were the aged, 11.4 percent, and whites, 10 percent. (Com-

---

[2]Measuring poverty is contentious. The official definition, which was established in the 1960s, uses the cost of a minimum amount of healthful food consumption. Noting that most people spent about one third of their income on food, the federal government multiplied food costs by three to arrive at the poverty level, with adjustments made for family size. Each year since, the poverty line has been adjusted only for inflation. The poverty line is attacked for being too low because it has not taken into account changes in consumption, mainly the costs of housing and child care. It is also attacked as being too high because it does not include the benefits of food stamps, Medicaid, and subsidized housing.

mittee on Ways and Means, 1991 — hereafter called *1991 Green Book*) Most of the increase (84 percent) from 1989 to 1990 in the poverty rate among families came in female-headed households. Although the poverty rate in 1990 among whites was 10.7 percent, nearly two-thirds of all poor people were white.

The poverty rate of individuals is generally higher than the poverty rate of families. The poverty rate in 1989 for families was 10.6 percent compared to 19.2 percent for individuals. The poverty rate for families with no member aged 65 or over was 11.5 percent, while the poverty rate for individuals under age 65 was 18.1. For families with some member aged 65 or over the poverty rate was 6.6 percent, while the rate was 22 percent for individuals aged 65 or over.

The rate of people living in poverty decreased from 30 percent in 1950 to 11.1 percent in 1973, but rose to 13.5 percent in 1990. Although little progress has been made in reducing the percentage of poor people since 1973, the past two decades show three major changes in the distribution of poverty.

- The most notable trend concerns the aged. Until 1982 the poverty rate for the aged was always higher, in most years much higher, than the overall poverty rate. Since 1982, however, the poverty rate has been lower for the aged.
- The second trend concerns children. From 1967 through 1979 the highest poverty rate for children was 16.6 percent. In 1980 the poverty rate for children increased to 18.3 percent and has since remained between 20 and 22 percent.
- The third trend concerns the percentage of poor persons living in female-headed families compared to those living in all other families. From 1959 to 1985 the number of poor persons who were members of female-headed families was always less than the number in all other families (the ratio was one to two as late as 1966), but since 1985 the opposite has been true. The percentage of poor persons who are individuals living in female-headed households increased nearly continuously from 26.3 percent in 1959 to 53.1 percent in 1990. Poverty has become concentrated in single-parent families: in 1989 nearly 65 percent of all poor families with children were headed by single parents.

Many poor people work. In 1989, nearly 28 percent of all poor families with children had one or more family members who formed a full-time equivalent (FTE) worker (i.e., the number of hours family members worked during the year was the equivalent of 35 hours of work per week for 50 weeks for one person). About 44 percent of all poor families with children had at least a half FTE worker. Poor female-headed families with children worked much less than poor families with children headed by a married couple. Over 55 percent of poor families with children headed by a married couple had at least one FTE worker, and nearly 75 percent had at least a half FTE worker. On the other hand, only 13 percent of the female-headed poor families with children had at least one FTE worker, and only about 28 percent had at least a half FTE worker. (*1991 Green Book*)

In 1990, 40.3 percent of poor persons 15 years and over worked and 9.4 percent worked year-round full-time. Neither of these proportions was significantly different from those in any year since 1978. (*Commerce News*, 1991)

Poverty is temporary for most poor people. Although 25 percent of all families were poor for at least one year between 1969 and 1978, fewer than 3 percent were poor for eight or more years. People who were persistently poor were in two overlapping groups, blacks and women who headed families. (Klein and Rones)

Analyzing the Issue

Between 1979 and 1989 there was an absolute increase in poverty. Using a definition of poverty that adds near-cash benefits (e.g., food and housing) to and deletes federal income and payroll taxes from the official definition of poverty, the number of poor people increased by 54 percent from 1979 to 1989, from 6.9 million people to 10.6 million people, compared to a 25 percent increase, from 25.2 million to 31.5 million people, using the official poverty definition. (*1991 Green Book*)

Population growth caused 38 percent of the increase in poverty, followed by the reduced effectiveness of means-tested welfare programs, 30 percent, changes in demographics, 26 percent, and changes in the reduced effectiveness of social insurance programs, 13 percent. Increased market income partly offset the above increases by 13 percent.

The importance of these causes of increased poverty change depending on the types of poor families. For individuals in all families with children, the reduced effectiveness of means-tested welfare programs was the most frequent cause of increased poverty, contributing 42 percent compared to the 32 percent contribution of average population growth. Market income actually increased poverty for this family type, by 16 percent. (*1991 Green Book*)

Impact of work, earnings, and family

Work, earnings, and social policy help explain the nature of poverty. A strong national economy with strong demand for jobs, low unemployment rates, and growing real personal incomes reduces the number of poor people. One estimate suggests that a reduction in the unemployment rate from 6 to 5.5 percent would reduce the number of poor people by about 2.5 million. (Lynn and McGeary) Between 1989 and 1990 the unemployment rate rose from 5.3 to 5.5 percent while the poverty rate increased from 12.8 to 13.5 percent. From 1969 through 1986, a remarkable consistency exists between the trend line of the annual unemployment rate and the trend line of the annual nonelderly poverty rate. They moved up and down at about the same time maintaining a three- to four-point differential. (Marmor, Marshaw, and Harvey)

Households with members who work have a much lower rate of poverty than households with members who do not work. While nearly 28 percent of all poor families with children had one FTE worker, over 93 percent of all nonpoor families with children had one FTE worker.

The relationship between work and not being poor is particularly strong in female-headed households. In 1989, only 15 percent of female heads of households who worked at least three-quarters time were poor, compared to over 91 percent who did not work. Nearly 80 percent of all nonpoor female-headed households with children had one FTE worker. (*1991 Green Book*) Education, marital status, and age of children were secondary variables that explain poverty among female heads of households. (Cautley and Slesinger)

The most striking difference between poor and nonpoor families is the percentage of families with only one earner. The more workers in a family, the less likely the family will be poor. In 1985, 12.2 percent of all hourly wage workers who earned more than $3.35 per hour and who were the sole worker in their family were poor, but only 2.8 percent of these workers were poor if any other family member worked. Similarly, 44.3 percent of hourly wage workers who earned less than $3.35 an hour were poor if they were the sole worker in the family, compared to only 8.2 percent in families with one or more other workers. (*1990 Green Book*) Seventy-six percent of all poor families with a working member had only one worker, while the majority of nonpoor families had two or more workers. (Klein and Rones)

Black workers have a poverty rate about three times higher than white workers, largely because their family structure is conducive to poverty. Families headed by black women are overrepresented among the poor not because they earn much less than white women (they do not), but because they are more likely to be the sole earner. Compared to whites, a higher percentage of black never-married women head families, a higher percentage separate after marriage, and a much lower percentage remarry. (Klein and Rones) In 1990, female-headed households constituted 75 percent of all poor black families compared to 46 percent of all poor Hispanic families and 44 percent of all poor white families.

The plight of blacks relative to family structure and poverty may not become any easier to resolve. In 1988, single women had 26 percent of all births, up from 18 percent in 1980, but 63 percent of black babies were born to single women compared to 34 percent for Hispanics and 18 percent for whites. In 1985, about 90 percent of all births to black mothers ages 15 to 19 were out-of-wedlock, compared to 45 percent for comparable white mothers. The birth rate per thousand unmarried black women aged 15 to 19 was 89 percent compared to 21 percent for comparable white women. (Vinouskis)

Completing high school and having out-of wedlock births affect family structure and poverty. White teenage women who complete high school and have no out-of-wedlock children have a 97 percentage chance of avoiding poverty at age 25; the percentage for black women is 87. But 22 percent of white teenage women who do not graduate from high school or have an out-of-wedlock birth will be poor at age 25; the percentage for black teenage females is a much higher 48. The "penalty" for leaving high school before graduation or having a child out-of-wedlock increased substantially from the 1960s to the 1980s in terms of both being poor and having a low median income. The higher percentage of women, especially black women, who never married by age 25 is the primary cause of this increased penalty.

Children are almost twice as likely to be poor after their parents separate than before the separation. Adjusted for family size, income for one-parent families with children declined by 26 percent after separation, and by 37 percent when the father departed. One reason is that only about 44 percent of the absent fathers were paying child support more than four months after the breakup. Fathers who left were less likely to be employed full-time than those who remained in households, 67 percent to 81 percent. Although the separated mothers worked more after the separation, the percentage working full time increased only from 33 percent to 41 percent one year after separation. The percentage of nonworking mothers dropped from 43 percent to 31 percent four months after separation, then increased to 43 percent one year after separation.

Broken families had only 83 percent of the income of intact families. Seventy-seven percent of white families remain in two-parent families, compared to only 37 percent for blacks. About 29 percent of children under age 15 did not live continuously with two parents from 1983 to 1986. (DeParle, 1991 b; U.S. Bureau of the Census, 1991 b) In March 1990, 15.8 million children lived in single-parent households, which represents 26 percent of all children but 60 percent of all black children. Nearly 39 percent of children in single-parent households were living with a divorced parent, while nearly 31 percent were living with a parent who has never married. (Barringer)

In 1989, only about one-half of women awarded child support received the full amount due. Of the remaining, one-half received partial payment and one-half received nothing. The award rate of child support payments ranged from 24 percent for never-married women to 72 percent for married, separated, or divorced women. The average amount of child support assistance was $2,995. (*Commerce News*, 1991 d)

While marriage, education, and out-of-wedlock births explain much of the poverty of white women, these factors do not fully explain poverty for black women. A much lower percentage of black teenage females who either did not graduate from high school or had an out-of-wedlock birth were employed, and a much higher percentage received welfare benefits. There was a significant shift from work to welfare among black teenagers who in the 1980s either left high school without graduating or had an out-of-wedlock birth compared to comparable black teenagers in the 1960s and white teenagers in the 1980s. (Duncan and Hoffman)

The connection of poverty, work, and family also appears in an analysis of unemployment insurance (UI). In 1985, the average family income of persons on long-term spells of UI was about 78 percent of their average monthly income before unemployment; this percentage drops to 56 percent if UI benefits are excluded. Nine percent of those who were on long-term UI spells had family incomes below the poverty level before unemployment occurred. This percentage increased to 19 during the UI spell, and would have been 46 if no UI benefits were received. UI benefits clearly contribute significantly to sustaining income and preventing poverty. Yet, if there was one other worker in a family with a person receiving UI benefits, the poverty rate was only 5 percent. If there was no working family member, the poverty rate was 40 percent, and would have been 85 percent in the absence of UI benefits. (*1990 Green Book*)

A similar relationship occurs holds in income after re-employment. About two-thirds of long-term UI recipients were re-employed in 1985. Nearly two-thirds of those re-employed had other workers in the family, and their average family income was 102 percent of their income prior to unemployment. In contrast, two-thirds of those who did not gain re-employment had no other earner in the family.

Employment trends suggest that multiple-earner households will become increasingly important if lower wage workers are to avoid poverty. Nontraditional employment (part-time, temporary, contract, and other nontraditional workers) grew rapidly during the 1980s, reaching 25 percent of the workforce by 1988. Nontraditional employment may expand its share of the workforce by the year 2000 because nearly all net job growth will occur in the services sector, where part-time employment is concentrated. Nontraditional workers, especially those who are involuntarily nontraditional, have fewer economic protections than full-time workers. They earn about 38 percent less, and while about 5 percent of families headed by full-time workers were poor in 1988, the percentage for families headed by part-time workers was 21. Twelve percent of families headed by part-time workers received public assistance, compared to 2 percent of families headed by full-time workers. Part-time workers are less likely to have health insurance, and when they do have it, it is most likely provided through a relative. Most part-time workers lack employer-sponsored pension plans, and a higher percentage are not covered by unemployment insurance or minimum wage standards. (GAO, 1991)

The connection between poverty and education and skills levels also must be noted. In 1987, nearly one-half of the young (under 30 years of age) families headed by a high school dropout lived in poverty (up from 25 percent in 1974), while only one in five young families headed by a high school graduate was poor in 1987 (more than double the percentage in 1974). In 1986, nearly nine of 10 children in families headed by a woman under 30 who had not graduated from high school lived in poverty. Although the poverty rate was 69 percent for those with a high school diploma but no college, it was 16 percent for those headed by a young woman with a college degree. (Porter)

Skills levels also have a positive relationship to earnings, as shown by scores on the Armed Force Qualification Test, which covers vocabulary, reading, numerical operations, and arithmetic reasoning. Earnings of dropouts vary depending on their basic skills. Women aged 20 to 24 years-old who in 1981 scored in the middle fifth of a national skills test had average earnings more than double those of dropouts whose test scores were in the lowest fifth. Dropouts with test scores in the highest fifth had earnings one-third higher than those in the middle fifth and nearly three times those in the lowest fifth. A similar pattern occurred among those with high school diplomas. Young women with scores in the middle fifth had earnings 50 percent higher than those in the lowest fifth. Those who scored in the top fifth earned 30 percent more than those who scored in the middle fifth and more than twice as much as those who scored in the lowest fifth. Overall, more than three-fourths of poor persons had basic skills below average for all persons in their age bracket.[3] (Porter)

Impact of public policy

Public policy also plays a role in poverty. Over 41 percent of poor people received governmental cash assistance in 1990, and 64 percent of poor people were in households that received some cash assistance or both. However, about 28 percent of poor people received no assistance of any type. (*Commerce News*, 1991 c)

The most "effective" (no notion of cost-effectiveness or efficiency is included) national antipoverty program is Social Security, which has a greater and more sustained impact on poverty than means-tested programs. In each year 1979 through 1988, social insurance removed 30 to 33 percent of individuals from poverty. Social Security accounted for about 89 percent of this amount.

Means-tested cash transfer programs are much less effective. From 1979 through 1988, these programs removed about 4 to 6 percent of people from poverty.

Food and housing programs are more effective than means tested cash transfers. From 1979 through 1988 these programs removed 6 to 10 percent of people from poverty. (*1990 Green Book*)

Means-tested transfer programs do a good job of targeting the poor. About 86 percent of these transfers went to poor people in 1984, compared to about 66 percent of in-kind transfers and 54 percent of all cash transfers. But a portion of all transfer programs, including means-tested programs, enrich people to incomes beyond the poverty level. About 25 percent of means-tested transfers raised incomes above the poverty line; the percentage for in-kind transfers was 40, and for cash transfers, 66. (Weinberg)

---

[3]A recent study of over 6,000 high school graduates six years after graduation concludes "formal training and employer-provided training remain important — more so than any of the other credential, skill level, or motivation variables. Indeed, for individuals with less than a 4-year college degree and similar with respect to educational attainment, skill level, and motivation as well as SES, gender, and race, the experience of formal training for their job is worth, on the average, $0.68 per hour more than their counterparts who did not receive such training, and the existence of employer-provided training for their present job is worth $0.57 more per hour." (Wolman, Lichtman, and Barnes, pp. 148-149)

Public policy changes caused the effectiveness of means-tested programs to decrease in the early 1980s. The percentage of people removed from poverty through means-tested cash transfer programs was relatively high in 1979 and 1980, 6.3 percent and 5.5 percent respectively, but dropped precipitously to 3.6 percent in 1983, and remained at about 4 percent from 1984 through 1988. The effectiveness of food and housing programs paralleled those of cash transfers in that their effectiveness was relatively high in 1979 and 1980, 10.2 percent and 9.1 percent respectively, but declined to 6.3 percent in 1983, and have remained at about 7 percent since 1984.[4]

Federal tax policy also contributes to poverty. In 1979 and in 1988, the payment of federal taxes increased the number of people in poverty by about 1.6 percent. The rate was much higher between those years, being 4 percent or above from 1981 through 1986. The percentage are even higher if persons in households with all persons aged 65 or more eliminated. In 1979, federal taxes increased the number of people in poverty by 2.1 percent, but this percentage quickly rose to 5.9 percent in 1981 before peaking at 6.1 percent in 1984. From 1981 through 1985, America was in the ironic, if not ridiculously tragic, situation of putting more people into poverty (considering all individuals) through federal taxes than of removing people from poverty through means-tested cash transfer programs.

The importance of unemployment insurance in maintaining income and preventing poverty was noted previously. Public policy changes, however, have helped make UI less effective in fighting poverty. In the 1975-76 recession about 75 percent of unemployed workers received UI benefits. From 1967 to 1981 the percentage of unemployed persons who were receiving UI benefits in the month of January dropped below 51 only once, to 48 percent in 1979. But by January 1989, this percentage had dropped

---

[4]The figures above are for all individuals. Eliminating all individuals in units entirely aged 65 or more still results in Social Security being the most effective antipoverty program, although less effective than indicated above, removing 21.6 people from poverty in 1979 and 17.7 percent in 1988. The percentage was in the 20 to 22 percent range from 1979 through 1984, but was around 18 percent from 1985 to 1988. As expected, means-tested cash transfers had increased effectiveness, but only slightly. They removed a high of 7.3 percent of people from poverty in 1979, but this figure, as might be anticipated, dropped continuously to 3.8 percent in 1983, and then rose to 4.9 percent in 1988. Food and subsidized housing remained more effective than cash transfers, although the small difference suggests that these programs collectively affect the elderly and the non-elderly similarly. The percentage of people removed from poverty was a high 12.5 percent in 1979 and 10.7 percent in 1980, but dropped in 1983 only to a low of 7 percent, and moved to about 8 percent from 1984 through 1988. (1990 Green Book)

to 35, although it rose to about 40 percent in 1990. Changes in state and federal policy accounted for one-to two-thirds of this change. (*1990 Green Book*) Additional statutory changes enacted in the 1980s increased the reasons for UI denial and substantially reduced the extended benefits program (i.e., providing benefits beyond the initial 26 week claim period). The increased use of part-time labor and the relative growth of employment in the South and West, where UI requirements are stricter, and in the service sector also contributed to the decreased value of UI. UI now provides about one-third less income protection and economic stimulus than it did in the 35 years before 1980. (Rowen)

Public policy clearly helped increase poverty and substantially influenced who became or remained poor. This society has chosen through Congress and the president to aid the elderly, primarily through increasing the value or coverage of social insurance programs, and to increase poverty among families with children, especially those headed by single parents, by reducing the value or coverage of means-tested welfare and unemployment insurance programs, and to a lesser extent through federal tax policy.

The Congressional Budget Office estimates put this pro-elderly policy into a broader context. In fiscal year 1985 the federal government spent $246 billion on programs for the elderly and $90 billion on programs for families with children under the age of 18. Spending for the elderly constitutes about 44 percent of the federal budget excluding defense and interest, while spending for families with children accounts for about 16 percent of the budget. The elderly comprise about 12 percent of the population, while families with children account for about 55 percent. (*1990 Green Book*)

A House Budget Committee study indicates that federal spending on programs targeted to children declined by about 4 percent in real terms between 1978 and 1987, while expenditures on programs for the elderly increased by about 52 percent. (*1990 Green Book*) Federal spending for the elderly in constant (1985) dollars per aged person continually increased from $3,390 in 1965 to $9,060 in 1985. Spending for the elderly rose from 15.9 percent of total federal outlays to 27.3 percent; from 31.9 percent of total federal outlays excluding defense and interest to 45.8 percent; and from 2.8 percent of GNP to 6.6 percent. Social Security and, more recently, Medicare account for most of the expenditures and increases.[5]

---

[5]The amount of spending for the elderly is understated because it does not include a portion of means-tested welfare programs, particularly Medicaid, they receive. In New York State, where spending for Medicaid increased from $7 billion in 985 to $12 billion in 1990,

Income Inequality

Describing the Issue

Income inequality among family types[6]

Although the average income for all families increased by 11.6 percent between 1979 and 1989, income for the lowest quintile fell by 2.1 percent, while income for the highest quintile increased 20.4 percent.[7] Major differences in income inequality occurred among different types of families.

- Families with children experienced much greater income inequality than families without children. The income of the lowest income quintile of families with children dropped 6.2 percent, while the income for the highest quintile rose by 17.4 percent. For all families with children, income rose by 7.9 percent.

---

the elderly represent about 13 percent of those eligible for Medicaid, but they receive 41 percent of Medicaid expenditures. On the other hand, families with children comprise about 46 percent of the eligible population but receive only about 13 percent of New York's Medicaid dollars. (Kolbert)

[6]Measuring income inequality is even more complex than measuring poverty. There are two primary considerations in measuring inequality. One is the definition of income. Does it include only cash income and, if so, what cash income? Is it measured before or after taxes? The second consideration is whether to adjust for family size and other considerations. For example, is a two-person family with an income of $15,000 as well off as a four-person family with an income of $15,000? Should a three-person family be weighted more than a two-person family to account for the fact that more people are included in the three-person family has more people?

The following description of income inequality uses cash income (earned income, cash transfers, interest and dividends, etc.) plus food and housing benefits (excluding the value of public and private health benefits) minus federal income and payroll taxes. This description uses standardized family size, based on the premise that a four-person family earning the same as a two-person family is less well-off (using official poverty standards as the basis for making adjustments). Finally, family size is weighted. The years used are 1979 and 1989, both peak economic years. Incomes are divided into quintiles using constant 1989 dollars. This analysis of income inequality relies on data in the 1991 Green Book, pages 1210 - 1260. Incomes and poverty thresholds are adjusted for inflation using the CPI-X1.

[7]The average household income increase is not an accurate measure of income changes for most Americans because so much of the increase is in the top quintile. For example, between 1983 and 1987 the top quintile had 52 percent of the post-tax income increase; more than 60 percent of households had less than the average increase. (Michel)

- The average income for all families headed by a person under age 35 rose by only 1.4 percent between 1979 and 1989. The income of the lowest quintile dropped 23.5 percent, while the income of the highest quintile increased by 11.4 percent. This group, families headed by a person under the age of 35, suffered the largest increase in income inequality.
- The average income for families headed by 35 to 49 years-old increased by 27.4 percent. No quintile lost income. The highest quintile gained 32.8 percent.
- When only families with children are considered, the average income of families headed by persons under age 35 fell by 2.7 percent. The average income of the lowest quintile decreased by 25.5 percent, while the highest quintile gained 7 percent. Families with children headed by persons aged 35 or over gained 13.2 percent in their average income. The only quintile with a loss was the lowest, 0.1 percent, while the highest quintile rose by 19.7 percent.
- When the race of the family head is considered, the average income of all families headed by whites grew by 12 percent, while that of all families headed by nonwhites grew by 19 percent. Income inequality grew more among nonwhites than among whites. The average income of the lowest white quintile decreased by 3.1 percent, the only quantile with a loss of income, while the highest income quintile gained 20.1 percent. For nonwhite-headed families, the lowest quintile lost 7.1 percent in average income and the highest quintile gained 25.1 percent.

The bad news about income levels since 1973 is brought more sharply into focus by comparing changes in the 26 years prior to 1973. Median family income (1987 dollars) rose from $15,422 in 1947 to $30,820 in 1973, just about doubling. (Marmor, Mashaw, and Harvey)

Asset inequality

Considering wealth rather than income generates a starker picture of inequality. The highest quintile in wealth or net assets[8] had a median wealth in 1988 of $111,770, compared to $35,750 for the median wealth of all households. Between 1984 and 1988, the median wealth for the highest quintile rose 14 percent after adjusting for inflation, but median wealth for all households did not change in this time period.

---

[8]Defined as the value of checking and savings accounts, real estate, cars, stocks, and bonds, and other assets (except the value of pension plans, jewelry, or home furnishings) minus debt.

While the median wealth of white households was $43,289 in 1988, it was only $4,169 for blacks and $5,524 for Hispanics. The median wealth for all married couples was $57,134; the median wealth for white married couples was $62,390, compared to $17,640 for black couples and $15,690 for Hispanic couples. The fact that a greater discrepancy exists between white and black medians than between white married couples and black married couples medians suggests that marital status offsets the lower median wealth of blacks. About 35 percent of all black households included married couples, compared to 60 percent for whites. The median wealth for female-headed households was $13,571, ranging from $22,100 for white female-headed households to $760 for black and $740 for Hispanic. The median wealth of elderly married people was $124,420, compared to about $12,500 for couples with a head of household under 35 years old.

A key component of wealth is home equity. About two-thirds of all households owned their homes, and the median equity was $46,110. In 1988, home equity represented 43 percent of the net wealth of the average household. (Pear; U.S. Bureau of the Census, 1991 a)

Asset inequality also appears to be growing. In 1983 households headed by a person under 35 had an average net worth of $45,700, but this figure dropped to $38,600 three years later. During this time, the average assets of households headed by persons 65 or older increased from $208,000 to $218,000. On average, the net worth of all households headed by a person under 55 grew poorer; all households headed by a person over 55 grew richer.

In 1963, households headed by a person over 65 represented only 19 percent of the population, but held 26 percent of the wealth. In 1986, this group represented 21 percent of the population, but its share of wealth increased to 33 percent. Meanwhile, the share of wealth of households headed by a person under 35 remained at 6 percent from 1963 to 1986, although their share of population rose from 18 to 23 percent.

Home equity explains part of this asset differential. Since 1973 homeownership rates have increased only among households headed by a person over 55, increasing from 76 percent to 80 percent from 1973 to 1990. However, homeownership rates dropped from 51 percent to 44 percent for households headed by a person aged 25 to 34 and from 23 to 15 percent for households headed by a person under 25. In 1991, 85 percent of homeowners 65 years of age of older own their homes outright, debt-free. As noted in the next section, lower earnings for younger workers also contributed to asset inequality. (Peterson)

Analyzing the Issue

Many possible culprits exist for the growing inequality in family income. This section examines two attempts to explain increasing income inequality. The first (*1990 Green Book*) examines only trends in incomes, benefits, and taxes, while the second (Bradbury) looks more broadly at' possible explanations for increased income inequality. The first is more detailed in the kinds of families reviewed.

The discussion of income inequality highlights earnings because in 1988 all income quintiles received most of their income from earnings, which were slightly less than one-half the poverty level for the lowest quintile to over six times the poverty income for the highest quintile. Average earnings were 3.1 times the poverty income for all families. The next most significant source of income for all families was investment income, averaging nearly 25 percent of the poverty income for all families, but ranging from less than 2 percent of poverty income for the lowest quintile to over 80 percent of poverty income for the highest quintile. Social Security income ranked third, and pension income fourth in source of income for all families.

In summary, changes in family earnings caused most of the increase in income inequality between 1979 and 1989. Average total family earnings for the lowest quintile rose by 1 percent, but increased by 16.7 percent for the highest quintile. For all types of families, both the average income earned by males and the average number of male earners in a family decreased in the lowest income quintile. This was more than offset by an increase in the average number of female earners in the lowest income family and by increased average female earnings. Although the average number of male earners in the highest income quintile decreased (at a rate higher than the lowest quintile's), much higher earnings per male worker more than made up for the decrease. Simultaneously, the average number of female earners and, especially, their average earnings increased in the highest income quintile. Each of these two factors, the higher average earnings of males and the higher total earnings of females, was equally important in raising the income of the highest quintile from 1979 to 1989, and substantially increasing income inequality. The increased earnings of primary adult female earners (the female with the highest earnings in a family) caused most of the earnings changes, and most of these changes occurred through a substantial increase in the percentage and number of adult females working in the higher income quintiles, especially in the highest income quintile.[9]

Causes of inequality by family type

Increased incomes of the primary adult female earner and decreased incomes of the primary adult male earner tended to be the most significant cause of income inequality.

- Earnings were the most significant cause of increased income inequality for families with children. The average earnings of primary adult males decreased for families with children. However, average primary adult male earnings decreased by 9 percent for the lowest quintile and rose by 13 percent for the highest quintile. Earnings of primary adult females were even more important in families with children than in all families. The average earnings of primary adult females in families with children rose by 43.5 percent, but they rose only by 10.3 percent for the lowest income quintile, compared to a very high 57.2 percent in the highest income quintile.

- Decreases in primary adult male earnings were the most significant cause of increased income inequality among families with children headed by married couples. Although the average primary adult male earnings rose by 4 percent for families with children headed by married couples, it fell by 3.4 percent in the lowest quintile and rose by 14.9 percent in the highest quintile. Each income quintile had fewer male earners per family in 1989 than in 1979. Increases in primary adult female earnings also added to income inequality, as average adult female earnings

---

[9]Between 1979 and 1989, the earned income of the primary adult females increased an average of 36.9 percent for all families. Earnings of the primary adult female increased in all quintiles, but the increases were proportionately higher the higher the income quintile. The smallest earned increase among high adult female earners was 12.8 percent for the lowest income quintile, but this jumped to 45.8 percent for the highest income quintile. Most of the increase in the earned income of high adult females was caused by increased average earnings rather than by increased labor force participation.

In 1989, a negative correlation existed between the average number of persons under age 18 in families and the earnings of income quintiles. This suggests females in higher quintiles were more able to work because they had fewer children or a smaller percentage of them had children. For example, the average number of children per family in the highest income quintile was .33, compared to .86 in the lowest income quintile. Also, females in the lowest income quintile may work less given the same average number of children per family as females in the higher income quintiles. While all women in the top four income quintiles in all families with children increased their labor force participation between 1979 and 1989, females in the lowest quintile decreased their participation.

increased by only 29.9 percent for the lowest quintile, compared to 58.3 percent for the highest income quintile. Although female earnings are less important in this family type than in other family types, the pattern of higher female earnings the higher the income quintile held.

- Among families with children headed by single mothers, the most significant cause of increased income inequality was the earnings of the primary adult female. The average income of the primary adult female dropped by 2.6 percent in the lowest quintile, but increased by 28.8 percent in the highest income quintile. The average number of female earners per family dropped from .45 to .41 in the lowest income quintile.

- Among nonelderly childless families, the average earnings of the primary adult male rose by 2.3 percent. These earnings rose by 9.7 percent in the highest quintile, but by only 2.1 percent in the lowest quintile. As with the other family types, the average earnings of the primary adult female also rose, by 27.4 percent, but rose much higher in the highest quintile, 43.7 percent, and increased by only 5.8 percent in the lowest quintile. Much of this additional female income was due to the increased number of female workers, especially in the highest quintile.

- For elderly childless families, increased income inequality was caused primarily by increased social security income (26.7 percent) and investment-related income (22.5 percent) in the highest quintile, and by reduced means-tested cash transfers (34.5 percent) and only a very slight increase in social security income (0.1 percent) in the lowest quintile.

A broader look at income inequality

The second analysis of income inequality also looks at income quintiles, but for the years 1979 and 1988. It excludes elderly families, does not consider taxes, does not standardize for family size, and does not weigh for individuals. In searching for causes of increased income inequality, it does consider not only changes in income sources but also changes in family composition and work patterns.

This second study suggests two significant reasons for increased inequality. First, the incomes of upper-income families increased substantially because more wives in these families increased their already high labor force participation rates[10] and because of the high real growth in the

---

[10]In 1988, 82 percent of the wives of husband-wife families in the highest income quintile worked compared to 49 percent in the lowest quintile.

earnings of male and female workers.[11] Second, the incomes of the lowest quintile declined because the earnings of primary male workers decreased.

Two secondary factors were important in increasing inequality. The most significant of these was the increased income value of education, especially post-secondary education. In the early 1970s, a 30-year-old male college graduate earned 15 to 20 percent more than a 30-year old high school graduate. By 1988 this differential had grown to 49 percent. (Levy) The one family in six whose head did not finish high school earned 29 percent less in 1988 than in 1973. (Passell, 1990)

Much of the increase in earnings returns to education occurred in the 1980s. Real wages declined by 12 percent between 1980 and 1988 for males with a high school education and 10 years of work experience, but increased by 20 percent for male college graduates. The increase was even greater for those with graduate education. (Kosters) Finally, the percentage of heads of families in the lowest income quintile who had not finished high school rose from 36 percent in 1979 to 43 percent in 1988. The economy of the 1980s clearly had a high demand for schooling and skills.

The other important secondary factor is the lower labor force participation rates of males in the poorest quintile, which dropped from 79 percent in 1979 to 73 percent in 1988, while the percentage in the highest quintile remained at about 98 percent. A recent federal report reinforces this point by noting that 45.3 percent of New York City residents over 16 were not in the labor force in the first half of 1988, and even this was better than the estimated 56.4 percent in Baltimore and 53.1 percent in Detroit. (Lueck)

The following factors reinforce the factors already mentioned: (1) the shifting mix of income sources, particularly the decreased value of transfer

---

[11]The increasing inequality of full-time, year round wage earners between 1978 and 1988 was pronounced and widespread, and included all racial and sex groups except black women. In almost all cases the top fifth of earners had most of the earnings gains and at the expense of the bottom three-fifths. Increased inequality in earnings among men were statistically significant in manufacturing and retail trade industries, and for women in manufacturing and professional and related services industries. Among detailed occupational groups, statistically significant increased earnings inequalities among men occurred in the category of salaried administrators and officials in private industry and in the category of salesmen (securities salesmen, insurance salesmen, and real estate salesmen as well as sales workers in retail and personal services); and among women, for all occupations, especially saleswomen. The earnings distributions among men employed as administrators, officials, and sales workers, which include about 22 percent of all male, full-time, year-round workers, were sufficiently powerful to influence the trend for all men. (Ryscavage and Henle)

payments for the lowest quintile and the increased value of dividend and interest income in upper quintiles; (2) the aging of the baby boom generation, with more middle-aged and, therefore, higher-income families; (3) the increased percentage of single-parent families, lowering the income in the lowest quintile; and (4) fewer manufacturing jobs, lowering the income in the lowest quintile.[12]

Welfare Dependency

Describing the Issue

It may be an understatement to say that there is a great deal of controversy and confusion about welfare. Part of the confusion stems from the sometimes sloppy use of the term "welfare," specifically the lack of distinction between programs with means-testing and social insurance programs, which have no "means testing" (i.e., no income and asset tests need to be met to receive benefits). Only the means-tested programs are welfare programs.

Size of welfare programs

When people talk about the "welfare state," they often include social insurance and welfare programs. Yet, the budgetary impact and size of social insurance programs and welfare programs are very different. In fiscal year 1986, the federal and state governments together spent $360 billion on social insurance programs (social security, public employee retirement, railroad retirement, unemployment insurance, workers' compensation, and several other small programs), with most, $270, billion, spent for social security benefits (retirement, disability, survivors, and Medicare). This $360 billion overwhelms the $149 billion the federal and

---

[12]Real weekly earnings of production workers in private nonagricultural industries declined from $186.94 in 1970 to $166.52 in 1989. People employed in low-wage work have lost ground just by standing still. (Schmidt) The only sector of the economy with average hourly earnings that are about what they were in 1973 is the finance, insurance, and real estate sector, the only sector that showed continuous growth during nearly all of the 1980s. The manufacturing and wholesale sectors were only slightly less well off in 1990 than in 1973, while retail trade, construction, and transportation and public utilities showed significant declines. Studies show that the loss of manufacturing jobs due to imports in the 1980s particularly hurt men with a high school degree or less. (Bluestone) However, wages are only part of a worker's income. In March 1990, hourly total compensation averaged $15.40, $11.14 in wages and $4.27 in benefits. Blue-collar workers earn a much larger percentage of their compensation in the form of benefits, and this is especially true of union workers. (Crenshaw) Chapter 3 discusses industrial aspects of income inequality.

state governments spent on all federal means-tested programs. The $149 billion includes $44 billion for Medicaid benefits, $18 billion (including administrative costs) for Aid to Families with Dependent Children (AFDC), $13 billion for food stamps, $13 billion for subsidized housing, $13 billion for supplemental security income (SSI), and $11 billion for various kinds of educational aid. (Marmor, Marshaw, and Harvey)

This fiscal year 1986 "snapshot" puts welfare in perspective relative to social insurance. Another perspective emerges by examining expenditure trends. Between 1965 and 1975, federal social welfare (a broader category than that used to generate the $430 billion figure above) expenditures rose from 5.6 percent of gross national product (GNP) to 11 percent. Since 1975, expenditures have stayed at 11 to 12 percent. In constant 1988 dollars, federal social welfare expenditures jumped dramatically from $141 billion in 1965 to $368 billion in 1975, and have risen since, reaching $520 billion in 1987.

A very different trend emerges when looking at AFDC. Total federal, state, and local AFDC benefit payments rose from 0.24 percent of GNP in 1965 to 0.60 percent in 1975, then dropped nearly continuously since 1975 to 0.36 in 1987. The federal share of AFDC expenditures as a percentage of federal social welfare spending dropped steadily from 8.6 percent in 1975 to 3.6 percent in 1987, while the federal costs of AFDC as a percentage of all federal spending dropped from 4.3 percent in 1975 to 1.7 percent in 1987. But AFDC costs are a relatively small share of means-tested expenditures. Total federal, state, and local expenditures for all means-tested programs rose from 1.9 percent of GNP in 1968 to 3.9 percent in 1978, then dropped only slightly to 3.6 percent of GNP in 1988. Federal expenditures for means-tested programs rose from 6.4 percent of total federal expenditures in 1968 to 14 percent in 1978, then dropped to 11.8 percent in 1988.

What happened was that Medicaid and SSI (which was completely federalized in 1974) were taking up a greater percentage of the federal government's means-tested expenditures. In constant 1988 dollars, total federal, state, and local AFDC payments were $6.2 billion in 1965, peaked at $21.1 billion in 1976, dropped to $15.8 billion in 1982, and then rose again to $17.1 billion in 1987. In short, in constant dollars total AFDC benefit payments have remained about the same, $18.1 billion, since 1971. On the other hand, federal Medicaid expenditures in constant 1988 dollars increased steadily from about $1 billion in 1965 to about $29 billion in 1988. Federal SSI expenditures rose, although not continuously, from about $9 billion in 1975 to about $12 billion in 1988 in constant 1988 dollars.

One important budget-related aspect of a discussion on welfare and social insurance is the financial contribution made by state governments. Although it may seem peculiar, the states' share of social insurance expenditures is lower than the states' share of welfare expenditures, 15 percent to 27 percent. States pay about 45 percent of the AFDC benefit expenditures. This helps to explain why AFDC payments have been relatively stable over the past 18 years while other means-tested expenditures have seen real increases. Both state fiscal constraints and the "closeness" of states to welfare may help prevent these expenditures from rising, unlike programs that are primarily or wholly funded or administered by the federal government.

Characteristics of welfare recipients

Until very recently, the AFDC recipient population level was remarkably stable. In 1990, there were about 11.4 million AFDC recipients (4 million families), about 34 percent of the number of poor people. About 7.7 million of AFDC recipients were children, although AFDC children numbered 59 percent of all poor children. These percentages have been about the same since 1974. (*1991 Green Book*) AFDC recipients as a percentage of total population dropped from 5.13 in 1972 to 4.35 in 1989. AFDC child recipients as a percent of the total child population remained at about 11 percent from 1972 through 1989, reaching a low of 10.48 in 1982. AFDC child recipients as a percent of children in poverty dropped from 81 percent in 1973 to 49.6 percent in 1982, but rose to 57.9 in 1989.

By March 1991, the AFDC recipient population reached 12.5 million, the highest ever.[13] The increase was caused by the recession, along with continued changes in social behavior, population composition, and public policy, such as rising birthrates, increasing immigration, broader eligibility requirements for Medicaid, welfare assistance outreach, and changes in unemployment insurance. Also, as more fully described below, a greater percentage of people who came on welfare in the 1980s compared to earlier years were those who were likely to stay on welfare for a long time. Thus welfare starts were increasing while welfare exits were decreasing.

---

[13]The number of people receiving food stamps reached a record 23.6 million in August 1991. About one of every 10 Americans now receives food stamps, compared to 1 out of 20 in 1970. The food stamp program cost $19.6 billion in FY 1991. The economy, changes in application processes, and changes in immigration laws contributed to the increase. (Butterfield)

The changing nature of the economy, with an increasing number of part-time jobs and few good employment opportunities for the low-skilled, may keep welfare levels high even when the economic recovery begins. Even so, because of severe budget problems many states are reducing the size or availability of public assistance. (Peterson)

In 1990, the average monthly AFDC payment per family was $389. In real dollars, the median state AFDC payment for a family of three was 42 percent less in 1990 than in 1970. The median state benefit for a family of four fell from $739 in 1970 to $432 in 1990 in constant dollars (*1991 Green Book*) The median state payment in 1990 for a family of three was 43 percent of the poverty threshold; the addition of food stamps raised this to 72 percent of the poverty threshold. Combined food stamp and AFDC payments are below the poverty threshold in all states except Alaska, California, and some counties in New York. In eight states these combined payments are less than 60 percent of the poverty threshold.

In 1989, two- or three-person families accounted for nearly two-thirds of all welfare families, but nearly every AFDC family had a child: 55 percent had two or more children, and 25 percent had three or more. In about 57 percent of AFDC families, the youngest child was five years old or less, and in 35 percent of the families the youngest child was under three. Fifteen percent of the female adult recipients were under 22 years of age; 20 percent were 22 to 25, and 20 percent were 26 to 29. About 38 percent of AFDC families are headed by whites and about 40 percent are headed by blacks. About 9 percent of AFDC families had earned income, averaging about $240 per month. (*1991 Green Book*)

Although from a macro perspective the AFDC program has been stable over the past 15 years, specific characteristics of the AFDC population changed, often dramatically, between 1969 and 1989:

- the average family size dropped from 4.0 to 2.9;
- the percentage of one-child families rose from 26.6 to 41.8, while the percentage of three-child or more families dropped from 50.2 to 25;
- "no marriage tie" as the basis for eligibility increased from 27.9 percent to 52.7 percent;
- the percentage of AFDC mothers under the age of 25 rose from 23.3 to 35.8;
- the percentage of recipient children under the age of 3 rose from 14.9 to 19.4;
- the percentage of AFDC mothers who work full-time fell from 8.2 to 2.5 percent;
- the percentage of AFDC families with no other income other than AFDC rose from 56 to 79.5;

- the percentage of AFDC families participating in the food stamp program rose from 52.9 to 85.2; and
- the percentage of AFDC parents who are black fell from 45.2 to 40.1. (*1991 Green Book*)

Some of these changes in AFDC recipient characteristics were caused by 1981 statutory changes that reduced AFDC eligibility and payments. One result of these changes was to increase the effective tax rate on earnings of AFDC recipients from about 32 percent to 70 percent; the tax rate on earnings also increased for food stamp recipients. (Burtless) The percentage of AFDC mothers working full-time dropped from 8.7 percent in 1979 to 1.5 percent in 1983, and the percentage of AFDC families with earned income dropped from 12 percent to 5.2 percent in the same period. Also, the number of AFDC recipients dropped from 11,160,000 in 1981 to 10,143,000 in 1982. (*1990 Green Book*)

The most significant change in AFDC recipients in the past 20 years has been the dramatic increase in the percentage of recipients who were eligible because they were not married. The characteristics of not-married 1989 AFDC recipients differed from the characteristics of other AFDC recipients as the following approximately show:

- 7.4 percent of other recipients owned or were buying their homes compared to 2 percent of the not-marrieds;
- 19.7 of other recipients lived in subsidized housing compared to 27.7 of the not-marrieds;
- 26.6 percent of other recipients were black compared to 54 percent of the not-marrieds;
- 28 percent of other recipients had children under the age of 3 compared to 42.2 percent of the not-marrieds;
- 27.5 percent of other recipients had been on AFDC continuously for more than 4 years compared to 32.9 percent of the not-marrieds; and
- 10.6 percent of other AFDC female adult recipients were under 22 years of age compared to 20.2 percent of the not-marrieds.

Length of stay on welfare

Two of the most controversial issues in welfare dependency are the length of time recipients remain on AFDC and the extent to which AFDC is inter-generational. Nearly 50 percent of the people who begin their first "spell" on AFDC receive AFDC benefits for less than 3 years, while only 17 percent receive AFDC benefits for 8 or more years. At any given time in a single spell only 14 percent of AFDC recipients receive assistance for less than 3 years, while 50 percent receive assistance for 8 or more years (75 percent for 5 or more years). About one-third of all spells on welfare

are followed by subsequent spells. When these multiple spells are counted the percentage of beginning AFDC recipients who spend less than three years on welfare drops to 30 percent, while the percentage of beginning recipients who spend 8 years or more on welfare increases to 65 percent (82 percent for five or more years). Thus, while those on welfare at any one time are predominantly long-term users, the typical welfare recipients is a short-term user. (*1990 Green Book*) A recent study of Chicago welfare recipients indicates a 70 percent probability that an AFDC spell for a black mother would last 5 years and a 60 percent probability of a 10-year spell. Overall, 40 percent of AFDC spells lasted two years or less, while 18 percent of the spells lasted 10 years more. Black and Puerto Rican mothers had much longer spells than Mexican or white mothers. (Tienda)

Studies in California and Texas, two states with very different welfare policies, are also consistent with national data. About 60 percent of single-parent AFDC recipients left AFDC within one year in California. Within six months of leaving AFDC, one-third returned to the programs; within three years one-half had returned. Two-parent families were more likely to leave and less likely to return. In Texas, more than 60 percent of AFDC recipients (all single-parents) left the program within one year, but about 20 percent returned within six months and another 20 percent returned within four years. (Porter)

Knowledge about inter-generational welfare dependency is sketchy. A 1984 study suggests only between 19 to 26 percent of daughters in high welfare families (families receiving at least 25 percent of average family income from welfare) become highly dependent on welfare during the time these daughters are aged 24 to 30. Yet, another study, done in 1989, shows daughters of mothers who received welfare have a much higher probability of giving early births and being on welfare than do daughters of mothers who although eligible, do not receive welfare. (Gottschalk) A third study finds receipt of AFDC by parents increases the probability a teenager will have an out-of-wedlock birth, even after controlling for effects of economic opportunity. (Duncan and Hoffman)

Analyzing the Issue

Welfare programs have a bad image; many people perceive welfare programs as unaffordable, unmanageable, and undesirable. (Marmor, Mashaw, and Harvey) AFDC, particularly, must fend off attacks it encourages dependency and rewards sloth and inappropriate behavior such as illegitimate childbirth. The Family Support Act of 1988, which begins to take full effect in 1991, tried to respond to some of these criticisms by emphasing employment, employment training, and childcare, and by creating a self-sufficiency goal, acknowledging welfare programs should help people become independent.

Several characteristics of the welfare program and welfare recipients are important relative to economic development. One is the high cost of getting off welfare; a second is the changing character of the welfare population; and a third is the way people get off welfare.

It has been neither easy nor practical to get off welfare. For example, in one state in early 1990, a mother with two children received $5,052 in AFDC benefits and $2,007 worth of food stamps for a total disposable income of $7,059 plus Medicaid benefits. If this mother worked 35 hours per week at $3.45 per hour, earning $6,000 per year, her AFDC and food stamp benefits would drop to $3,672. Although she would receive an earned income tax credit of $840, she would have to pay a social security tax of $459 and $1,800 in work expenses such as child care, and transportation. Her total disposable income would be $8,208, only $1,229 more than if she remained on welfare. If she took a better paying job at $4.95 per hour for an annual income of $10,000, her total disposable income, including a $953 tax credit, would have been only $8,701, about $1,600 more than if she had remained on welfare, and she would no longer be eligible for Medicaid.

The Family Support Act tried to rectify this situation. Beginning in April 1990 such a family qualifies for 12 months of Medicaid, and the state must offer Medicaid to all children up to age six whose family income is not above 133 percent of poverty.

A second issue related to economic development is the changing character of AFDC recipients. Research has identified characteristics of welfare recipients who have AFDC spells lasting more than 10 years. At the beginning of their first spell, these recipients have the following characteristics: under age 22 (32.8 percent will have spells lasting 10 or more years); black (32 percent), not married (39.3 percent); the youngest child under three (31.9 percent); and the recipient did not work in past two years (31.2 percent). It is estimated that over 40 percent of beginning recipients who have never married and begin AFDC at age of 25 or less with a child less than three years old will spend 10 or more years on AFDC. (*1990 Green Book*)

As indicated by data presented earlier, the characteristics of the AFDC recipient population in the aggregate increasingly fit the long-spell probability. Between 1979 and 1990 the percentage of not-married AFDC recipients increased from 31 to 52.7, the percentage of mothers under the age of 25 increased from 32.1 to 35.8, and the percentage with children under three increased from 18.9 percent to 19.4 percent. These are percentages of the AFDC population as a whole, not the incremental additions to the welfare population over the past 10 years. Thus, unless these trends change the number of people on welfare should increase simply because fewer people will be exiting welfare.

Third, the reasons why people get on or off welfare have a bearing on economic development. While in the aggregate divorce or separation are the single biggest reason why people are on welfare, out-of-wedlock births is the current single biggest reason. One study finds women living in states with higher AFDC benefits are more likely to have out-of-wedlock births. While most earlier studies suggest high welfare benefits are not related to out-of-wedlock births, several very recent studies conclude a relationship does exist. (Duncan and Hoffman; Jencks) Although the illegitimacy ratio is much higher among blacks than whites with the same amount of education, more years of schooling decreases the likelihood of out-of-wedlock births. Twelve years of schooling drops the illegitimacy ratio for whites from 38 percent to 14 percent and for blacks from 83 percent to 62 percent. Sixteen or more years of schooling drops the rate to 2 percent for whites and 21 percent for blacks. (Jencks) A decline of earnings triggers about 15 percent of entries to welfare, and other reasons (including unidentified), 10 percent.

The most important reason for getting off welfare is marriage (35 percent). Twenty-six percent get off welfare because of earnings increases; 11 percent because children leave the parental home; and 28 percent for other reasons (including unidentified). (*1990 Green Book*) A study of welfare recipients in Chicago showed that while work was the single leading reason for welfare exits, it accounted for only 10 percent of the exits. (Tienda)

AFDC recipients with more education and prior work experience are more likely to leave AFDC because of increased earnings. Additionally, women who had 12 or more years of education and who had worked at least two years before being on AFDC were more likely to earn more than $6,000 in their first year off AFDC. (Porter) In Chicago, blacks with a mother who had a high school education were 50 percent more likely to get off welfare. (Tienda)

The difference between registration and employment as a result of participating in WIN suggests some of the difficulties that might face the JOBS program in the Family Support Act.[14]

In summary, the characteristics of the welfare program and of welfare recipients, especially those who have started on welfare during the past 10 years, pose a significant challenge to economic development policy, which could enable adult welfare recipients to become part of the economic mainstream.

The Urban Underclass and Ghetto Poverty

Describing the Issue

The concept of the underclass is controversial because it is difficult to explain and to measure. There are also concerns that the phrase "underclass" evokes inaccurate beliefs about poor minorities or ghetto residents.

Although there is no single accepted definition of the underclass, people with the following characteristics are generally considered members: permanently unemployed people; women who are persistently poor (for at least eight years), with prolonged welfare dependency and high rates of out-of-wedlock births, usually starting in their teen years; children who are persistently poor with high drop-out rates; and persons with

---

[14]Prior to the Family Support Act, the welfare system had some experience with job training and job placement, primarily through the work incentive program (WIN), which was established in 1967. Although all states became involved in WIN, it was not well-funded (funding dropped from $365 million in 1981 to $110 million in 1987), and states were limited in their ability to provide skills assessments, training, or job placements. WIN was somewhat cost-effective — each dollar spent saved about two welfare dollars. About 35 percent of WIN registrants received unsubsidized jobs; about 19 percent left welfare because of employment; and 61 percent of those with unsubsidized employment kept their jobs for six or more months. (1990 Green Book) Between 1983 and 1985, 34 percent of the registrants were black, but only 25 percent of the job entrants were black; although 52 percent of the registrants had less than 12 years of schooling, only 40 percent of the job entrants had less than 12 years of schooling. (1990 Green Book)

Also, over a 32-month period one of seven adults (19 years or older) who did not have a high school diploma received either AFDC, general assistance, or SSI compared to fewer than one in 20 for those with a high school degree but no college. More than one-half of those 19- to 23- years-old and on public assistance had below average scores on a test of basic academic skills, and more than one-half scored in the lowest 5 percent on a basic test of 23- year old receiving public assistance scored inthe lowest 5 percent on the basic skills test as among those in the middle. Seventeen- to 21-year old AFDC mothers had reading abilities averaging below the sixth-grade level. (Porter) Also, the average IQ of welfare mothers aged 22 to 30 is 86 compared to 100 for all women in this age group. Most welfare mothers would not qulity for the Armed Forces. (Rich)

disproportionately high rates of criminal behavior or criminal victimization. (GAO, 1990) The underclass is a group of people living close to one another who are isolated from the mainstream with little or no opportunity for upward mobility, and thereby creating, in an arguably controversial conclusion, an environment that destructively feeds on itself and continually expands.

Part of the controversy surrounding the term underclass deals with its implication that members of the underclass have problematic behavior that is culturally based. This leads people to "blame the victim," rather than acknowledge the impact of economic circumstances or racial discrimination. Further, members of the underclass are usually black or Hispanic in urban neighborhoods. The underclass also is perceived as a set of very poor people permanently impervious to improvement through public policy.

William Julius Wilson, the sociologist whose writings have highlighted the underclass issue, does not think a culture of poverty causes the black underclass. He thinks the cause is a dramatic transformation in the structure of the urban economy which has caused unemployment among black men. Black male unemployment, according to Wilson, explains their poverty and unmarriageability, which, in turn, has led to the decline of the family and a perpetuation of the black underclass. A 1990 study of inner city Chicago reported black males with steady jobs are twice as likely to marry as black men who are not in school, in the military, or at work. (Orfield)

Another view blames the existence of the underclass on changing attitudes toward sex, divorce, and parenthood, led by the upper classes' relaxation of moral constraints and its strivings for individual freedom. While this change may have benefitted well-educated and high-income persons, it has had a devastating affect on the poor and less educated. Christopher Jencks believes that the moral norm requiring a man to marry a woman he has impregnated lost much of its force between 1960 and 1990 as women's earnings rose and their ability to control their own fertility increased. (Jencks) For example, a study of men 20 to 27 years-of-age who had fathered a child as a teenager found being Hispanic or black was strongly associated with not getting married, even after controlling for the effects of other characteristics of the father or his parents. (Vinouskis)

The percentage of black women who will never marry is estimated for 1990 at 25 percent, triple the rate of 1960. The 1990 rate for black women is three times that of white women, although the figures for both black and white women were about equal in 1960. About 22 percent of black men had never married by their late 30s, compared to 14 percent for white men.

Additionally, black females outnumbered black males by about 1.5 million according to the 1990 census. (Vobejda)

But another recent analysis concludes there is no persuasive explanation of family formation trends in recent decades. (Lerman) and one other recent study suggests lack of economic opportunity does not clearly affect family structure. (Osterman) Nonetheless, high urban poverty areas have a demographic imbalance: they have a high incidence of female-headed black families because they have a high absence of black married males. (Gramlich) This is partly due to the exit from inner city areas of working and middle class blacks, but also partly due to alcoholism, substance abuse, imprisonment, and homicide. The key concept in the underclass, according to Wilson, is not a culture of poverty, but of social isolation.

Most observers believe that the underclass is growing and that poor blacks are becoming more geographically isolated, but the increasing geographic concentration of poverty appears to be confined mostly to large northeastern and midwestern cities. Estimates of the size of the underclass vary, ranging from 2 to 6 million people, or about 1 to 3 percent of the total population (or about 5 to 13 percent of the total poverty population). A detailed analysis of the 1990 census should add substantially to the knowledge of the underclass (although decennial data cannot deal with behavioral aspects of an urban underclass definition).

To deal with a concept that is easier to measure, the concept of "ghetto poverty area," is often used. It is defined as a census tract the poverty rate is 40 percent or more.[15] (Jargowsky and Bane) Using this definition, about 9 percent of all residents lived in ghetto poverty areas in 1980, but this included 21 percent of all blacks, 16 percent of all Hispanics, but only 2 percent of all non-Hispanic whites. However, 10 metropolitan areas accounted for nearly half of the ghetto poor in 1980. Mincy (Kasarda, 1991) found 70 percent of the residents of extreme poverty tracts in the 100 largest central cities in 1980 were black, and fewer than 10 percent were white.

The number of people living in ghetto poverty areas increased by 66 percent (from 975,000 to 1,615,000) between 1970 and 1980, and four cities

---

[15]Erol Ricketts and Isabel Sawhill argue the term underclass is not meaningful if it cannot be distinguished from poverty, including persistent and spatially-concentrated poverty. (Ricketts and Sawhill)

(New York, Philadelphia, Chicago, and Detroit) accounted for two-thirds of the increase. Another analysis shows the 30 largest cities added 527 ghetto poverty census tracts between 1970 and 1980, and 91 percent of these additional census tracts were in the Northeast or Midwest. (Kasarda, 1991) The number of ghetto area poor apparently increase through a process by which some census tracts adjacent to ghetto poverty tracts become ghetto poverty areas through a complicated interaction of dispersion, poverty, and racial segregation.[16]

The small size of the underclass is misleading because the underclass may be imposing high costs on the rest of society. Loic J. D. Wacquant and William Julius Wilson suggest that ghetto poverty areas provide their residents with deteriorated housing, schools, businesses, recreational facilities, and other community organizations; remove the economic and social buffer of a stable middle class to economic downturns; loosen if not destroy ties to the workworld; and deplete the social networks of parents and friends. (Wacquant and Wilson) A very high concentration of urban poverty may overwhelm government, resulting in crowded clinics, failing foster care, ineffective law enforcement, and neglected services. (DeParle, 1991) This fosters a belief among many Americans that government programs, especially government antipoverty programs, do not work, and clearly are not worth paying for with increased taxes.

One of the biggest conceptual problems in dealing with the underclass is the lack of longitudinal data. Are people who live in poor neighborhoods persistently poor? Are they the same people who were poor in the same area at an earlier date? Are they trapped?

One longitudinal analysis suggests that about 15 percent of poor white persons leave high poverty tracts (40 percent poor) over a three-year

---

[16] An analysis of the urban underclass that used multiple behavioral indicators found that 2.5 million people lived in underclass tracts (Kasarda, 1991; Ricketts and Sawhill) and that most of these tracts were in northeastern and midwestern cities. While the number of people living in poverty increased by only 8 percent between 1970 and 1980, people living in these underclass tracts grew by 230 percent, from 752,000 to 2,484,000. Another behavioral analysis (Kasarda, 1991) found 1.33 million "severely distressed" people living in the 95 largest cities in 1980, with children comprising about 58 percent. About 40 percent of these severely distressed people lived in New York (25 percent), Chicago, and Philadelphia. Nearly 60 percent were black and one-quarter Hispanic. In some cities, blacks comprise 95 percent or more of the severely distressed population (Washington, D.C., New Orleans, Memphis, and Jackson), while only in a few cities are one-half or more of the severely distressed people white (Akron, Des Moines, Grand Rapids, Spokane, St. Paul, Wichita, and Worcester). In some cities, Hispanics make up two-thirds or more of severely distressed people(Albuquerque, Austin, El Paso, San Antonio, and Santa Ana).

period. When they leave these tracts, or when they leave middle-income tracts, they move up. About 11 percent of blacks leave underclass areas. For persistently poor people, however, the entrance rates are higher than the exit rates, so that underclass tracts become poorer over time and the share of poor living in underclass areas increase, and it appears that the population level living in underclass tracts decreases. (Gramlich) But our understanding and knowledge about the dynamics of urban underclass areas and people is unclear. We do not know whether an exit from an underclass area is good, bad, or indifferent; we do not know what causes exits and entrances for different groups; and we do not know the fate of an underclass area when its role models leave, with their places taken by very low-income persons without steady jobs.

Little research has been done on the extent to which living in under-class or ghetto poverty areas affects peoples ability to become part of the economic mainstream, in part because it is difficult to separate this factor from the affect of poverty or race or other factors. The sparse analysis that does exist suggests two conclusions.[17] First, neighborhood characteristics affect teenage sexual behavior. Holding race and family background con-stant, girls aged 16 to 19 are substantially more likely to have children out of wedlock if they lived in poor neighborhoods than if they lived in average neighborhoods.[18] (Jencks and Meyer) Second, neighborhood charac-teristics, at least high welfare dependency, reduce men's chances of ob-taining well-paid jobs in adulthood. (Corcoran et al.)

Although less certain than the preceding two conclusions, the per-centage of high-status workers (professional or managerial) in a neighbor-hood seems to affect schooling, especially for black males. In 1970, when 5.5 percent of the workers in a neighborhood had high-status jobs in 1970, the dropout rate for black males was 14.6 percent, and rate declined continually to about 6 percent as the percentage of high status workers increased to 28 percent. As the percentage of high-status workers dropped from 5.6 percent to 3.4 percent, the dropout rate exploded to nearly 35

---

[17] A study of welfare in Chicago also showed residence in a neighborhood with a poverty rate of 40 percent or more significantly lowered welfare exits for blacks, while residence in a neighborhood with a poverty rate of 30 percent or more significantly lowered exits for whites. (Tienda)

[18] This suggests, to some, that poor girls chose to have babies because they believe they have nothing better to look forward to. (Passell, 1991 b)

percent from 14 percent. A similar pattern occurred for teenage childbearing, especially for blacks in cities. (Crane)[19]

Analyzing the Issue

Analyzing the underclass is important to economic development not only because of the costs of the underclass to society, but also because economic reasons are used to explain the development, maintenance, and growth of the underclass. Skills and spatial mismatches are keys in analyzing the underclass, and crime is also an important factor. A spatial mismatch occurs when jobs once held by inner city residents move to or increase in the suburbs where they are unaccessible to inner city residents. A skills mismatch occurs when job changes in the inner city make it impossible for people with low skills to obtain decent paying jobs.

Spatial mismatch

One of the biggest issues in analyzing the underclass or ghetto poverty is whether the intense concentration of poverty in inner city areas results in a spatial mismatch whereby employers are less willing to hire black workers, and black workers are less able to find jobs. Spatial mismatch is difficult to prove. For example, if middle class blacks leave poor urban neighborhoods, unemployment rates in these neighborhoods will probably increase, but not necessarily because of spatial mismatches.

The spacial mismatch theory is based on the dramatic change in central cities from manufacturing centers with relatively well-paying jobs requiring low levels of skills and education to information processing centers with well-paying jobs requiring high levels of skill and education. According to the theory, this has devastating consequences for black families, especially black men, because black labor in central cities is characterized by a very high percentage of persons who have not completed high school. (Kasarda, 1989) As John Kasarda has said: "Throughout our history spatial mobility and economic mobility have gone hand in hand. Now for the first time that connection has been broken." (Suro)

---

[19]Neighborhoods may have a stronger affect than schools. Students in schools with low socioeconomic status tend to drop out in the same proportion as students in schools with higher socioeconomic status, although teenage pregnancy occurs more frequently among students in schools with low socioeconomic status. (Mayer)

The relative increase in well-paying, low-skill jobs in suburban areas, unavailable to inner city minorities, compounds the problems associated with the deindustrialization of central cities and the apparent drop in these jobs in the cities. One-half to two-thirds of the employment decline of less educated blacks in the 1970s has been caused by the changing job structure of central cities, especially the loss of manufacturing jobs.[20] (Kasarda, 1991) Anecdotal evidence suggests when manufacturing firms go to new technologies and operating processes they move to fairly sparsely settled areas where land costs and labor costs are relatively minimal. The increasing importance of very small or flexible business — some evidence suggests that using flexible production or operating processes is associated with downsizing and outsourcing, which may also hurt urban black male workers — and the increasing amount of privatization of the state and local government employment may also adversely affect black male employment. Also, blacks likely are overrepresented in metropolitan areas that are slow growing. (Johnson and Oliver)

---

[20]Kasarda (1991) shows that manufacturing's share of earnings in constant 1980 dollars dropped between 1970 and 1987 in the five largest central counties (data are not available for central cities, although they are conterminous for New York) as follows: Chicago, 31.8 percent to 19.5 percent; Detroit, 41.3 percent to 38 percent; New York, 18.7 percent to 8.9 percent; and Philadelphia, 25.3 percent to 13.2 percent. During the same period, the share of workplace earnings held by finance, insurance, and real estate and services for these same counties went from 24 percent to 38 percent for Chicago; from 19 percent to 26 percent for Detroit; from 36 percent to 53 percent for New York; and from 26 percent to 43 percent for Philadelphia.

Even more striking are the differences between central city and suburban ring changes in manufacturing employment between 1977 and 1987. For Chicago, central city manufacturing employment dropped by 60 percent but increased by 11 percent in the suburban ring. For Detroit, central city manufacturing employment dropped by 51 percent compared to only a 5 percent drop in the suburban rings. For New York, central city manufacturing employment dropped by 58 percent, but increased by 86 percent in the suburban ring. In Philadelphia, central city manufacturing employment dropped by 64 percent, while suburban ring manufacturing dropped by only 10 percent. The picture is even more devastating if trade employment is considered.

Kasarda also examines four large cities in the growth belt. While their central city economies are doing much better than those in the above northeastern and mid-west cities, the suburban rings are outstripping central cities in terms of manufacturing employment growth. The percentage differential between central city and suburban ring manufacturing growth is 182 percent for Atlanta, 14 percent for Los Angeles, and 331 percent for Phoenix. Only in Dallas-Fort Worth did the central city outperform the suburban ring. And even here, from 1972 to 1982 Dallas manufacturing jobs dropped by nearly 18 percent, while manufacturing jobs in such suburbs as Plano and Irving rose by 363 and 309 percent, respectively. (Suro)

In examining 45 large metropolitan areas, Johnson and Oliver found manufacturing employment declined by nearly 10 percent, and job growth in the suburbs exceeded central city job growth by about 56 percent in 34 central cities. Central city job loss in producer services (finance, insurance, and real estate), social services (medical, education, and government), and manufacturing and construction were particularly noticeable. Only nine metropolitan areas had job growth and no loss in manufacturing jobs.

Unlike Kasarda's more limited analyses, Johnson and Oliver's analysis does not suggest a sunbelt versus frostbelt breakdown. While the high-growth metropolitan areas are concentrated in the South and on the West Coast, some slow growth-high job dispersion metropolitan areas are in the South and West, e.g., Los Angeles, San Francisco, Miami, Jacksonville, Denver, and Nashville. Geographic dispersion of jobs, especially in producer and personal services, rather than deindustrialization, seems to be the most significant economic variable in distinguishing metropolitan economies from one another.

Johnson and Oliver's analysis suggests that job growth and job dispersion account for one-quarter to one-half of urban black male joblessness. Slow employment growth also negatively affects black unemployment rates, unsurprisingly, but the effect seems relatively modest. (Holzer) Cities with job growth have lower rates of black male unemployment, non-labor force participation, and total black male joblessness than cities with slow or no employment growth or employment decline. Tight labor markets unquestionably benefit young adult males, especially young black men. One study shows that a 1-point decrease in area unemployment rate increases youth employment by 1.9 points and black youth employment by 4.3 points. Tight labor markets also increase earnings for black youths, but these findings also suggest unemployment rates need to drop as low as 3 or 4 percent to produce these benefits, and it is unlikely many areas can sustain low unemployment rates. (Freeman)

Employment declines in 52 large metropolitan areas during 1970 to 1980 affected all males, especially the young and least educated. Within each group, blacks were affected more adversely than whites. The declines were greatest in the Northeast and Midwest. Industrial shifts might explain only 10 or 15 percent of overall employment declines in the 1970s for males, but they may explain one-third to one-half for young black dropouts. Overall, demand in metropolitan areas has a larger affect on blacks than whites. The demand shifts away from less skilled blacks and whites also lowered annual earnings.

Cities with high rates of job dispersion have higher black male unemployment rates, idleness (percentage of black males neither in school or at work), and total black male joblessness (percentage of black males neither employed nor in the labor force). In these areas, there is more intense competition for entry-level jobs. This diminishing job availability weakens labor force participation. Educational advancement alone is not likely to improve the economic situation of spatially-concentrated minority people who are isolated from employment opportunities, especially when the cities where they live have low and declining levels of employment growth. (Moore and Laramore)

A recent examination of spatial employment trends reinforces the spatial mismatch concept. Between 1965 and 1985 total employment in the continental United States rose by about 70 percent. About 35 percent of all job growth occurred in urban counties in large metropolitan statistical areas (MSAs). Most of the balance of the job growth was nearly equally spread, about 19 percent each, among suburban counties, small MSAs, and "exurban"[21] counties, while rural counties gained only about 7 percent. Manufacturing employment grew only about 10 percent during this period of time; however, urban counties *lost* an amount of manufacturing jobs equal to 26 percent of all the manufacturing jobs that were gained, while exurban counties gained 61 percent of all manufacturing job growth. Suburban counties collared 21 percent and small MSA counties 18 percent of all manufacturing job gains, and rural counties, 27 percent. (Nelson)

Spatial employment trends varied noticeably among regions. Exurban counties substantially benefitted, and urban counties substantially lost in the Northeast and Midwest. In both regions, exurban and suburban counties substantially outpaced urban counties in total job growth, manufacturing job growth, and population growth. Urban counties in the Northeast captured only 21 percent of all job growth compared to 31 percent for exurban counties, while the comparable figures for the Midwest were 17 percent for urban counties and 24 percent for exurban counties. In both regions, exurban counties had a greater share of total job growth, manufacturing job growth, and population growth than either suburban or small

---

[21]Exurban counties may be within or outside of MSAs. For all MSAs except those of less than 500,000 (small MSAs), exurban counties are all MSA counties outside of the central city and all MSA counties defined as metropolitan (suburban) in 1960. For MSAs of less than one million, exurban counties are outside MSAs but within 60 miles of the outermost circumferential limited-access highway, or within 70 miles of the center of the central city, whichever defines the larger area. For MSAs with more than one million people, exurban counties are outside MSAs but within 80 miles of the outermost circumferential limited access highway, or within 100 miles of the center of the central city.

MSA counties. In the South, urban counties gained a greater share of total job growth than exurban counties, 39 percent to 22 percent, but a smaller share of manufacturing job growth, 22 percent to 37 percent. The respective shares of population growth were at the same, about 32 percent. Urban counties were strongest in the West, but the geographical constraints (mountains and ocean) on exurban growth and the very large size of counties make the analysis misleading.

In the large northeastern and midwestern metropolitan areas the percentage of unemployed blacks with less than a high school education was lower in suburbs than in central cities during 1968-1970, 1976-1978, 1980-1982, and 1986-1988. Unemployment rates for black males increased in each of these periods, but it was always lower in the suburbs than in the central cities. This suggests that segregation per se does not explain city-suburban joblessness. "Growth in low-skill job opportunities in closer proximity to poorly educated black suburban residents would seem a more plausible explanation of the somewhat lower suburban rates." (Kasarda, 1991)

Research suggests that spatial mismatch also affects Puerto Ricans in New York City and Mexican Americans in Los Angeles (Ortiz)

Skills mismatch

The skills mismatch theory focuses on a shift of jobs from well-paying jobs that do not require much education, sophistication, or specialized job skills. For example, the average years of schooling in 1984 for urban workers in manufacturing and personal services industries was 12.7, but these industries had job losses in central cities between 1970 and 1980. On the other hand, the average years of schooling was 15 for persons employed in industries that had the most job gains in central cities from 1970 to 1980 (producer and social services). This suggests the loss of well-paying jobs in central cities affected less-educated and less-skilled workers. (Moore and Laramore)

It is instructive to note the differences between central city households in census tracts where the poverty rate is 40 percent or higher and those in census tracts with poverty rates under 20 percent. In Chicago, 62 percent of high-poverty tract households have less than a high school education and 67 percent have no vehicle, compared to 37 percent with less than a high school education and 29 percent with no vehicle present in low-poverty tracts. In Detroit, the same percentages for high-poverty tracts are 62 and 58 compared to 37 and 15 in low-poverty tracts. In New York, the percentages are 63 percent and 82 percent compared to 33 and 49; and in Philadelphia the percentages are 64 and 67 compared to 39 and 27.

(Kasarda, 1991) The differences are even more dramatic for the four growth belt cities. Consequently, the relative growth of employment opportunities requiring either higher education or personal transportation adversely affects blacks who live in ghetto poverty areas.

Between 1970 and 1980 the city of Chicago lost over 230,000 jobs where the job holder had a high school degree or less, but gained over 160,000 jobs where the job holder had at least some college. The comparable figures for Detroit are minus 168,000 and plus 46,000; for New York, minus 596,000 and plus 372,000; and for Philadelphia, minus 150,000 and plus 375,000. (Kasarda, 1991) Suburban residents probably held many of the high-education jobs. Yet, in each of these cities the percentage of unemployed black males with less than a high school education is more than 50 percent, while the percentage of all workers with less than a high school degree is about 22 percent. On the other hand, the percentage of black males who have a college degree ranges from 6 to 10, while the percentage of job holders with a college degree range from 20 to 28. This clearly suggests a structural mismatch that may impede any development effort in large cities to employ black males.

The well-noted and documented increased earnings inequality of the less educated young, especially drop-outs, lends credence to the skills mismatch theory. The real wages of male high-school drop-outs aged 25 to 34 who worked full time decreased by 21 percent between 1972 and 1986. The falling labor force participation rates of males aged 16 through 18, which dropped from 87 percent in 1978 to 77 percent in 1987, also lends credence to the skills mismatch. Clearly, during the 1980s labor demand shifted, both within and among industries, away from less educated workers, especially black males.[22]

Technological change, more imports, and outsourcing and relocation of work abroad may all lower manufacturing employment and adversely affect black male employment, particularly for the less educated. This does not indicate that U.S. manufacturing industry is dying. Between 1970 and 1989 manufacturing's share of national output declined very little, but manufacturing's share of male employment dropped from 30 percent to

[22]Jencks doubts the reality of the skills mismatch theory because the chances of finding a steady job also decreased from 1964 to 1987 for college students. (Jencks) Employment and earnings gains among black young males increased in Boston's low-unemployment rate era in the 1980s, although Boston is a heavily white-collar city. (Osterman) Boston also is the only large northeastern city that had no increase from 1970 to 1980 in the level of ghetto poverty among blacks. (Jargowsky and Bane)

20 percent. (Holzer and Vroman) Nor does this mean blacks are or were overrepresented in manufacturing employment. In 1970, about 44 percent of all black males and 40 percent of all white males were employed in manufacturing but blacks in manufacturing had a relative wage premium of about 20 percent compared to their wages in other sectors of the economy. The shift away from manufacturing employment has been slow to resolve itself via economic equilibrium in part because of the high "reservation" wages sought by those who are displaced from high-wage manufacturing jobs.

Nonetheless, simply educating undereducated and unskilled blacks may be ineffective. Unlike with whites, with blacks there is little relationship between the percentage of high school graduates and labor force participation and unemployment. Even if the key problem is the quality of inner city schools, according to Thomas S. Moore and Aaron Laramore, "the segregation and concentration of the black work force within areas of slow employment growth are likely to render educational differences and gains less consequential regardless of the quality of schools or the hiring practices of employers....educational advancement alone is not likely to improve the economic situation of that population as long as it remains concentrated in central cities with low and declining levels of employment growth." (Moore and Laramore, p. 655)

Impact of crime

Black male joblessness may also be related to crime. Richard Freeman (Freeman, 1991 b) suggests crime among disadvantaged black males became so pervasive in the 1980s, it is now a major and adverse determinant of their economic lives. Although crime data is far from perfect, several studies suggest one-third of all arrests and one-half of all incarcerations involve blacks. Over two-thirds of all prisoners and three-fourths of all black prisoners aged 18 to 24 have less than 12 years of education. Among blacks, 41 percent of 18- to 24- year-old drop-outs and over 75 percent of 25 to 34 year-old drop outs are under the supervision of the criminal justice system. "An extraordinary proportion of the nation's disadvantaged youths are seriously involved in crime," says Freeman. (Freeman, 1991 b, p. 7)

Studies also suggest tight job markets are not sufficient to have a positive affect on black youth crime. Unfortunately, crime has a very adverse and long-term affect on getting a job. Having been in jail or on probation reduces the chances for employment by one-half to two-thirds. At the start of the 1980s, few youths believed that crime pays more than legal activities, but by the end of the decade youths generally agreed that illegal activity paid more than legal activity, a statistic possibly explained by increased drug use.

Freeman estimates disadvantaged youths receive $8.00 to $30.00 per hour, tax free from crime. Most youths also place a high value on the nonmonetary aspects of crime, especially autonomy and peer esteem. Both the pay and the working conditions of crime are better than what most disadvantaged youths feel they can get from legal work, notwithstanding the risk. Decreased opportunities for legitimate employment for less educated men and increased opportunities from drugs led to increased crime among disadvantaged youth in the 1980s. This spawned the likelihood for long-term disaster for the current generation of criminally-active disadvantaged youth.

Urban-Rural Differences

Some states must design an economic opportunity strategy for rural areas, others for urban, and still others for both. The strategies must address the differences between rural and urban poverty, and differences among rural areas such as sparse populations and limited institutional richness.

During the 1980s, poverty became more of an urban phenomenon than a rural one. In 1959, 56 percent of poor people lived outside metropolitan areas, but by 1985 only 30 percent did. About 27 percent of poor people lived in central cities in 1957, but this percentage increased to 41 in 1985. The incidence of poverty in central cities rose from 14.2 percent in 1970 to 18.6 percent in 1987, higher than the nonmetropolitan poverty rate of 16.9 percent and much higher than the suburban poverty rate of 8.5 percent. (Lynn and McGeary) From 1989 to 1990, the poverty rate did not increase in a statistically significant way in nonmetropolitan areas, but increased from 12 to 12.7 percent in metropolitan areas.

Urban poverty is becoming more firmly entrenched. The proportion of urban residents who escaped poverty each year dropped from 37 percent in 1975 to 23 percent in 1982, largely because the typical urban poor person was further below the poverty line in 1982 than in 1975 (e.g., the fraction of urban poor with incomes less than three-quarters of the poverty line increased from 50 percent to 63 percent). (Lynn and Mc-Geary)

Several important differences between rural (nonmetropolitan) and urban (metropolitan) poverty exist. First, the percentage of poor persons in female-headed families is much higher in urban areas than in rural areas, 41 percent compared to 29 percent (1986), while the percentage of poor persons who were members in other families (generally, married couples with or without children) is much higher in rural areas than in urban areas, 51 percent compared to 35 percent. Second, the percentage of poor families with no workers is only 33 percent in rural areas, compared to 44 percent in urban areas. The percentage of poor families with two or more workers is 29 percent in rural areas, compared to 17 percent in urban areas. Third, 44 percent of all blacks in rural areas are poor compared to only 31 percent in urban areas and 33 percent in central cities. (*1990 Green Book*)

In 1980, over one-third of female heads of households in central cities were under 30 years old compared to under one-fourth in rural areas. Nearly 40 percent of female heads of households in central cities had children less than 6 years old compared to 29 percent in rural areas. Nearly one-quarter of female heads of households in central cities were never married, compared to less than 10 percent in rural areas. Over 36 percent of female heads of households in central cities did not work, compared to about 28 percent in rural areas. About 36 percent of rural female heads of households younger than 30 work full-time, compared to about 27 percent in central cities. (Jensen)

The impact of welfare varies between central city and rural areas. In 1987, about one-half of poor central city families received welfare compared to only about 30 percent of rural poor families. (Jensen) While the mean welfare income for central city welfare families was nearly $4,000, it was slightly under $3,000 for rural families. (SSI shows a different pattern. Relatively more rural poor persons and families are likely to receive SSI, but the average SSI benefit in rural areas is less than that in central cities.)

Welfare assistance is less helpful in dealing with poverty in rural areas than in central cities. The percentage of poor families with pre-welfare income below the poverty line that is brought up to the poverty line by the addition of welfare is only 1.9 in rural areas, compared to 4.8 in central cities. In another example, the mean proportion of pre-welfare poverty gap that is closed by welfare is 15.9 percent in rural areas and 31.4 percent in central city areas. There is little rural-urban difference in the ability of SSI to ameliorate poverty because of the countervailing effect of utilization rates and benefit levels.

The primary reason welfare in rural areas has a relatively low ameliorative impact is that rural poor persons are less likely to receive welfare. Fewer rural poor persons receive welfare because they are (1) more likely to have an employed family head; (2) more likely to be in a family headed by married couples; (3) less likely to have children present; (4) less likely to a non-white head of family; (5) more likely to have an older head of family; (6) more likely to own their own home; and (7) less likely to live in a state that offers AFDC-Unemployed Parent Assistance. (Jensen)

In one way, however, urban and rural poverty seem to be converging. Poverty in rural areas has always been the result of low wages and a shortage of jobs, especially jobs with upward mobility. Now low wages and job shortages are plaguing poor people in urban areas as well. In both urban and rural areas, community characteristics affect the economic success of individuals within these communities regardless of the individuals' characteristics. Location now affects economic opportunity. (Tickamyer and Duncan)

A Policy Context

This review of poverty and related issues leads to three conclusions. First, the connection between employment and family is critical to preventing or eliminating poverty. Most people who work are not poor, particularly if more than one family member works. At the same time, long-term unemployment or the prospect of substantial underemployment, especially among black males, helps create broken families or prevents the formation of families. Once a broken or unformed family plummets into poverty, escape becomes very difficult. Children who grow up in a female-headed household are more likely to live in poverty, drop out of school, and have other problems that decrease their ability to earn a good livelihood. "[D]amage in the ghetto labor market in one generation feeds a set of mechanisms that tend to carry it into the next generation in the form of uneducated and ill-prepared workers." (Orfield p. 27)

Although in the U.S. we may have turned a policy corner by making self-sufficiency an important welfare goal, the welfare system may not be able to meet this goal if it goes it alone.

Second, the American economy began a major transformation in the early 1970s that reduced the number of well-paying manufacturing jobs in central cities, and increased the number of jobs requiring high education and skills levels. Net job growth is primarily occurring in the suburbs, especially the outer suburbs. This change adversely affected young families and minorities, and federal policies simultaneously exacerbated the situation. At least when Nero fiddled, he did not add fuel to the fires in Rome.

Although federal policy may have improved in the past three or four years, its approach to poverty is still timid and, at times, counterproductive. Preoccupation with the elderly has placed children and young adults in much greater jeopardy than before. The federal government's lack of concern about mobility, and its preference for concentration in place, not only may make serious problems more serious, but also limits an exploration of policies that could significantly affect long-term poverty.[23]

Third, and this is a statement of the obvious, resolving the issues discussed in this chapter will be extremely difficult. Many poor people and most people in the underclass may not have the education, work skills, work experience, and supports, such as day care, to be immediately employable, fully productive, and quickly earn enough to escape poverty in today's economy. Therefore, human investment programs, such as education, health and drug control, and employment and training programs for adults and young people are essential. But programs such as early childhood or pre-school education and programs targeted to primary schools have long-term benefits. Although some of these human investment programs are successful, most are costly, and they do not work miracles.[24]

Economic development strategies may be ineffective because most firms that locate in poverty areas probably will offer only low-paying, low-wage jobs with few of benefits and opportunities for advancement. Also, subsidies to these firms may substitute for private financing, with these firms undertaking activities they would undertake without any public subsidy. Finally, it may be impossible to find the few firms that may be able to offer well-paying, long-term employment.

Nonetheless, this report advocates that economic development and human development must work hand-in-hand to achieve the linked goals of growth and equity. This should be a priority agenda item for state policymakers. The limits of a bifurcated approach, that relies on macro-

---

[23]Federal policies may have helped create or sustain ghetto poverty areas. For example, there appears to be a positive correlation between the location of public housing units and new construction Section 8 units and areas of concentrated poverty; mass transit subsidies probably help higher income commuters more than central city poor people; and federal infrastructure programs and tax policies favor new construction over rehabilitation and reinforce the market forces that push the suburbanization of jobs and people. Also, some evidence suggests high welfare benefits may hold back recipients from moving to a close-by state with lower benefits but a stronger or more growing economy. (McGeary)

[24]One of the most significant disagreements in discussions of the underclass concerns appropriate policy responses. Some argue the most appropriate response is a series of a very expensive programs emphasizing job creation, job training, childcare, and related topics that are made available to all persons adversely affected by structural changes in the economy. Others argue that race-specific policies, with some programs targeted solely to ghetto communities, are absolutely necessary if the underclass or disadvantaged problem is to diminish. (See Book Review Forum)

economic strategies to maintain the health of the mainstream economy and income maintenance and social services to aid those unable to support themselves, are increasingly clear. A faltering economy blocks social progress, while economic progress is limited by our inability to bring new people and products into the marketplace. It is doubly unfortunate that economic development efforts are not benefiting the poor. We are missing opportunities for expanding economic access to the poor. Even more important, we are not diminishing the "isolation" of these communities and individuals.

3

Economic Opportunity And State Economic Development Activities

This chapter focuses on current state economic development practices that could be used in a state antipoverty strategy. The chapter first addresses "supply-side" activities that try to make production factors, especially labor, more attractive to businesses in ways that would also benefit poor people and distressed areas. The second part of the chapter describes "demand-side" activities that help create new economic investment which benefits poor people and distressed areas. Although the division of economic development activities into supply side and demand side is not perfect, it does help frame different state economic development initiatives.

Supply-side Activities

Supply-side activities help create a business climate attractive to firms that are free to locate, relocate, or expand through branch plants or other forms of firm growth. The most common supply-side activities involve tax policy — usually exemptions, abatements, or credits — and various forms of credit assistance — usually low-interest debt financing. Less frequently, supply-side activities include regulatory policies and labor policies, usually related to unemployment and disability insurance. Most supply-side activities are not targeted to distressed areas or disadvantaged people, but some activities have an antipoverty orientation, particularly labor-related activities involving poor people.

The first part of this chapter focuses on activities designed to improve the quality of labor, especially activities that increase the skills and workforce readiness of poor people. Next is a brief review of wage and tax subsidies, followed by a discussion of geographically-targeted business or employment subsidy programs, including enterprise zone programs.

Developing the Labor Force

Labor has not been an important component of state economic development activity. Much of the old "smokestack chasing" activity considered labor important only when its price was low, and the attractiveness of a state's business climate often was based on a non-union, low-wage, hard-work-ethic labor force.

As the nation's economy changed, economic development policy began focusing on the need for an educated work force. Yet, workforce skills and training still remain a minor part of economic development. Few parties are interested in acting alone to improve education and training of the workforce. Businesses are reluctant to spend substantial amounts of money for fear that once their employees are trained, they will work somewhere else. This is particularly true for the literacy training and remedial instruction needed by low-wage employees. Because turnover is high among low-wage employees, few firms offer them literacy training. (*SGPB Alert*)

Another reason workforce education and training is not more common is the "systematic undervaluation in this country of how much difference it can make when people are well educated and when their skills are continuously developed and challenged." (Dertouzos et al. p. 82) Consequently, management treats workers "as a cost to be controlled, not as an asset to be developed." (Dertouzos et al., p. 83) Although businesses spend about $30 billion yearly on formal training, about one-half of what government spends, only one-third of this amount is spent on non-college educated workers, and only 8 percent on front-line workers. (Stone) Less than 0.1 percent of the workforce receives basic skills training. (Citro) About one-half of 1 percent of employers contribute nearly the entire $30 billion; fewer than 200 companies spend more than 2 percent of their payroll on formal training. (Commission on the Skills of the American Workforce) In Japan, new auto-assembly workers receive about 300 hours of training in their first six months compared to about 50 for their U.S. counterparts. Small companies — who are most likely to employ the young and minorities, workers who may most need and use training — rarely provide formal training for their workers. (Stone)

Finally, many workers themselves do not want training. In a survey of two states, over one-third of the workers said they would attend classes only if their employers required them to do so. (Stone) The vice president for training and education at Motorola, a corporate leader in employee education, recalled that the first mistake the company made "was to assume that once we described the courses, the people who needed them most would sign up to take them. They didn't." (Wiggenhorn, pp. 75-76)

The excuses that workers give for not wanting or making use of training are no more reasonable than the excuses many businesses give for not providing more training. Together, business and worker disinterest about training "creates a contract of complacency between workers and employers. Slowly but surely, that contract is destroying the effectiveness of U.S. companies, the standard of living of U.S. workers, and U.S. competitiveness." (Stone, p. 54)

Vocational education and customized job training

Workforce skills and training development usually includes one of three sets of activities: vocational education, customized job training, or employment training. Vocational education has long suffered from a reputation for inflexibility, excessive bureaucracy, and irrelevance to current private sector needs. It also is stigmatized for what is widely seen as poorly-skilled clients. Although academically disadvantaged students take more vocational education courses in secondary schools than do academically advantaged students, "the most disadvantaged have less access to a wide range of intensive programs." (McDonnell and Grubb, p. 28) Some vocational education is postsecondary, usually provided through community colleges, but attrition rates are high in this kind of training.[25]

One study suggests specific skills "developed through technical schools are either not germane to business needs or are of questionable value to labor-force enhancement. In some cases, business leaders are answering their skill development needs through on the job training....Businesses frequently indicated that they had very specific skill needs that are generally being addressed through internal training programs as opposed to vocational/technical schools." (Glaser and Pisciotte, p. 172) Although vocational education has been supported by the federal government for over 70 years and enrolls about five million students annually, it "has a very disappointing performance and is not generally viewed as a viable preemployment training system. Employers do not see vocational high school programs as a prime source of skilled or even trainable workers. Indeed, often the fact of having participated in a vocational program stigmatizes workers in the eyes of employers." (Dertouzos et al., p. 85) An effort to upgrade the skills of metal workers in Massachusetts found "the technology that was revolutionizing the workplace was not being taught [in area vocational/technical schools]. The same technology that had bypassed the workers had also bypassed some of the teachers." (Forrant, p. 28)

---

[25] A survey of 1980 high school graduates showed that 42 percent of those who enrolled in community colleges left without earning a degree or a certificate. Only 9 percent of blacks, compared with 20 percent of whites and 21 percent of Hispanics, earned a degree or certificate after four years. (McDonnell and Grubb)

Customized training, which trains a labor force in specific skills for a specific firm, is a more common component of economic development than vocational education, although the same institutions often provide both services. A 1984 Congressional Budget Report indicated 39 states had customized training programs, and 33 states used these training programs as an incentive to attract businesses. States offered to screen and train workers. In about 75 percent of these programs, states paid all costs, although the payment of costs varied. For example, Pennsylvania's Customized Job Training Program pays all costs, rather than its normal 80 percent, for firms that locate in economically distressed communities or hire unemployed or disadvantaged people. States usually operate these programs through their vocational education or college system, sometimes through specially created institutes. (Eisinger) Most of these programs are small. For example, Massachusetts' Bay State Skills Corporation, one of the best known state training institutions, spent only $5.6 million in 1988. (McDonnell and Grubb) By 1990, states spent a total of only $1 billion dollars on customized training. (Commission on the Skills of the American Workforce)

Customized training has certain advantages over vocational education from an economic development perspective. It provides a direct link to employers, which helps place workers. When firms contribute equipment, as they often do, they can ensure that the training is up-to-date — in most states, the funds for equipment are minimal. (Grubb and Stern) Customized training also presents opportunities for combining general education and specific skills training, although much current skills training may be too short (one to four months) and too focused to do this. Finally, customized training may benefit small- and medium-sized firms that cannot afford to provide training themselves.

Questions exist as to whether customized training benefits disadvantaged persons and distressed communities. Little data is available on the extent to which customized training programs recruit and work with poor people. One recent, nonrandom study of community and junior college related customized training showed businesses chose participants about one-half the time, the training agencies about one-quarter, and both, one-quarter. (Grubb and Stern) About one-half the training took place at colleges; about one-quarter at the businesses, and about one-quarter, at both places. Colleges provided all the instructors in about 60 percent of the cases, and material and equipment in about one-half the cases. This study suggests there may not be a substantial opportunity to recruit poor people into customized training slots, and that access to colleges and businesses, through geographical proximity or good transportation, is important. Otherwise the involvement of poor people will be limited. Using customized training to create employment opportunities for poor people has potential, but it requires aggressive initiative by the customized training system.

No hard data is available because these programs generally are not evaluated on performance measures, but most state customized job training programs are seen as business recruitment and expansion endeavors, not as major initiatives to combat joblessness or upgrade the labor force. (McDonnell and Grubb) They usually are not linked to JTPA or vocational education, because state economic development practioners want to avoid red tape and overcome negative images of the traditional government-sponsored training programs. As one state government representative said, "Most firms have not dealt with state government before. Employers associate JTPA with welfare and unemployment, and think that the unemployed are lazy." (McDonnell and Grubb, p. 46)

A few states do link customized job training to disadvantaged persons or distressed communities. Illinois' Prairie State 2000 Authority is one example. Its Individual Training Assistance Program provides educational and vocational training vouchers to unemployed persons and employed workers who need additional skills for continued employment. Priority is given to unemployed persons. To receive a voucher, an applicant must be enrolled or must intend to enroll in a certified training program, must have vocational goals directed toward acquiring marketable skills, must meet certain unemployment insurance-related criteria, and must not receive JTPA training while receiving voucher assistance. A variety of organizations can operate the training program: a public school, a community college, private or public nonprofit organizations, or vocational or technical schools. The key criteria for certification as a training program is to provide training in semi-technical or technical fields that reflect current labor market need and to develop marketable skills. No more than 50 percent of the training can be basic education. Unemployed recipients can use their vouchers over 24 months to cover training expenses up to $2,000, including tuition, fees, and supplies. A recipient who does not complete the training, must reimburse the authority, unless the authority finds the recipient did not complete the training for good cause.

Another issue is the extent to which customized training simply substitutes for what a business would otherwise do. Because demand for non-managerial and nonprofessional employees is relatively insensitive to wages, businesses that frequently use customized training "may be those for which training is least effective as a way of increasing employment, and which increase employment only by reducing wages substantially." (Grubb and Stern, p. 36)

Customized job training is ineffectively and infrequently used with small businesses. In the study of college-related training referred to above, about two-thirds of the clients of customized training were single firms, and two-thirds of these were national or international companies and only one-third were local or regional. In the South, most customized training programs train workers for entry-level jobs in manufacturing firms the states recruited; few serve small businesses. (SGPB Foresight) Yet, the small firms have neither the incentive nor the resources to train their workers. Only Illinois, through its Employment Training Assistance program, provides training to small firms that have few resources for training. (McDonnell and Grubb)

Customized training is likely to have more positive effects on employment and earnings than conventional vocational education programs, and may be more valuable from an economic development perspective. But if all costs are subsidized, public cost may outweigh public gain. The most potential for customized and related training may be with small businesses which are important jobs generators. Because they attract entry-level workers and are training grounds for larger firms, they have the greatest training needs. They also are least able to meet these needs. State training may be particularly valuable for small firms that have not adopted the best or most effective technologies because they cannot afford limited qualified labor. Obtaining additional skilled workers through training could lead to overall increases in employment. (Grubb and Stern) Apparently there has been a limited ability to target vocational or customized job training this way.

Illinois' Prairie State 2000 Authority illustrates one option. It's Employer Training Assistance Program provides grants or loans to employers who are increasing the number of jobs by (1) expanding their business, (2) locating a new business, (3) introducing more efficient technology that will result in greater output per employee, (4) expanding into new markets, or (5) expanding exports from the state. Also, a firm is also eligible if the employees who will receive the training are threatened with layoff unless the training is made available. A firm can use the loan or grant to pay for training expenses, including salaries and benefits of training staff, contractual services, overhead, materials and supplies, equipment, and travel. Up to 25 percent of the cost of training an individual who is continuously employed full-time for one year can be credited toward partial repayment of the loan. Loan terms and amounts are flexible. Grants can pay for up to 50 percent of the training costs, except the authority holds a minimum of 50 percent of the grant until the trainee has been employed for 90 days after completion of the training. The trainee is limited to 18 months of training, and the training program must be completed within 24 months.

JTPA

From the perspective of assistance to poor persons, most efforts at developing the work force have focused on short-term job training, mostly through JTPA and its predecessor or through the work programs related to welfare programs. The federal government spends about $6 billion annually on 13 different employment and training programs, with most of this money spent on the JTPA program. JTPA was specifically designed to make job training for the disadvantaged more responsive to the needs of the private labor market by requiring heavy private sector participation, performance standard accountability, and short-term training leading to job placement.

JTPA offers several incentives to business, including recruitment, testing, selection, customized job training, and subsidized placements for up to six months. JTPA funds are distributed to states largely through a formula based on population and unemployment rates and are channeled through two separate and programmatically distinct components — Title IIA, providing employment and training services for those certified as economically disadvantaged, and Title III, aimed at dislocated workers. The great majority of federal funding passes through the state to local Service Delivery Areas (SDAs). This money is administered by Private Industry Councils (PICs) which are composed of community leaders with particular emphasis on the private sector. The local nature of JTPA gives the PICs authority in choosing whom to serve and how, subject only to the restrictions of performance standards and the local economy. In some communities, JTPA is heavily on-the-job training-oriented (OJT), while in others the emphasis is on classroom training. In some cases, community colleges provide much of the training, while in other community-based organizations provide much of the training.

Although Title IIA programs have met individual placement and cost goals, they have been less effective in linking economic development with job training for the disadvantaged. Distribution of the bulk of funds by formula to local SDAs has limited flexibility and impaired statewide integrated planning. Also, the emphasis on performance standards has led SDAs to focus primarily on individual placements rather than on long-term economic growth. States rarely impose standards on SDAs that go beyond federally-mandated requirements and usually do not collect data on local programs. (McDonnell and Grubb)

JTPA IIA programs also have been ineffective in dealing with problems of the more disadvantaged portions of the population — those who read below the eighth-grade level and those without recent work experience. Although JTPA programs serve people without recent work experience, people on welfare, blacks and Hispanics, and people with little schooling, pressures to achieve high placement rates have led individual SDAs to serve the most job-ready among the disadvantaged, ignoring the needs of the least employable.

In addition to setting relatively high academic requirements for entry, JTPA programs may have discouraged the disadvantaged by failing to provide remedial education, support services, or stipends for training and work experience. One study concludes that more than one-fourth of the less job ready "received only job search assistance, and 88 percent of the high school dropouts [in the sample] received no remedial education." (McDonnell and Grubb, p. 36) A preliminary investigation by the General Accounting Office found white participants were more likely to receive classroom and OJT, and black participants were more likely to receive only job search assistance. Women received more classroom training than black men, but much of this training was for lower-wage occupations. (Swoboda) JTPA's OJT activities also have been criticized for helping to train low-wage employees for firms that would have provided informal training without JTPA funds. In program year 1987 (July 1987 through June 1988) the employment rate for adult "terminees" after 13 weeks was 66 percent and for welfare terminees, 57 percent. The average weekly earnings of adult terminees was 53 percent of the average weekly wage in all industries. (Redman)

JTPA programs have been changing. Declining unemployment rates and decreased funding have forced JTPA programs to find and train a more disadvantaged population. At the same time, new state and federal initiatives in education and welfare reform have made employment a priority, encouraging closer ties between these institutions. Finally, the pressure to find and train new workers has led some states to make affirmative efforts that use a variety of funding mechanisms to tie the systems together. For example, Pennsylvania's JTPA program gives priority to persons with multiple barriers to employment, and California uses a portion of its JTPA funds for its welfare reform program.

Welfare to work: what worked?

Rigorous evaluations of welfare-related training programs indicate the extent to which and why these programs have been successful. The Manpower Demonstration Research Corporation (MDRC) evaluated several state welfare employment programs during the 1980s, mainly job search assistance and work experience programs that exempted mothers with children under six years-old. [26] MDRC found these programs to be marginally successful. One year or more after participation, the employment rate among participants was 3 to 8 percentage points higher than nonparticipants. One year after entering the program, the average earnings of participants was 10 to 25 percent higher than the earnings of nonparticipants. Also, AFDC benefit payments often dropped due to increased earnings. The earnings increases occurred primarily because more participants than nonparticipants worked and only secondarily because working participants obtained better paying jobs or jobs with longer hours than nonparticipants. Other research has produced similar findings. (Porter)

These programs are inexpensive, ranging from $100 to $1,000 per person served, and more than pay for themselves. They also show that many welfare recipients are eager to take jobs that leave them little better off. (Passell, 1991 a; Rich, 1991 b) But employment and earnings gains are likely not to materialize in rural communities with very high unemployment. (Gueron)

Another facet of the evaluations found welfare employment programs have the least impact on the most job-ready because the most job-ready participants find employment on their own, even without the employment programs. As a result, there is little net increase in earnings or employment due to the training programs. [27]

---

[26]In the 1980s, most state employment-related welfare programs provided less intensive services, such as job search and limited support services, and tended to exclude from participation recipients with the most severe barriers to employment. A GAO study found that in 1985, 50 percent of the state programs provided job search assistance, 3 percent provided remedial or basic education, 2 percent provided vocational skills training, and less than 5 percent provided other education or training assistance. A 1986 Urban Institute study found all states offered job search only, 13 states offered job search plus one other activity; only 11 states offered a full array of services. (Porter)

[27]This conclusion is drawn from MDRC evaluations that divided participants into three groups based on job readiness. The most job ready were persons who were first-time AFDC applicants. Persons who had received AFDC payments in the past were considered moderately job ready, while persons who currently were receiving AFDC payments were

Although low-cost or low-level service programs are not very success-ful for people who have many barriers to employment, several intensive welfare employment programs designed for the least employable have been relatively successful. The effects of intensive training and education also may become more apparent and increase over time. (Porter) A GAO study of JTPA suggests that intensive skill training was effective for less job-ready participants. Studies of Massachusetts' Employment and Train-ing Choices program and several other AFDC employment programs all conclude that more intensive services have a greater effect on the less job ready than do less intensive services such as job search assistance.[28] (Porter)

Although neither the largest nor most comprehensive of welfare programs, Massachusetts's employment and training effort (ET Choices), is clearly a model. Welfare recipients are provided an extensive array of services designed to promote employability, including basic skills training, access to higher education, advanced skills training, and day care and other support services. Nearly 70 percent of those on welfare in fiscal year 1987 in the state attended an ET orientation session, and 50 percent par-ticipated in at least one component. ET participants were similar in age, sex, race, average monthly grant, age of youngest child, and family size to the total adult welfare population in the state. (Nightingale et al.)

In a state with rapid job growth and labor shortages, ET had placed over 42,000 AFDC recipients and applicants in jobs as of January 1988 and saved the state an estimated $130 million in welfare payments in 1987.

---

considered least job ready. Those in the middle group had the largest earnings, with the positive results continuing to the end of the three-year evaluation, but there were no significant reductions in AFDC payments. Persons in the least job-ready group had fewer increases in earnings, possibly due to the low-cost services being provided. (Porter)

[28]Participants in the "Supported Work" program of the late 1970s were more likely to work, earn higher hourly wages, and experience large reductions in their AFDC payments and food stamp benefits compared to non-participants. Supported Work provided a sup-portive work environment and gradually increasing job responsibilities to persons who had received AFDC payments for at least three years and had little or no recent job experience. The TOPS (Training Opportuniities in the Private Sector) program in Maine was also successful. TOPS included a sequence of pre-vocational training, work experience, and then on the job training during which time employers received a subsidy for part of the wages. The AFDC Homemaker-Home Health Aide Demonstration was also successful. This program contained four to eight weeks of training in homemaking and health services skills followed by a year of subsidized employment. The Baltimore Options Program also appears successful. Options offers basic literacy training, high school equivalency preparation, job skills training, work experience, and job search assistance.

Although only established in 1985, ET choices has reduced welfare rolls by 5 percent, the average length of stay on AFDC by 29 percent, and the average monthly welfare grant by 8 percent. The employment rate for ET participants was about 8 percent higher than the comparison group, and earnings were 32 percent higher. The median hourly wage was $5 ($10,900 annualized at a 40-hour work week) $5, compared to the average annual welfare grant of $6,500. About 72 percent of the job finders were still employed 12 to 16 months after leaving ET to take a job (38 percent in the same job, 34 percent in a different job). About 48 percent of the jobs provided health coverage.

The Urban Institute's evaluation of ET's components are consistent with earlier evaluations of work-welfare programs. The most intense training-related activities, which included supported work experience and occupational training, had strong positive impacts on AFDC duration, monthly grant, employment, and earnings. (Nightengale et al.) The impact of job search was greater in ET than in other programs, probably because unlike other programs, ET used job search selectively. Nonetheless, the impact of job search appeared to be short-term. While participation in basic and secondary education tends to extend the length of time on welfare, remedial education tends to result in a longer duration of employment.

In programs with voluntary participation, selling the program is important. But voluntary programs can be successful, as illustrated by Massachusetts' ET program, where the percentage of AFDC recipients participating in ET was about the same as mandatory programs in Michigan and Texas, although ET had more resources. Voluntary programs do not necessarily involve mostly the job ready. Some evidence suggests voluntary programs may be more effective than mandatory programs, and voluntary programs may sustain good management better than mandatory programs. Despite high initial costs, the structured, transitional, paid work experience of the 15 sites participating in the National Supported Work Demonstration showed positive long-term effects for very disadvantaged welfare recipients that were cost-effective to taxpayers. (Gueron)

The evaluations of employment programs for AFDC fathers is very mixed. There is no evidence that either low-level or high-level services have increased their employment or earnings, but this issue has been investigated less than with AFDC mothers. Generally, AFDC fathers are among the most job-ready AFDC recipients. Some suggest that state policy should give low priority to using scarce resources on AFDC fathers, but concentrate these resources on high-need AFDC mothers. (Porter)

Gueron and Pauley summarize a decade of MDRC welfare to work evaluations by saying these programs increased the earnings of poor families and saved money, but did not eliminate welfare or poverty. Within a given budget, welfare to work programs face a trade-off. "Providing mandatory job search to large numbers of people may maximize welfare savings and job-holdings, but by itself usually will not get people better-paying jobs or benefit the more disadvantaged. Providing mainly higher-cost, more intensive services to a selected population can get people jobs with somewhat greater earnings, but will produce lower welfare savings per dollar invested." (Gueron and Pauley, p. 12)

Two other conclusions also should be noted. One, the earnings gains, which ranged from $268 to 658 annually for low-cost, broad-coverage programs and $591 to $1,124 annually for higher-cost, targeted programs, were sustained for at least three years after program enrollment. Two, for nearly all the low-cost, broad-coverage programs, the "payback" period to the public (i.e., savings in transfer payouts and increased taxes that offset the cost of the welfare to work programs) was rapid, two to five years. (Gueron and Pauley)

JOBS

The Family Support Act has made welfare programs a potential major resource for economic opportunity. The key feature of the FSA was the creation of the Jobs Opportunities and Basic Skills Training (JOBS) program. Each state must establish a JOBS program that consists of education, job training, and job readiness activities, including at least two of the four following activities: job search, work experience, grant diversion, or on-the-job training. The FSA also requires states to have a two-parent AFDC program, and effective in 1994, requires a parent in each AFDC-UP (unemployed parent) to participate at least 16 hours per week in a work activity. It increases Medicaid coverage; strengthens child support payments; and increases or expands the level of income or services to AFDC recipients, among other changes.

The FSA was a compromise between liberal and conservative perspectives on welfare reform. Partly because of this, opinions about the legislation differ. Some believe the legislation made radical revisions in welfare policy, while others think the revisions were modest. Most of the skepticism focuses on the expectation the requirements for expanded coverage and benefits are routine changes the welfare bureaucracy can and will easily make, while the requirements for training are not only relatively modest but are much more difficult to implement. For example, about one-half the welfare caseload is exempt from JOBS; the required

1995 participation rate is only 20 percent; work is not required; prior training and work experience with the JOBS target population shows limited success in generating participation; and there is some question about how or whether sanctions, either against nonparticipants or states, will work. The challenge from this perspective, and a challenge many feel will not be met, is both one of implementing an effective training - support service - employment program and of ensuring an effective employment demand for the participants of the training.[29]

FSA also did not adequately address the problems of fathers of children receiving public assistance. While the FSA places mandates on and provides resources to mothers, it does not require or provide for the employment, education, or skills upgrading of fathers. As noted earlier, employment has increased for black women, but black men are increasingly detached from the labor force. While the median earnings of white and black females were equal by the mid-1970s, the median earnings of employed black males was only 65 percent of that of white males, and virtually no improvement has occurred since. "In the early 1970s, the black male employment-to-population ratio exceeded the black female employment-to-population by 54 percent. By 1989 the former exceeded the latter by just over 20 percent." (Mincy and Wiener, p. 11)

AFDC recipients who are not exempt[30] must participate in JOBS at a rate of 7 percent of the nonexempt caseload in 1990, gradually increasing to 20 percent of the caseload in 1995. JOBS funds, which are authorized to increase from $600 million in 1990 to $1.3 billion by 1995, must be targeted to families that are most likely to have long stays on welfare: custodial parents under 24 years of age with no high school diploma and who are not enrolled in a high school preparatory course or out of work

---

[29]Welfare reform always has to hurdle a dilemma: welfare discourages work since more work means less assistance, and increasing assistance to fight poverty further decreases work incentive. Liberals tend to emphasize the need to reduce poverty over reducing dependence, while conservatives tend to emphasize reducing dependence over reducing poverty. Liberals tend to believe that most welfare recipients want to work, but do not have the education and skills for self-sufficiency employment. Conservatives believe that welfare recipients are unwilling to work and have unrealistic expectations about their job prospects. (Gueron)

[30]Those who are exempt include ill or incapacitated persons, persons needed in the home to care for a household member, parents caring for a young child, persons working 30 or more hours per week, children under the age of 16 or attending school, women in at least the second trimester of pregnancy, and persons residing in an area where the program is not available.

for the last year; adults in families receiving AFDC in 36 of the prior 60 months; and adult recipients whose youngest child is within 2 years of ineligibility. At least 55 percent of funds must be spent on these three groups or the federal match is reduced.

States must make an initial assessment of each client, develop an employability plan, inform recipients of grounds for exemption, and give people a chance to volunteer for the program. Mutual duties and obligations may be contracted for, and case management must be assigned. Sanctions must be applied to those recipients who without good cause fail to participate in JOBS. Welfare recipients who are participating in JOBS are guaranteed the provision of child care and reimbursement for work-related expenses, such as transportation. Medicaid coverage is extended for one year to families who leave welfare because of work. By October 1, 1992, states must have programs available in each jurisdiction of state.

JOBS emphasizes education much more than the work-welfare programs of the 1980s. Early JOBS evidence indicates states are emphasizing intense education and training, including postsecondary education, and are moving away from a focus on job search and community work experience. In March 1991, 11 percent of welfare families were participating in the JOBS program. Of these, 33 percent were enrolled in a basic education course, 11 percent were enrolled in a post-secondary school, 16 percent were learning a technical skill, 15 percent were in miscellaneous school programs, 21 percent were in programs to help them quickly find work, and only 4 percent actually had jobs. (DeParle, 1991 c) Fewer than one-half the states are using work supplementation programs, in part because of statutory constraints on the use funds for this purpose.

According to one analyst, the JOBS program faces three major hurdles. (Sanger) First, it is very expensive because it targets the very disadvantaged who need extensive assistance. Massachusetts' ET program cost about $80 million in fiscal year 1988, with nearly 80 percent paid by the state. Intensive assistance costs at least $2,000 to $4,000 per participant. A question, then, is whether states and the federal government will continue to provide this level of resources. Two relatively successful intensive demonstration programs, the AFDC Homemaker-Home Health program and the National Supported Work program, had estimated net costs (1985 dollars) of $6,000 to $12,500. (Gueron and Pauley)

A second hurdle is the cost of support services, especially child care. In addition to the cost of administration and development, successful work-welfare efforts have required states to spend substantial additional money to pay for added services. Providing transitional benefits is important to sustaining employment. The Urban Institute study of ET suggests health insurance coverage was associated with job retention, although health insurance may also be associated with good jobs. Child care — its affordability, availability, quality, and administration — is perhaps the biggest challenge facing states in the early years of the JOBS program. Rural areas, especially, have a shortage of child care.

The cost of funding adequate day care can be enormous. Some states are allocating more than $50 million to supplement available federal day care money. In fiscal year 1987, ET cost an average of $1,433 per participant. This includes only direct costs, and does not include the costs borne by other programs, such as JTPA and student financial assistance. Nearly half was for child care, although only 14 percent of the participants and 28 percent of the job holders used ET's child care vouchers.

Preschool GAINS (California's welfare demonstration program) participants used child care resources four times as much as those nonparticipants with school-age children. The child care experience in work-welfare programs is new because many pre-FSA employment training programs screened out those who needed child care. (Porter) Even if adequate funds were provided for day care, questions arise over whether an adequate number of day care slots can be provided. Facility development and rehabilitation is expensive, and affordable locations are infrequent. Adequate care can also be held back by the lack of trained workers.

Yet, as was the case in Massachusetts' ET program and California's GAIN program, early evidence indicates transitional child care is being underutilized, perhaps because of a heavy reliance on unsubsidized informal child care.[31] Finally, states are flagging as an administrative problem the integration of as many as 14 funding resources for child care. (American Public Welfare Association)

---

[31]The extent to which unaffordable or unavailable child care prevents employment is unclear. One study suggests that young women do lose employment because they cannot find satisfactory child care, and this seems particularly true for women in low-income families (less than $15,000 in 1988) who have a child aged 1 year or younger. (Venum and Gleason) Another study suggests about 1.1 million mothers aged 21 to 29 were out of the labor force in 1986 because of child care problems. These mothers accounted for 14 percent of all mothers in the 21 to 29 age group and for 23 percent of all mothers who were out of the labor force that year. This study suggests that lower income mothers who are single parents and who have no high school degree are most vulnerable to being out of the labor force because of lack of child care. To an extent this is due to the relative cost of child care, which takes 26 percent of a poor mother's weekly income compared to 8 percent for a non-poor mother. However, only a minority of poor mothers pay for child care. This study also suggests that mothers with children ages 1 to 5 and mothers with three or more children are most

The third hurdle the JOBS program faces is administrative. "The delivery of employment-related services to welfare recipients is one of the most complex tasks faced by public administrators," one practitioner said. "It requires coordination and integration of education, training, job search and job placement, support services, and financial assistance ... delivered by different agencies each with their own goals, expertise, culture, procedures, funding streams, and personnel systems... service quality must be high, client flow among services must be efficient, and payments and paperwork tracking of clients and reimbursements of them must be timely." (Sanger, pp. 673-674) The question is whether the states have the managerial and budgetary resources to respond to this challenge.

JOBS is a mandatory program, phased in over time. Evaluations of seven mandatory state welfare-to-work programs suggest a participation rate of 50 to 60 percent is probably the maximum possible. (Gueron). Although mandatory programs can make people participate, they cannot make people take jobs. Pennsylvania's demonstration program involved only 5 percent of the mandatory population. About 30 percent of the welfare population participated in California's GAIN program; but of 100 typical registrants, 66 did not even attend an orientation session, and only 11 percent received education or training. Only 30 percent of those involved in Florida's Project Independence received training. Sanctions, such as temporarily stopping or reducing welfare payments, or paying a third-party all or part of a welfare grant, were rarely invoked. In 1987 California sanctioned less than 4 percent of GAIN participants, while Texas sanctioned less than 2 percent and Michigan less than 6 percent. (McDonnell and Grubb)

Not only do total costs, which can range from $2,500 to $10,000 per participant, and participation rates challenge JOBS, but also the cost of living. Because of high housing costs and a shortage of subsidized day care, jobs may have to pay at least $10 per hour to prevent participants from falling back onto welfare. About 50,000 GAIN participants had jobs as of June 1989, but only 14,000 were earning enough money to move off welfare completely. (McDonnell and Grubb) Low-paying jobs do not necessarily lead to higher-paying employment for welfare recipients. Fewer than

---

likely to be out of the labor force than mothers with children one year or less in age or with one or two children. For low-income mothers in poor neighborhoods, the most unmet need for child care for children under 3 years of age. (Catten) Security and safety fears may heighten a reluctance to seek widely child care providers in these neighborhoods.

one-third of the welfare recipients who were employed at a wage of $5.50 per hour or less in 1984 went on to a higher-paying job; nearly one-half the recipients who took low-wage jobs became unemployed or returned to AFDC when the job ended. (Porter)

Near the end of 1991 early evidence reflected some of the difficulties JOBS was confronting. In FY 1991 more than one-third of the federal job funds available to states were unused because states were unable to match the full amount available. Thirty-nine states said JOBS was difficult to operate in rural areas because of insufficient transportation and 36 states indicated shortages in infant care made serving teen parents difficult. (Rich, 1991 c)

By 1991 it also was clear that most JOBS activities could not be appropriately linked back to the evaluations of earlier welfare to work programs. None of the MDRC studies examined the effectiveness of education or classroom training of the kind occurring in JOBS. Also, none of the studies tested the impact of continued childcare and Medicaid services. None of the programs studied would have met the participation standards required of the JOBS program in 1995. The costs of support programs may reduce the total savings that otherwise occurred when people took low-wage jobs through the demonstration programs. (In FY 1991, about $356 million of federal monies was being spent for childcare and related services.) Little of the research on prior programs addressed whether intensive services can be more successful with long-term welfare recipients than lower-cost services, particularly in providing earnings gains. As mentioned earlier, the research of AFDC-UP eligibles is very limited. Finally, past studies provide very little guidance on the relative effectiveness or appropriateness of an up-front job search approach to screening versus the front-end assessment approach being used in JOBS or on the various approaches to care management. (Gueron and Pauley)

The education-skills training-job placement-earnings link

Linking basic education with specific occupational skills training may be more effective for AFDC recipients than sequential or unlinked basic education and skills training, and employment training programs that begin with and stress tangible jobs skills may be more successful than those that begin with and stress basic education.

The Center for Employment Training (CET) in San Jose, California, focuses on skills training tied to specific jobs in the local job market. The training is available to all participants, with basic education offered within the context of job training. It includes hands-on skills training complemented by counseling, child care, and other support services. One year after entering the program, 46 percent of the welfare mothers were employed, compared to 36 percent of the welfare mothers in the control group. Their average monthly pay was also much higher than the control group's, $416 compared to $283. These differences were statistically significant. Although not significant, the average monthly public assistance income was $291, compared to $306 for the control group. The average cost per person for the program in 1985-1986 was $3,600. (Burghardt and Gordon)

The CET program was one of four community-based employment training programs to help low-income single mothers move from welfare to work. All were part of a well-researched program funded by the Rockefeller Foundation. Each of the four programs (the other three were in Atlanta, Washington, D.C., and Providence) had control and treatment groups, and each program provided a comprehensive array of services, generally outreach and recruiting, assessment, remediation of basic reading, math, and communication skills, job-skill training, job-search and job placement, child-care assistance, and counseling. Each program served low-income minority, single mothers who had low levels of education, a lack of work experience, the need for care for young children, few family resources, and high dependence on public assistance.

Of the four programs, CET was the only one that integrated basic education with job skill training. Reading and math skills were taught concurrently with job skill training, as they pertained to the job skills being learned. The other three programs used the traditional approach placing women in remedial education classes before job skill training. Researchers concluded CET was more effective than the other three programs when program effects were measured 12 months after participants started in the program, and that these differences may continue to hold 30 months after the start of training. (Burghardt and Gordon)

According to the research, several other aspects of CET's program may have contributed to its success. The CET training simulated workplace conditions, used instructors with recent experience in industry, phased skill offerings in and out in response to demand, and used an open-entry and open-exit, self-paced, competency-based training — all of which quickly moved applicants into training, avoided unsettling testing, and permitted individual attention to participants. CET relied heavily on an industrial advisory board that kept the program informed on what skills were needed and how to teach them, and served as an informal placement network. CET also had a strong counseling and placement service. (De-Parle) CET provided more on-site services than the other programs, especially day care. The other three organizations acted more like brokers, helping participants access services elsewhere. Finally, CET was a large organization dedicated to employment training, and it ran the program as an integral part of its overall operations. In the other programs, the sponsoring organizations were smaller, had no single dedication to employment training, or operated the program as an adjunct to their major operations.

The study of the four programs drew the following conclusions. First, sustained and intense outreach and recruitment are important; participants did not come forward on their own. Second, the assessment process should be rapid, convenient, and free of intimidating hassles. Third, basic education should be provided with job-specific skill training and conducted within the skill training as much as possible. Fourth, job training should be tailored to the abilities and interests of the participants, with open entry and exit, a self-paced process, competency-based curriculum (rather than academic style testing), and training for a variety, or at least a cluster, of occupations. Fifth, the job training should not only help participants, but also should provide a quality employee to employers through continuously close linkage to the local labor market, industry-experienced instructors, only job-ready participants going on job interviews, active marketing to employers, and follow-up assistance after placement. Sixth, child care should be provided or arranged, and not just referred, and child care programs should be comprehensive and flexible. Finally, other services must be provided in a supportive fashion, meaning locating services in one place, having instructors who can function as counselors, and having specialized counseling resources available.

As mentioned earlier, the average cost per participant in the CET program was $3,600, but this includes the 20 percent of participants who received only assessment and counseling. Considering the cost from recruitment to job placement and adjusting for inflation produces a 1991-1992 cost estimate of about $5,400. The allocation of cost among major activities in CET's program suggests a framework for looking at other programs. CET spent a greater percentage, 30 percent, of total costs on education and training than each of the other three programs. CET also spent much less on administrative and indirect costs than the other three programs, 18 percent compared to a range of 36 to 45 percent. CET's administrative costs were low because its large size gave it economies of scale, and it fully integrated the program into its ongoing operations. Finally, CET's share of costs for support services, 25 percent, and child care, 27 percent, were nearly as large as the share of costs for education and training.[32]

On-the-job training: a closing comment

Specific skills may be the primary labor concern of the business community, but businesses have "specific work-skill needs that are not presently being addressed. Consequently, many businesses have developed internal training programs to meet their labor skill needs....The apparent attraction of OJT programming is that it addresses specific employment needs." (Glaser and Pisciotte, p. 173) The Aetna Life Insurance Company, for example, attempts to fill 6 percent of its entry level positions from Hartford's inner city through a four-month training program. The first two months are on such basics as how to write a sentence, followed by two months of specific job training. The training salary was $13,500 in 1989, with increases to $14,500 to $16,000 upon completion of the training. Aetna's cost is $7,000 to $10,000 per employee. (Bennett)

Since 1983, the Federal Reserve Bank of Boston has offered training to about 200 inner city employees. The training encompasses basic education, clerical training, and supervised work experience and counseling prior to placement in clerical work. About one-third of the trainees have been unmarried women with children; about two-thirds of the trainees have completed the program. Graduates stay longer than other entry-level employees, and their earnings keep pace with their peers at least for five years following training. The success of the program is due to the combining of specific skills and general education, supervised work experience and counseling, a self-paced instructional program, ongoing connections with community agencies to recruit applicants, and good communications with supervisors to develop job placements. The per person cost of the training in 1987 was about $7,000. An assessment of the program concludes that unmarried women with children need child care and high school dropouts require special services. (Hargroves)

OJT appears to be related to wage levels, especially with women and blacks. One of the reasons women and black men have lower earnings than white men even when educational levels are similar is that "blacks and women were seldom in jobs in which they were currently receiving train-

---

[32]Early MDRC evaluations of the Minority Female Single Parent Demonstration suggest the superior performance of one site may be due to job skills training being integrated with remedial education and open to all regardless of educational skills and strong links to employers. (Gueron and Pauley)

ing." (Klein and Rones, p. 8) Based on data from 1969 to 1980, training young workers significantly increases their wages, by about 10 percent in the first year after training, but by about 17 percent if training is provided by the business. Research on later years showed a 12 percent increase in earnings from company training. (Hargroves)

The importance and effectiveness of on-the-job training has also been noted in the JTPA program. The U.S. Department of Labor reports that in 1988 83 percent of OJT participants in Title II-A entered employment compared to 56 percent for classroom training, 78 percent for job search assistance, and 53 percent for work experience. The average hourly wage on termination was $5.09 compared to $5.33 for classroom training, $4.99 for job search assistance and $4.30 for work experience. (Alegria)

OJT also can reach out to high-need populations. In Georgia's JTPA OJT component in 1988-1989, 25 percent of OJT enrollees were black, compared to 7 percent of labor force; 17.7 percent were handicapped, compared to 6.6 percent of the labor force; 52 percent were dropouts, compared to 27 percent of those registered with the Georgia Department of Labor; and 40.9 percent were not in labor force at all. (Dellinger)

The model of linking basic education with specific skillstraining in a employment context is similar to the education, training, and employment pattern in Japan and West Germany, which rely on on-the-job training to develop both general and specialized skills. In contrast, in this country formal educational institutions provide most of the specialized work skills and on-the-job training provides little more than cursory task-related instruction. The MIT report mentioned earlier recommends the expansion of the employment-based approach in this country because it develops skills that are broader and more relevant to the present and future needs of firms, leads to more effective organizational arrangements and processes within firms, and effectively retrains the workforce. (Dertouzos et al.) Japan and West Germany do not have a high employee turnover, one of the fears businesses in this country have about providing company training. In fact, there is evidence that company training, both general but more particularly specific, lowers turnover rates. (Hargroves)

Accessing Company Employment

One way to provide jobs for disadvantaged persons is to make them more attractive to employers through remedial education, vocational education, or job training. Another approach is to provide incentives for firms to hire the disadvantaged. Negotiating with firms to hire disadvantaged persons on a project-by-project basis when these firms are receiving public subsidies is one example of this approach. Another example is subsidizing firms to hire the disadvantaged through tax incentives or wage subsidies.

Hiring agreements

Hiring agreements are arrangements in which government or other interested parties reserve a certain percentage of employment in an economic development project for targeted populations. This targeting has included women, minorities, and residents of certain geographical areas. When properly designed and managed, hiring agreements can provide employment to low income individuals without imposing undue burdens on business.

Perhaps one of the bestknown hiring techniques is "first source hiring," which helps channel jobs to low-income people. The concept has several variations, but it basically consists of requiring firms receive public contracts or subsidies (such as industrial revenue bonds, CDBG-supported development projects, or tax increment financing) to hire or interview, more low-income workers. A low-income labor pool becomes the firm's "first source" for new hires.

The local governmental employment and training agency usually negotiates a contract with a firm, specifying the number and types of positions covered by the first source agreement. The employer submits written job descriptions for these positions, listing, minimum qualifications, wage rates, hours, and duration of employment. The employment and training agency usually recruits candidates for these positions. The employer retains the final hiring decision, but must attempt to fill these positions from the candidates referred by the employment and training agency. For example, through Pennsylvania's Contractor Partnership, each company that receives a contract from the Department of Public Welfare informs the department how many new jobs or vacancies will be created, and must make a good faith effort to fill 25 percent of the new jobs with qualified welfare clients participating in various welfare to work programs. Although local governments usually use first source agreements on "bricks and mortar" development projects, the idea can be adopted by other units of government for any type of development with a public subsidy.

Hiring arrangements have also been worked out between community organizations representing the disadvantaged and developers or employers, who see such cooperation as being in their mutual interest. Employers and developers need labor and community organizations need jobs. Many community organizations operate job banks, job placement services, or job training programs, so they are well-connected to the pool of workers, and are adept at screening out unsuitable employees. This occurs most frequently around a commercial development project (such as a neighborhood shopping center) or a major expansion of a hospital, educational institution, or other facility. Community organizations look for jobs on the construction crews and permanent jobs with the retail or service firms.

Tax incentives and wage subsidies

Tax incentives can be used to induce firms to hire disadvantaged workers. This incentive can take the form of either a tax concession or a direct wage subsidy. The economic assumption is that if there is an inadequate demand for labor at certain wages, by reducing the cost of labor through a subsidy, employers will hire more workers. A federal example is the Targeted Jobs Tax Credit (TJTC), which gives employers a tax credit of up to $2,400 for hiring welfare recipients, disadvantaged youth, Vietnam veterans, ex-convicts, the handicapped, and the elderly.

New York's Training and Employment Assistance Program (TEAP) diverts welfare payments to provide wage subsidies to businesses. (Corporation for Enterprise Development) TEAP places AFDC and New York's Home Relief recipients into private, entry-level jobs. The employer pays participants prevailing wages for up to six months, and receives a wage subsidy of $250 per month for AFDC recipients and up to the whole grant for Home Relief recipients. Payments are made from the recipient's welfare grant, usually supplemented by TJTC. Participants remain eligible for Medicaid during the subsidy period. TEAP uses written agreements between employers and local social service districts specifying the type of work, length of training contract, and hourly wage. Employers are not obligated to retain the recipient after the contractual trial period is over, but most do.

Between November 1981 and March 1987, TEAP enrolled 11,649 welfare recipients, 49 percent of whom were retained as regular employees in occupations ranging from clerical and sales to managerial and paraprofessional duties. Hourly wages ranged from $3.35 to $7.40, averaging $4.00. Aside from a $300,000 administrative appropriation in its first year, TEAP received no state funds beyond the diverted welfare grants, and is thus virtually cost-free.

TEAP is a job placement program that helps state and federal welfare recipients gain access to decent low- and medium-wage jobs, while offering firms a screened, subsidized workforce they can test with no strings attached before offering permanent employment. The intent of programs like TEAP is not to guarantee jobs but to guarantee equal access to opportunity for people often excluded from the mainstream labor market. A 1984 comparison of 449 TEAP clients to employable Home Relief recipients in non-TEAP districts during a 12-month period found that more than one-half the TEAP clients transferred to unsubsidized jobs following their TEAP contracts. (Corporation for Enterprise Development)

In April 1991, the New York State Department of Social Services proposed a similar plan for home-relief (general assistance) recipients. The state would pay up to 90 percent of the home-relief grant to an employer who hires a home relief recipient for one year and makes an effort to continue employment after one year. The employer would be required to pay the difference between the subsidy amount and the prevailing wage for the job, which would be at least one-half the worker's salary. The plan would be mandatory for all employable home-relief recipients (about 115,000 of the state's 315,000 home-relief recipients are considered employable) who have stayed on the rolls for six months. Those who declined a job offer would be removed from the rolls for 75 days. Business representatives appeared to doubt the efficacy of the proposal, saying the home-relief recipients needed training in both social and employment skills, not just a job, and that it would be difficult for businesses to abandon preconceived notions about welfare recipients. (Sack)[33]

A recent study of the federal Targeted Jobs Tax Credit (TJTC) describes several problems with trying to provide wage subsidies to firms that hire poor people. (Bishop and Kang) The study explains why in 1983 businesses claimed tax credits for only about 10 percent of the eligible youth they hired. The most significant reason for the lack of participation is the high administrative cost of participating in the program: complicated eligibility rules make it difficult to identify and recruit eligible disad-

---

[33] As for financial incentives for firms hiring the disadvantaged, an interesting experiment was the use of a direct wage subsidy rather than a tax subsidy. Passed in 1983 in response to the state's worst depression since the 1930, the Minnesota Emergency Employment Development (MEED) Act began as a two-year, $70 million program to create temporary jobs in government and nonprofit agencies, and permanent jobs in the private sector. The program was made permanent by the 1985 legislature under the new name (dropping "emergency" and adding "Economic") with a $27 million appropriation for the July 1985 to July 1987 biennium. The program was terminated in 1989.

The MEED program offered employers up to $4 an hour in wage subsidies and $1 an hour in benefits for 26 weeks for hiring people who had been state residents for at least one month, were unemployed, and were ineligible for unemployment insurance or workers' compensation. Since 1984, priority was given to state welfare clients in areas of higher unemployment particularly workers in households with no other source of income, farm households that demonstrate severe financial need, and persons eligible for general assistance or AFDC.

vantaged workers. Therefore, much of the participation that occurs is passive. Employers hire, then certify after the fact. Consequently, TJTC actually created few job opportunities for disadvantaged persons. The second major cause of nonparticipation is the stigma attached to being a member of the TJTC target group. Most businesses believe TJTC-eligible persons make poorer new hires than non-TJTC persons. Most employers do not know whether they have hired someone on welfare or another kind of disadvantaged person. They do know, obviously, when they hire people in order to take advantage of the tax credit.

The study concludes the TJTC program provides a substantial windfall and the program is fairly cost-ineffective. The dilemma is the more targeted a program is, the greater its relative administrative costs are and the greater the stigma placed on the targeted group. If the targeting is very broad, the program becomes cost-ineffective. The study suggests wage supplements to employees are likely to be more effective and less costly than wage subsidies to employers.

Assistance to Targeted Areas

Most of the states' traditional, or supply-side, emphasis on assisting disadvantaged persons or distressed areas has been through economic development activities that are geographically targeted to areas of distress or decline. The targeted financial assistance generally includes capital subsidies, tax abatements, and public works grants. Their objective is to increase employment of disadvantaged persons by locating or expanding businesses in distressed areas, based on the belief that these businesses would hire the disadvantaged residents.

Targeted financial assistance

State targeted financial assistance to distressed areas has had limited success. Few state credit assistance programs are available and they are in a limited number of distressed areas. The U.S. Advisory Commission on Intergovernmental Relations estimated that in the early 1980s about a dozen states provided debt financing on a geographically targeted basis. (Eisinger) Most states, however, make their economic development resources available statewide.[34] Targeting to areas of distress can be

---

[34]The extent to which a state is able to target its economic development resources may depend on the relative strengths of the governor and the legislature and of the major political parties. States with strong governors in the same party that controls the legislature tend to provide more targeting. When the legislature and the governor's office are split among parties and the legislature is strong, targeting is less likely. (Hanson)

problematic, in part because it often conflicts with targeting to areas of growth potential or with sectoral targeting, such as recent emphases on developing high tech firms.

New York's experience with geographical targeting is typical. Its Job Development Authority was created in 1962 to make loans only in labor surplus areas; five years later it was expanded statewide. About 38 percent of its loans, $308 million, went to Long Island, one of the state's most prosperous areas with about 17 percent of the state's population. One recent study concluded "JDA loans tended to follow, rather than lead, the geographic patterns of new economic activity in the state....The ability to prepare financing prospectuses, generate business plans, lobby industrial development agencies, and organize effective underwriting of public debt securities was skewed toward areas of relative concentration of growth." (Mauro and Yago, p. 77) A similar fate befell the Urban Job Incentive Program, a tax credit program that began in 1968 and was limited to the poorest neighborhoods in New York's six largest cities. It was geographically expanded in 1970, and renamed the Job Incentive Program. It was expanded again in 1975, then expanded statewide in 1976, before being eliminated in 1983. (Mauro and Yago)

State assistance of industrial and commercial site development through such activities as industrial parks or land banks usually are not used in distressed areas. (Eisinger) The best known and most widely used targeted financial assistance programs are those associated with tax abatement and tax increment financing (TIF). These programs began in a concerted way in the 1950s as a way to use local resources to help finance development in "blighted" areas. Tax abatement enabling legislation permits localities to fully or partially waive the taxes on developed parcels of land. The best known tax abatement program is Missouri's Chapter 353 program. TIF programs permit localities to require that the payment of taxes on developed parcels above the original pre-development value be set aside in a special account that is used to pay off locally-originated bonds. The proceeds are used to pay for land acquisition, clearance, or development. California and Wisconsin are the two states that have made most use of TIF.

After reviewing studies of tax abatement in Missouri, Michigan, Ohio, and New York, Eisinger concludes abatements "tend to be awarded to corporations or developers capable of undertaking large-scale projects with potentially dramatic development impacts," and the tax subsidy is a small part of the overall financial package. (Eisinger, p. 152)

Enterprise zones

Enterprise zones are the most recent and best known targeted state economic development programs. Enterprise zones are geographical districts in which state and, usually, local governments provide special tax and regulatory incentives to promote job creation and economic development. These incentives include full or partial relief from state income taxes, reduction in the unemployment insurance tax, and property tax deductions. In Eisinger's view, enterprise zones reflect a transition from traditional supply-side activities to newer demand-side activities.

Enterprise zones try to make tax and regulatory incentives, and often credit assistance work to the advantage of distressed communities. They are usually much more targeted than tax abatement or TIF programs. Most enterprise zone programs try to benefit a place where development occurs, assuming the benefits will accrue to those living or working in the zone, rather than directly to benefit the residents of the zone. Connecticut enacted the first enterprise zone program. By the mid-1980s it contained a variety of incentives: low-interest loans and venture capital, a 50 percent reduction in corporate business taxes for 10 years, property tax abatements, a sales tax exemption of $1,000 for manufacturing firms for each new job created, and a special job training program for zone workers.

Evaluating enterprise zones is very difficult because it is impossible to isolate the affect of zone incentives on development activity. Also, the variety of forms and content taken by enterprise zones belies their common name. Yet, there have been several thorough evaluations of enterprise zones, which present a mixed picture at best.[35] A 1989 evaluation of New Jersey's enterprise program surveyed 478 businesses that qualified for assistance for at least one full year in one of the state's 10 zones. Evaluators obtained other information on zone businesses from state records. The study (Rubin and Armstrong) found only 5 percent of the businesses declared the zone incentives as the only reason for their location or expansion in the zone, 27 percent indicated zone benefits were the primary reason for their activity, 38 percent said zone benefits were a secondary reason, and 30 percent reported zone benefits had no impact on their investment decisions.

---

[35]In the face of many negative assessments and evaluations of state enterprise zone programs, some argue the policy is not flawed; rather, program design is flawed and implementation weak or ineffective. (See Hororwitz)

Using results from businesses that said zone benefits were the only or the primary cause of their investments, the study did a cost-benefit analysis that compared total state and local taxes directly generated by zone businesses and jobs created directly by zone businesses to the total direct costs of the program to the state. The study concluded for every $1 the state spent, it received 70 cents in state and local taxes. The state's cost per job was $13,070. When the study calculated the secondary and tertiary affects of business investment and employment, the fiscal return per dollar spent jumped to $1.70, and the cost per job created dropped to $3,171.

The evaluation indicated the most important enterprise zone incentive was the state sales tax exemption on personal property. The two other sales tax exemptions, on materials and on services, were of middling importance. The remaining three incentives were relatively unimportant: (1) a $1,500 corporate business tax credit for each full-time employee who had been a zone resident and who was unemployed for at least the previous 90 days or was dependent on public assistance; (2) a $500 credit for employing a zone resident who did not meet the $1,500 requirements and who was not employed immediately before; and (3) a phased unemployment insurance rebate for new employees earning less than $4,500 per quarter.

The study gave the following reasons for the businesses' responses to zone incentives: many firms are not eligible for corporate tax benefits, sales tax benefits are earned as a matter of right, and the corporate income tax and UI rebate require firms to hire specific kinds of employees and require extensive recordkeeping. In explaining why the credits and rebate were not used, many businesses said they cannot hire the type of employees required and still conduct a profitable business, and many firms suggested a better trained labor force would improve business conditions in the zones.

The evaluation also linked the use of incentives with characteristics of the firms that located or expanded in the zones. One-third of the firms had fewer than 10 employees and three-quarters had fewer than 50 employees. About 31 percent of the businesses located in the zones relocated there or started since the zone program began. Twenty-six percent were startups and about 6 percent were relocations (44 percent from within the state). Fifty-four percent of the firms were in the wholesale or retail trade or the services sectors. Twenty-nine percent were in manufacturing, 9 percent in finance, insurance, or real estate, and the balance equally split between construction and transportation, communication, and public utilities.

Small firms generally reported the zone incentives had no impact on their investment decisions. This was true for nearly one-half of the firms with fewer than 10 employees, and for about 20 percent of the firms with 10 to 49 employees. Generally, the zone incentives were more important to the larger firms. Also, the zone incentives were most important to construction firms.

Finally, the contribution to employment, payroll, and investment made by the construction, trade, and services firms was generally much below their proportionate share, while the contribution made by finance, insurance, and real estate (FIRE) firms was substantially above their proportionate share. Although FIRE firms represent only 9 percent of all zone firms, they undertook about 55 percent of all the investment by zone firms. Manufacturing firms contributed to employment and payroll above their proportionate share, but their share of investment was less than proportionate.

A 1990 evaluation of Virginia's enterprise zone program suggests "investment in zone properties has been negligible when compared to the total in localities with zones" and "neighborhood revitalization has not been an integral element in the development of rural zones." (Virginia Department of Housing and Community Development, p. v.) In comparing the zones to a control locality, the study concluded zones "have not been significantly more cost-effective than the control locality in job creation" (p. 11) and the zones "are not magnets for investment." (p. 12)

The study found rural zones were less effective than urban zones in creating employment and generating investment. Additionally, a survey of zone firms found 36 percent of the urban zone firms said the zone had no influence on their business decisions, compared to 17 percent of the rural zone firms. The study also showed sales tax refunds (55 percent of state revenues forgone were from sales tax refunds) were used much more frequently than either the general tax credit (37 percent) or the unemployment tax credit (only 8 percent).

A study of Illinois' enterprise zone program concluded about one-quarter of the businesses that invested in a zone were not aware of the zone or the benefits available. About 43 percent of those that invested in a zone did not use any zone incentives, and 19 percent said the incentives had little influence. (Redfield and McDonald) The sales tax exemption and the property tax abatement were the two most used incentives, the investment tax credit was less important, and the job tax credit was hardly used.

A lack of data made it impossible to quantify zone costs and benefits. Slightly over one-half of the reported job creations came from existing businesses, with retail and wholesale trade being the primary source of reported job creation. The general purpose zones did not attract new manufacturing firms. Most new investment occurred in wholesale and retail trade. Zone designation had no effect on the general decline of manufacturing jobs or on overall employment trends.

Finally, the Illinois study notes the continual expansion of the number of zones. The initial legislation capped the number of zones in the state at 48. But statutory amendments increased the number to 82 in 1990, with an additional seven zones authorized but not yet designated. Other amendments increased the maximum area of zones. The 82 zones range in size from one-half square mile to 15 square miles; zone population ranges from 205 to 162,000; zone per capita income ranges from $5,800 to $21,500; and zone unemployment rates range from 0.9 percent to 21 percent. The study suggests zone designation became demand-driven rather than need-driven and indicates local officials and business leaders "do not view zones as creating new firms, products, and markets which make the economic pie larger for everyone. Rather, they view their communities in competition for a fixed number of firms and investment dollars." (Redfield and McDonald, p. 27) The report recommends creation of no new zones; linking incentives to job creation; increasing state and local marketing of zones; and targeting to areas of greatest need.

An evaluation of Indiana's enterprise program examined the affects of the program on employment and investment from 1981 through 1989 by comparing enterprise zone cities with similarly situated cities. (Papke) Because there were no statistically significant differences between the two sets of cities, the study concluded: "Any general claims of a positive linkage between the EZ tax incentives and employment and investment should be subject to serious skepticism and doubt. The analysis here would indicate that the tax concessions awarded participating businesses are, in fact, 'gifts' provided as compensation for the profit-reducing characteristics of zone location." (Papke, pp. xv-xvi) The study estimated the cost per job ranged from $3,600 to $5,600.

Other aspects of the evaluation showed results similar to other studies. For example, retail firms dominated the industrial structure of zones, and accounted for 35 percent of participating businesses, but manufacturing firms had the greatest impact. Although manufacturing firms accounted for only 21 percent of the participating firms, they accounted for 59 percent of zone employees, 63 percent of zone resident employees, and the largest total payroll for both zone employees and zone resident employees. Manufacturing industries that required fewer skills, like furniture and wood products manufacturing, hired proportionately more zone resident employees than higher skill manufacturers, such as electronic equipment and instruments. Nonetheless, 74 percent of the total income of zone participants came from within their zones, and only 10 percent came from outside Indiana, meaning there was little export base activity to sustain and multiply economic activity.

Forty-five percent of participating businesses employed fewer than 11 employees, a figure that partly reflects the dominance of retail trade, as 61 percent of all retailers employed fewer than 11 people. Although manufacturing firms tended to be the largest employers — 25 percent had more than 100 employees — 21 percent employed fewer than 11 people. A greater percentage of retail trade firms took advantage of zone incentives than the larger manufacturers and wholesale distributors. But the largest firms accounted for 54 percent of the value of all subsidies, although they represented only 8 percent of all the participating businesses.

The study showed zone residents employed in participating businesses had much lower annual wages than nonzone residents employed in these businesses, $11,746 compared to $20,434. In 1988 only 14 percent of the new jobs created by participating zone businesses were filled by zone residents. The author noted "...making job opportunities available in economically depressed areas does not ensure the hiring of unemployed area residents. They either lack information about job openings, motivation, or the required occupational skills. No amount of fine-tuning of the tax system will produce significantly improved productivity and standards of living for zone residents without major changes in the ways schools and businesses train and retrain workers and in job search and relocation programs." (Papke, p. xi)

Like the New Jersey study, the Indiana study showed a relatively low utilization of the only tax incentive, the employment expense credit, aimed at hiring and retaining zone residents as employees. Only 77 of 949 zone businesses claimed this tax break, and the tax savings (costs) represented only 3 percent of the total tax savings (costs). On the other hand, the nontargeted inventory tax credit accounted for 87 percent of all the tax savings.

After studying eight different enterprise zones in eight different states, a recent study concluded that the typical enterprise zone program "is unable by itself to adequately address the necessary factors found to be important in most business location decisions." (Dabney, p. 334) The basic point is that zone incentives usually do not make up for higher costs in such areas as insurance, transportation, and access to raw materials as well as for poor amenities and behavioral factors.

These enterprise zone evaluations, and the evaluations of geographically-targeted credit asssitance programs, support Eisenger's conclusion on geographically-targeted supply-side programs: "...many business firms simply believe that needy communities or distressed zones within otherwise healthy jurisdictions are particularly unattractive locations for investment....no inducement will be sufficient to make it [a firm] locate within a state in a place characterized by such severe handicaps as above average unemployment, blighted real estate, rapid population and industrial out migration, deteriorating infrastructure, declining services, and above average poverty." (Eisenger, p. 175)

Generating Employment and Ownership Opportunities — Demand-side Activities

During the 1980s, most states shifted their economic development emphasis from supply side to demand side. To be effective in the aggregate, economic development must be demand-side related, expanding demand by increasing exports or decreasing imports. A supply-side approach focuses on making firms and workers more efficient and effective, expanding the supply of goods. When supply and demand are matched, there is much less likelihood of price increases and inflation. Demand-side economic development must be sector specific. Focusing on retail and wholesale trade and many business and personal services will not raise aggregate demand or employment. It is difficult, and uncustomary, to try to identify import reducing or export producing firms. Yet, demand side activities do take risks, not only in identifying specific firms or sectors, but by becoming a partner, by trying to develop or even create markets, and by taking equity positions in firms.

Demand-side activities generally revolve around three major sets of activities: providing venture capital, helping to develop high-tech firms, and promoting exports. Demand-side activities mostly focus on small or new businesses. This portion of the chapter reviews economic development activities designed to support minority businesses, create new businesses, nurture entrepreneurs, and sustain or expand existing businesses.

A Focus on Startups and Small Businesses

"Just a decade ago the idea that small enterprises might be seen as the key to economic regeneration, and a road to renewed growth of employment and the fight against mass unemployment, may have seemed eccentric or even absurd. Today, this view seems much less far-fetched. On the contrary, many observers from different traditions and political orientations embrace the idea, though they may disagree on why and how small firm expansion and dynamism have arisen." (Loveman and Sengenberger, p. 1)

Importance of small businesses

Ninety-eight percent of all businesses covered by the 1987 economic census employed fewer than 100 people and 96 percent employed fewer than 50 people, while less than 1 percent employed 500 or more people. While businesses with fewer than 100 employees accounted for 40 percent of all sales and receipts, businesses with 500 or more employees accounted for 50 percent of all sales and receipts. The manufacturing sector contains larger firms than other economic sectors. The largest 267 manufacturing companies, each employing 10,000 or more, accounted for 48 percent of sales and receipts for the entire sector. Service companies were most numerous, 38 percent of all companies surveyed, while retail firms were second, 28 percent. Although manufacturing firms accounted for only 8 percent of all companies, they employed 31 percent and their sales and receipts comprised 37 percent of all surveyed businesses. (*Commerce News*, 1991 b)

Nonetheless, since in the early 1970s, the percentage of manufacturing employment working in firms with fewer than 100 people has increased, a phenomenon occurring in most of the industrialized world. This phenomenon seems to be part of a worldwide and long-term trend and is significantly independent of business cycles and changes in industry sub-sectors.[36] (Loveman and Sengenberger) Within manufacturing, as well, almost none of the shift to smaller firms is the result of the growth of industries where employment traditionally has been concentrated in small firms. (Pior)

---

[36]The analysis of small business is controversial. For example, there are two different explanations for the increasing importance of small firms. One explanation is that the increasing importance of small firms is a technological response to changing economic conditions: the increased importance of market niches in a global economy, rapidly changing markets, and reduced-scale technologies. These changes have reduced dramatically the importance of mass production, market expansion, and extensive division of labor into very narrowly defined jobs. Under these conditions, small firms are superior performers, primarily because of their superior ability to increase efficiency by promoting flexibility. Another explanation holds large corporations have decentralized or spun off smaller units to take advantage of lower costs, especially lower labor-related costs, of small businesses. While evidence exists for both explanations, the worldwide nature of this change leads most analysts to place more importance on the importance of flexible production to competition.

Small manufacturing businesses are very important to America's ability to compete globally. To succeed in today's global economy, companies must bring new products to market quickly because market niches, not mass markets, and flexible production technologies, not mass-production techniques, dominate the economy. These characteristics place a premium on decentralized production. The 355,000 manufacturers with fewer than 500 employees produce about 46 percent of value-added. (Howard) Small manufacturing firms likely will be more important in the future. Between 1980 and 1986 employment in manufacturing firms with more than 500 employees declined by 11 percent (1.8 million jobs), while firms employing fewer than 100 increased their employment by nearly 8 percent (326,000 jobs). (Howard) In looking at plants (a business facility at geographical location; a firm — busines ownerhip — can have more than one plant), Davis and Haltiwanger found that the coworker mean (the number of workers at the average employee's workplace) fell from 1,139 in 1967 to 665 in 1985, a 42 percent decline. In the manufacturing sector, the coworker mean fell from 2,239 to 1,587 between 1967 and 1986. Most of this decline in the manufacturing coworker mean occurred between 1967 and 1972, and occurred primarily in the areospace and defense industries. The shift away from large plants is wide-spread among all 2-digit (SIC Code) manufacturing industries. (Davis and Haltiwanger)

Although employment in the United States is based in a very fluid economy — "In the average year during the early 1980s, one in every eight jobs was newly created, while one in nine was destroyed." (Leonard and Jacobson, p. 300) — new business create more than one-half the new jobs, and firms with fewer than 50 employees create almost all new net manufacturing jobs. (Hatch, 1988) Overall, 88 percent of net job creation from 1981 through 1985 occurred in firms with fewer than 20 employees. An additional 40 percent of jobs were created by the expansion of existing firms.[37] (Loveman and Sengenberger)

---

[37]Job generation analysis is also controversial, with many questions about reliability of data and methodology. The notion of "net job creation" is particularly elusive. While small businesses contribute significantly to job generation relatively (as a percentage of net job creation), their absolute contribution is modest. Job losses in large firms are very high — high enough in manufacturing to more than compensate for the job creation in small firms. Also, a relatively small number of firms contribute to job loss and job creation. One study determined the 18 percent of firms with the fastest growth created 86 percent of net new jobs in 1981-1985. Additionally, job growth decreases with age given size, and vice versa. An argument can be made that the specific contriubtion of small businesses to net job growth varies by definition, time period, specific industry, and location. (White and Osterman) The

Small businesses are important to the economy, and small manufacturing firms may be critically important to our economic competitiveness. Self-employment and micro-businesses also are becoming more important. Entrepreneurship has been recognized as an important source of new jobs and economic vitality. Nonfarm, unincorporated self-employment increased by 63 percent between 1970 and 1988, compared to a 48 percent increase in company jobs. In 1988, 7.6 percent of all nonagricultural workers were self-employed. In 1987, the earnings of self-employed workers were nearly equal that of company workers. (*SGPB Alert*, 1990) According to the Small Business Administration, sole-proprietor and micro-businesses rose in number from 9.73 million in 1980 to 13.0 million in 1986, and the numbers are still increasing. A recent survey of 3,000 businesses by the National Federation of Independent Business indicated that 50 percent of all new businesses had two employees or less, and only 10 percent had more than 10 employees. (Rifkin)

Recently, policymakers have begun to apply this principle to low-income neighborhoods and people. The low-income population has its share of people with entrepreneurial talent who, given the opportunity and the support, can create jobs and help revitalize severely distressed communities. Self-employment through small and micro-business creation can give people with little formal education the opportunity to earn more than the minimum wage, and it can provide flexibility in work hours beneficial to their family structure. Owning a small business is an important avenue to building wealth. Owners of small businesses are about as wealthy as owners of large businesses, although their incomes probably are lower. (Brown, Hamilton, and Medoff)

Besides being important generators of jobs and avenues to wealth, small businesses have several characteristics that make them especially important to economic opportunity. Small businesses tend to be labor intensive, hire local people, employ less-skilled people, use local suppliers, and become more involved in community affairs. Small businesses often face constraints not faced by large businesses, and these constraints inhibit

---

significance of small business contribution to net job growth may rest largely with the importance of new firms, which almost always are born small. (Brown, Hamilton, and Medoff) Perhaps the soundest conclusion is this: "a conservative view of the job generation literature suggests that small firms account for at least their share of employment creation, but the net new jobs result from a very dynamic process of expansion and contraction within the small firm sector. Large employment gains occur only in a few small firms, as most small firms start and remain small throughout their existence." (Loveman and Sengenberger, p. 31)

their creation, expansion, and viability. The remainder of this chapter covers these major constraints: the lack of access to, or the high cost of, capital, weak or inexperienced management, and the lack of economies of scale.

Disadvantages of small businesses

Small businesses have weaknesses that policies must addressed in an economic development policy. First, small firms are more likely to go out of business than large firms. One study shows 40 percent of firms with one to 19 employees survived from 1969 to 1976, compared to 65 percent for firms with 20 to 99 employees, 70 percent for firms with 100 to 499 employees, and 80 percent for firms with 500 or more employees. Another study concludes the failure rate between 1967 and 1982 for manufacturing firms with five to 19 employees was 13 percent higher than for firms with 20 to 99 employees, 34 percent higher than for firms with 100 to 249 employees, and 105 percent higher than for firms with 250 or more employees. (Loveman and Sengenberger)

The average years of tenure by firm size are 4.5 (1 to 24 employees), 5.2 (25 to 99), 6 (100 to 199), 6.8 (500 to 999), and 9 (1,000 +). (Loveman and Sengenberger) From 1965 through 1969, the quit rate per 100 employees was 3.5 for small manufacturing firms (firms one standard deviation below the mean) compared to 1.9 for large manufacturing firms (firms one standard deviation above the mean). (Brown, Hamilton, and Medoff)

Second, wages tend to increase with firm size. In 1983, the average wage in firms with 10 to 99 employees was 77 percent of the average wage in firms with 100 to 499 employees and 57 percent of the average wage in firms with 1,000 or more employees, respectively. The discrepancy appears to be growing over time.[38] While these wage discrepancies tend to exist in all industrialized countries, they are larger in the U.S. (Loveman and Sengenberger) The wage premium for workers in large firms (500 or more workers) was more than 30 percent in the following industries: transportation, construction, manufacturing, and communication. (Brown, Hamilton, and Medoff)

---

[38]In 1974, firms sized 20 to 99, 100 to 249, and 250 to 499 all had about the same average wage, which was about 72 percent of the average wage of firms with more than 1,000 employees. By 1984 the range of the average wage among the smaller firms had widened slightly and was about 65 percent of the average wage of firms with 1,000 or more employees. (Loveman and Sengenberger)

The differences in wages according to business size needs further elaboration because they link back to the discussion of income inequality in Chapter 2. Davis and Haltiwanger, analyzing more than 300,000 manufacturing plants, found that wage inequality in the manufacturing sector rose by 20 percent between 1975 and 1988. Further, they found that most of this rise in wage inequality occurred within experience - education - gender groups. Thus, they concluded factors other than differences in education, experience, or gender were causing most of the increased inequality. They discovered that characteristics of manufacturing plants caused much of the increased wage inequality.

Three characteristics of manufacturing plants especially stood out. First, as pointed out earlier, manufacturing plants have become substantially smaller. Second, among most 2-digit codes manufacturing plants have become more specialized. Third, the employee structure within manufacturing plants has shifted away from operation, or production workers, and toward managerial and professional, or nonproduction, workers. Most of this shift occurred between 1967 and 1972; since 1977 there has been a substantial shift toward production workers. This shift was accompanied by increased educational attainment of the manufacturing workforce. Specifically, workers with less than 12 years of schooling accounted for 40 percent of manufacturing hours between 1967 and 1969, compared to only 20 percent between 1985 and 1987; the percentage of manufacturing hours accounted for by manufacturing workers with at least some college rose from 20 percent to 37 percent between 1967 and 1987.

In analyzing further these characteristics, they concluded: "Mean wages are higher at larger plants, older plants, multiunit plants, more energy intensive plants, more specialized plants, and more capital intensive plants. The most striking differentials involve plant size. The average wage gap between plants with more than 5,000 employees and plants with 20 to 49 employees is $4.92 per hour for production workers and $3.06 per hour for nonproduction workers. These size-wage gaps are quite large relative to the average wage of $8.56 for production workers and $12.96 for nonproduction workers. Large size-wage gaps occur within detailed manufacturing industries as well." (Davis and Haltiwanger, p. 147)

When changes in plant-wage structure were examined over time, "real hourly wages rose steadily for most plant sizes over the 1963 to 1986 period. Much larger wage increases took place at larger plants...In 1967 production workers at plants with 20 to 49 employees earned, on average, $3.40 less per hour than their counterparts at plants with more than 5,000 employees. By 1986 this wage gap rose to $6.31." (Davis and Haltiwanger, pp. 154-155) The size of this 1986 gap is large considering the mean hourly wage of $9.18 for production workers.

Third, non-wage compensation tends to be lower in smaller firms. Larger firms provide more vacation and sick leave, and better health insurance, life insurance, and retirement benefits than smaller firms.[39] Blue-collar nonunion employees in small firms are most likely to be adversely affected by a lack of fringe benefits. (Brown, Hamilton, and Medoff)

Finally, workers in smaller establishments tend to get less formal training. In 1982, the percentage of employees who received formal training in small establishments (1 to 99 employees) was about 11 percent, compared to 26 percent for establishments with 500 or more workers. (Brown, Hamilton, and Medoff)

On top of lower wages and fewer fringe benefits, employees in small firms tend to work more hours per week than employees in large firms, and tend to do more tasks than workers in large firms. (Loveman and Sengenberger) A survey of metalworking plants in the Springfield, Massachusetts, area found one of the reasons workers who were being laid off from large companies (firms over 1,000 employees) were not being hired by small firms (less than 100 employees) even when these small firms needed experienced workers was "...in large firms, you have a limited number of workers who have very rigid, limited skills....most...could run a drill press, lathe, and milling machine, but could not set up those machines, read blueprints, or do any kind of shop mathematics. The small and medium sized firms that were growing needed workers who had a broad range of skills." (Forrant, p. 29)

Why do small firms tend to pay less and offer fewer or less valuable fringe benefits? A very small part of the reason is larger firms tend to hire

---

[39] In 1986, 75 percent of firms with 500 or more employees provided vacation, sick, health, life, and pension or 401(k) benefits compared to only 7 percent of firms with fewer than 500 employees. In the U.S. in 1983, 35 percent of the employees in firms with 1 to 24 employees had health insurance, compared to 65 percent in firms with 25 to 99 employees, 75 percent in firms with 100 to 199 employees, 79 percent in firms with 500 to 999 employees, and 86 percent in firms with 1,000 or more employees. (Lovemen and Sengenberger) While nearly all firms that offer health insurance covered hospital room and board, surgical care, lab procedures, and physician hospital care, only the larger firms covered office visits, home health care, maternity care, mental health, and similar benefits. Long-term disability insurance was provided by 69 percent of firms with 500 or more employees, compared to 9 percent for firms with fewer than 500 employees. (Brown, Hamilton, and Medoff)

workers with more education than small firms: in 1983, 44 percent of the workers of firms with 500 employees had more than a high school diploma, compared to 37 percent in firms with fewer than 500 employees; at the same time, only 13 percent of the employees in the large firms had less than a high school diploma, compared to 22 percent in the small firms. Also, a greater percentage of the employees in small firms were under the age of 25 or were women. (Brown, Hamilton, and Medoff) This suggests because small firms tend to hire younger and less experienced and less educated workers, their payroll per employee is lower. (It also may be a partial explanation for higher quit rates as employees under the age of 32 are more mobile than older employees). Yet an analysis of skills composition suggests overall skill differences between small and large firms are minor, and are not a significant cause of wage differentials. (Loveman and Sengenberger; Brown, Hamilton, and Medoff)

Davis and Haltiwanger suggest that in the manufacturing sector large plants have been increasing the skill levels of their workforce more than small plants. Their suggestion is based on the crude distinction between production workers and nonproduction workers, with large manufacturing plants adding more nonproduction workers, who have higher educational and occupational skills, than small manufacturing plants. In essence, large manufacturing plants have increasingly relied on nonproduction workers. However, problems with data methodology relative in nonproduction workers limit the force of their conclusions.

Second, smaller firms have more part-time employees.[40] They tend to be paid less on an hourly basis than full-time employees and tend to receive smaller and fewer fringe benefits. In 1983, hourly wage rate for firms with 500 or more workers was $8.41; for firms with fewer than 500, it was $5.89.

The coverage by pension or retirement plans even more striking: the percentage of employees covered for firms of various sizes was 17 (1-24 employees), 41 (25-99), 64 (100-199), 74 (500-999), and 88 (1,000 +). (Loveman and Sengenberger) In 1986, 79 percent of firms with 500 or more employees had a pension or 401(k) plan, compared to 16 percent of firms with fewer than 500 employees. (Brown, Hamilton, and Medoff) In 1987, only 23 percent of firms with fewer than 25 employees offered pension benefits, compared to 89 percent of the firms employing 1,000 or more workers. (Census Bureau News Release CB91-240, July 19, 1991)

Firms with 500 or more workers were more likely to provide vacation time (95 percent) and sick leave (91 percent) than firms with fewer than 500 workers, vacation (58 percent) and sick leave (36 percent).

[40]The proportion of part-time employment by firm size is 32 percent (1-24 employees), 17 (25-99), 16 (100-199), 14 (500-999), and 12 (1,000 +). (Loveman and Sengenberger)

(Brown, Hamilton, and Medoff) This difference is too great to be explained by the fact that smaller firms have a greater share of part-time workers.

Third, unions are more prominent in large firms than small firms. In 1983, 4 percent of firms with 1 to 24 employees, 14 percent of firms with 25 to 99 employees, and 19 percent of firms with 100 to 499 employees were unionized, compared to 30 percent of firms with 500 or more employees. Small firms tend not to be unionized primarily because of the cost to the union. Nonetheless, unionization plays a very minor role in wage differentials. Employees in large nonunion workplaces earned 30 percent more than workers at small workplaces, and workers in large union firms earned only 14 percent more than unionized employees in small firms. (Brown, Hamilton, and Medoff) Davis and Haltiwanger and others also emphatically conclude that union variables have very little impact on plant-wage differentials. (Davis and Haltiwanger)

Small firms also are younger firms, and, as mentioned earlier, wages tend to increase as a firm ages. Because small firms tend to go out of business much more quickly and regularly than large businesses, part of the wage differential in small firms may be an age differential.

Another possible explanation is the small firm's reduced ability to control or substantially influence market uncertainties. This leads to higher costs, with small firms being less able than large firms to pass these costs on to their customers. (Zipp)

A plausible explanation for lower wages and fringe benefits in small firms rests in the diseconomies of small scale. For example, in 1985 bank charged fixed interest rates of 14.1 percent for short-term loans of $1,000 to $24,000, and 13.5 percent for loans of $25,000 to $99,000, but only 9.1 percent for loans of $1 million or more. The discrepancy in interest rates was even larger for long-term loans. The fixed interest rate on long-term loans of less than $100,000 was 16 percent, compared to 10 percent for loans of $1 million or more. Similar differentials existed for loans with floating interest rates. Thus, small firms may face a significant financing penalty when they borrow small amounts of money, especially for long-term loans.

In 1982 large manufacturers paid 19 percent less for coal, 26 percent less for electricity, and 6 percent less for natural gas. It is unclear whether these discounts continuously occur. Finally, small firms (fewer than 500 workers) paid about 10 percent more for monthly health premiums than large firms (500 or more workers). The administrative cost per worker of setting up and administering a health care plan also is much higher in small firms. (Brown, Hamilton, and Medoff)

Because labor productivity is higher for larger firms, the smaller capital-labor ratios in smaller firms are insufficient to offset substantially lower wage costs. (Loveman and Sengenberger) If productivity is lower in small firms because of low capital investment, and these firms operate in a competitive environment, they will be unable to pay wages commensurate with large firms.

It is unlikely that workers choose lower-paying positions in small firms because jobs in small firms are intrinsically more interesting or challenging. Research shows workers do not consciously trade high wages for more satisfying jobs. Recent research does suggest small firms provide more interesting and creative work than medium or large firms and employees in small firms report higher levels of job satisfaction and variety. (Zipp)

Overall, the reasons for wage differentials among firm sizes and among plant sizes rests in two basic characteristics of our changing economy — although, as will be noted, these conclusions are not definite, and more research is needed. One conclusion on which most analysts seem to agree is that technological change requiring a higher-skilled and more educated workforce is a major cause of wage inequality. Technological change probably is the single most important cause of wage inequality.

Other causes of wage inequality are important, however, and serve to complement the impact of technological change. One of these possible causes of wage inequality is the likelihood that weakening barriers to international trade has led to increased outsourcing of intermediate goods that are low-skill labor intensive. Second, it is very possible that changes in the demand for products has led to increased wage inequality. This "product-demand" rationale has two components. First, product demand for nonmanufacturing products, especially for products of nonmanufacturing industries requiring a highly educated workforce, has increased relative to demand for products of manufacturing firms. Second, within manufacturing, there appears to have been a shift to products of detailed, high-quality workforce manufacturing industries and away from products of manufacturing industries employing less-skilled workers. In this last case, trade growth might be causing important changes in the distribution of employment across manufacturing plants and firms with different characteristics. Finally, there is some speculation that productivity and technical change may relate more to managerial ability or other sunk costs than to skills of the workforce — "automobile plants that make a transformation from the American to the Japanese manufacturing system (such as the California NUMMI factory) have achieved significant gains in productivity while using the same workers." (Davis and Haltiwanger, p. 196)

Concluding observations on small and mid-size businesses

From an economic development perspective and from the perspective of designing a state economic opportunity strategy, this section leads to several major points. Small firms, especially firms employing fewer than 100 people, are important net generators of jobs. Small firms, especially small and mid-sized manufacturing firms, are important to our economic base and exports. Third, if small and mid-sized firms are to grow and thrive economically, they need to make appropriate technological and managerial adaptations. Fourth, small and mid-sized firms tend to compensate workers at a much lower level than large firms. If employees of small and mid-sized firms are to receive increased compensation, the owners and managers of these firms will have to adopt appropriate technological and managerial innovations, and the workforce of these firms must be skilled enough to use and work within these technological and managerial changes. These accomplishments may help small and mid-sized firms overcome diseconomies of scale and increase their longevity, both of which are apparently related to their ability to increase employee compensation.

Providing Credit Assistance

Poor access to capital can hinder the growth of many businesses and is one of the two most frequently cited reasons why so many businesses fail. Evidence suggests there are "capital gaps" where qualified small businesses, able and willing to pay the risk-adjusted market rate of capital, are denied appropriate financing due to imperfections in the capital market. These market imperfections arise from discrimination, perverse or counterproductive regulation, the disproportionately high information and transaction costs associated with smaller loans, and the risk aversion of lenders. Consequently, smaller businesses have difficulty raising capital, especially if they are located in poor neighborhoods or operated by women, minorities, or other "nontraditional" entrepreneurs. Even larger businesses may have problems getting financing if they are in poorer neighborhoods, where lenders think the costs and risks of doing commerce are higher. The capital access problem is particularly acute for new, young, and rapidly expanding businesses, the very enterprises that create the majority of the new jobs in our economy.

Most businesses require a mixture of equity and debt. The major advantage of equity to the business owner is that, unlike debt, it has no repayment schedule. Especially with young or growing businesses, too much debt can result in high loan repayments that cannot be met out of current cash flow. This can cause the business to fail. On the other hand, few businesses can meet all their capital needs without loans.

Conventional sources of financing are not structured to handle the risks or the costs of working with disadvantaged entrepreneurs. Even federal small business finance programs are often too risk averse and cost conscious. Usually, the administrative costs of very small loans is similar to the costs of very large loans. Also, loans to startups and to very small businesses often cannot rely on character lending (considering primarily the strengths of the person requesting the loan). Thus, there are few incentives to make small, risky loans.

Only relatively small amounts of capital are necessary for many startups and very small businesses, especially for low-income entrepreneurs. The National Federation of Independent Businesses estimates that in 1985 nearly one-fifth of business startups required less than $5,000, nearly one-third required $10,000 or less capital; and only about one-quarter required more than $50,000. Only 45 percent of small business startups get capital from a conventional lending source. (*SGPB Alert*, April 1990) Most of the loan funds discussed later provide financing for very small business ventures, and the loans are quite small. Few micro-enterprise funds provide loans larger than $10,000. Most conventional lenders and business finance programs are not capable of lending such small sums; they are structured to finance much larger deals. Fortunately, financing programs have emerged to make capital more accessible to very small businesses.

Programs that make equity available to low-income entrepreneurs are particularly important because the friends, family, and associates of the poor are usually too poor to help finance a new business. Because equity is so risky for the investor, very few financing programs that serve low-income entrepreneurs provide pure equity capital. Instead, they provide "near-equity" to entrepreneurs. Near-equity or equity-like financing are terms frequently applied to that which take a second or subordinate position in a loan package or that have very flexible terms with a delayed repayment. This "near-equity" functions like equity by leveraging additional debt.

With equity or near-equity financing programs, three factors are critical. First, the programs must accurately select and screen potential borrowers. Funds that invest in incapable entrepreneurs rapidly lose their capitalization and go out of business. Subordinated lending and equity, is often rolled-over, rather than repaid. Therefore, such loans require ever increasing amounts of capital for the lender as it seeks to maintain liquidity and adequate capitalization for additional lending. Second, funds must offer technical assistance, either directly or through an outside agency. Third, providing support services to very disadvantaged entrepreneurs can be crucial to program success. Starting a business places great demands on the entrepreneur. For the low-income entrepreneur who faces greater barriers and lacks the financial resources to pay for help, additional support services may be necessary.

To be most effective, these programs must be conducted in conjunction with entrepreneur training programs, technical assistance, and, for firms employing a substantial number of poor people, skills training. Because financing programs have to provide technical assistance and support, it is unrealistic to expect them to become financially self-sufficient. Most will require ongoing subsidies.

The rest of this section covers financial assistance to the kinds of businesses that can provide economic opportunity to poor people or distressed areas. Attention first is given to minority business development not only because of its potential contribution to creating employment opportunities for poor minority workers and creating assets as a means of self-sufficiency, but also because many of the points made, especially about the limits of minority business development as an antipoverty strategy, are relevant to other business assistance ventures, entrepreneurship, small business development and other business ventures.

Minority business development

Blacks are substantially less self-employed than whites. In 1976 about 12.3 percent of all whites over age 21 were self-employed, compared to 4 percent of blacks. (Bates and Duncan) The number of black-owned firms increased by 37 percent from 1982 to 1987, from 308,260 to 424,165, and their receipts increased by 105 percent, to $19.8 billion from $9.6 billion. Yet in 1987, black-owned firms represented only 3 percent of all firms and accounted for only 1 percent of total gross receipts. Blacks owned nearly 4 percent of all firms with annual receipts of less than $5,000, but owned less than 1 percent of firms with receipts of $1 million or more. In Maryland, which leads the nation in black-owned businesses per 1,000 residents, 1987 annual receipts for black-owned firms averaged $33,000 compared to $169,000 for all firms; only 12 percent of black-owned firms in Maryland had paid employees, compared to 23 percent of all firms. In 1983 a U.S. Department of Commerce report identified four reasons for the slow growth of black businesses, which are probably still valid today: limited market demand, limited access to capital, limited efficiency, and racial discrimination. (Pyatt)

Efforts to use the fulcrum of entrepreneurship to help minorities become self-sufficient should proceed with caution. Low earnings and self-employment often go hand in hand. Also, historically minority entrepreneurs have struggled to stay in business. For example, typical entrepreneurship endeavors in the black community have been in small food stores, beauty parlors, and barbershops located in black neighborhoods, serving a largely local and black clientele. These kinds of businesses have been declining for a long time.

Over the past 20 years minority entrepreneurship has become more successful. In 1980 minority entrepreneurs aged 65 or less had education levels and earnings that exceeded those of minority employees, $16,105 for self-employed males compared to $11,235 for male employees. While personal services and retailing accounted for over one-half of all minority enterprises in 1960, the growth in minority businesses has been outside personal services and retailing, and primarily in business services; finance, insurance, and real estate; transportation and communication; and wholesale trade. (Bates and Duncan) Emerging minority business firms tend to be larger, have lower failure rates, and generate more jobs compared to traditional minority businesses. One reason for this changing nature of minority firms is that more highly-educated blacks are going into nontraditional lines of business.

The potential for upward mobility and earnings represent only one advantage of small business ownership. Another is its importance as a source of employment. In 1981 41 percent of employees worked for businesses that had less than $5 million in annual sales. (Bates and Duncan) More important, employment patterns of small businesses tend to represent their ownership patterns. For example, nonminority firms in minority areas tend to employ more nonminority employees than minority employees. But minority firms, especially black firms, employ predominantly minority employees. The probable reason for this is that family and social networks play the key role in hiring and employment in very small firms. Since there are many more nonminority small firms than minority small firms, minorities often do not have the same opportunity for employment in small businesses.

The use of different job search techniques often explains job opportunities. Whites tend to find jobs by referrals from friends and relatives, blacks by walking in and applying. To the extent that blacks are segregated in poor areas with few nonwhites and few job opportunities, their ability to find jobs deteriorates substantially. A very important aspect of black business ownership is that black firms heavily rely on black employment even when they are located in nonminority areas. An examination of 28 large metropolitan areas in 1982 showed that about 90 percent of black firms employed 75 percent or more minorities, while nearly 58 percent of white firms employed no minorities. When looking soxly at firms located in minority neighborhoods, nearly one-third of the white firms employed no minorities, while over 93 percent of the black firms employed 75 percent or more minorities. Even in nonminority neighborhoods, nearly 80 percent of black firms employed 75 percent or more minorities. (Bates and Duncan)

Although there is a perception that minorities, especially Asian immigrants, receive much financial support from informal associations of family and acquaintances, this is not true. Commercial bank loans are the most common source of startup capital for Asians. (Bates and Duncan) Also, selling primarily to buyers of similar ethnic or racial background is neither a means to capital nor a marketing success. Asians particularly are much less likely to sell to minority customers than are blacks or Hispanics. In fact, selling to minority customers is associated with firm termination, which is logical because minority customers tend to have low incomes. Asian firms tend to be more successful than black or Hispanic firms for three reasons. Asian firms rely less on minority customers, Asian businesspersons tend to have more education and assets than black or Hispanic businesspersons, and Asians tend to go into business more frequently or stay in business longer because language difficulties block access to alternative means of income. (Bates and Duncan)

Human and financial capital appear to be the keys in determining minority business startup. High levels of educational attainment and larger asset holdings are related to higher rates of self-employment. The most widely-cited barrier to black entrepreneurship is the lack of equity capital. In 1988 the median black family had less than 10 cents in wealth compared to every $1 in wealth for the median white family. (U.S. Bureau of Census, 1991 a) Lack of personal wealth in combination with discriminatory treatment by commercial banks continue to stunt the growth of black businesses. Blacks have lower rates of business formation than other minorities because they have lower levels of net worth, lower educational achievement, are somewhat younger and less likely to be married, and have fewer opportunities for business startup. Accounting for differences in education and wealth and demographic considerations, blacks and Hispanics start up businesses less frequently than do Asians. (Bates and Duncan)

A key business development strategy relates to the kinds of businesses being nurtured for startup. In 1982, black firms compared to white male firms were overrepresented in retail trade (27 percent to 22 percent) and personal services (13 percent to 3 percent), and underrepresented in manufacturing (2 percent to 9 percent) and construction (7 percent to 13 percent). Manufacturing is much more capital intensive than personal services. Personal services and retail operations also tend to be much less profitable than manufacturing. (Bates and Duncan)

The state of Maryland has one of the most effective state minority business programs. The Maryland Small Business Development Financing Authority is located in the Maryland Department of Economic and Employment Development, but thinks of itself as a profitable "revenue center" within the department. While the authority obtains general funds from the legislature for its programs, its administrative and operating costs are more than paid for by fees (application fees range from $100 to $400), interest on loans, and interest on unexpended funds. Its identification as a revenue center is more than rhetoric, for it sees itself as a business operation that must and should meet market tests.

The authority operates four programs. The one most important to minorities, in the eyes the authority's executive director, is the Equity Participation Investment Program (EPIP), especially its business acquisition component. EPIP provides equity or debt financing for the acquisition of profitable businesses by "socially or economically disadvantaged persons." The business that is the target of the acquisition must (1) have been in existence for at least five years, (2) have been profitable for at least two of the previous three years, (3) have sufficient cash flow to service the debt and ensure return on the authority's investment, (4) have the capacity for growth and job creation, and (5) have a strong customer base. Applicants must have a minimum net worth of $75,000 (or the enterprise must have this net worth) and three or more years of successful experience with management responsibilities.

The authority's EPIP financing must complement financing from other sources. EPIP's investment is limited to the lesser of $500,000 or 25 percent of the total investment in the enterprise acquiring an existing business. The authority intends to recover its investment in seven years. When debt financing is provided, the rate of interest is equal to the market rate; when equity is used, the pegged rate of return is between 10 and 22 percent. The authority pays attention to the structure and eventual liquidation of its investment. Its funds can be used for many purposes, including purchase of machinery and equipment, leasehold improvements, furniture and fixtures, inventory, working capital, real estate acquisition, and construction or major renovation.

The authority gives priority to the acquisition of manufacturing firms and wholesale distributorships. It thinks these industries are particularly desirable in the Washington, D.C. and Baltimore region and substantially underrepresented in terms of minority ownership. Opportunities usually occur when nonminority owners want to cash out their investment or owners want to retire and have no relatives interested in the business.

The EPIP franchising component provides debt or equity investment for franchise ownership. It is similar to the acquisition program, except that EPIP's investment is limited to 45 percent of the total financing or a maximum of $100,000, whichever is less.

In addition to the equity participation program, the authority operates three other programs. The contract financing program provides loans, loan guarantees, or equity participation to firms for working capital and the acquisition of equipment to begin, continue, or complete work on federal, state, or local government or public utility contracts. The loans or guarantees cannot exceed $250,000 and the loan term is usually the duration of the contract. The financial institution must pay 1 percent of the loan amount as a guaranty fee. The long-term guaranty program provides loan guarantees and payments of interest subsidies (to lower the rate by as much as 4 percent) on loans used for working capital, improvements to real property, and installation of equipment and machinery. Loans for real property cannot exceed one-half the total loan amount. Otherwise, loan guarantees cannot exceed 80 percent of the loan, up to $400,000, and the loans cannot exceed $500,000 with terms of one to 10 years. Three-fourths of 1 percent of the loan amount is payable by a financial institution at closing and annually. Finally, the surety bond guarantee program guarantees **up** to 90 percent reimbursement for losses incurred as a result of a contractor's breach of a bid, performance, or payment bond of not more than $1 million on any government or utility contract. The standard contractor guaranty fee is one-half of percent of the bond amount and the standard surety guarantee fee is 20 percent of the bond premium. Some of the eligibility requirements for this program include employing fewer than 50 full-time employees or having a gross annual sales of less than $10 million and a limit on subcontracting no more than 75 percent of the contract.

Three points need to be made about the operation of the authority. First, it sees itself as doing economic development, not providing a social service. Its businesslike operations and success have enabled it to work well with the state legislature and the corporate or mainstream business community, resulting in joint ventures and encouraging the business community to view minority business development as good economic sense. Second, the authority relies heavily on accounting and auditing. Although its staff undertakes many activities, including financing analysis, nearly all the staff members are accountants. Companies are audited intensely and regularly. This helps prevent the authority from investing in bad ventures, and allows the authority to identify problems early, while they may be easily treated. Third, the authority provides its own training (under contract) especially in financial management. It encourages applicants and funded businesses to participate in an intense three-day, hands-on training program, and it also makes referrals to the University of Maryland's Total Quality Management Program.

Entrepreneurial and micro-business development

Several recently established self-employment programs are targeted to poor people or poor communities. Oklahoma's demonstration program, the Self-Employment and Entrepreneurial Development System (SEEDS) began operating in early 1988. It is based on the premise that a self-employment and entrepreneurial development program can help meet the employment needs of low-income people. Through SEEDS, the Oklahoma Department of Commerce provides financial support and technical assistance to local community action agencies who establish a micro-business development revolving loan program. A Community Services Block Grant setaside of $250,000 initially capitalized SEEDS, and the legislature appropriated $180,000 for training and technical assistance.

SEEDS begins with a detailed screening of potential applicants to assess their basic business skills, such as previous business experience, individual motivation, and marketing research. Once selected, an applicant undergoes a customized competency-based business management training course. The training uses existing educational, business, and economic development resources, but adds additional components if necessary. Training sessions cover recordkeeping, cash flow projections and analysis, marketing and advertising, salesmanship, customer relations, legal considerations, inventory control, credit and collections, production scheduling, operations management, and business operations planning. As part of the training, the potential entrepreneur prepares a business plan, is exposed to various financing arrangements, learns how to package a loan application, and prepares a schedule for getting technical assistance.

After completing the training and preparing a viable business plan, the participant is eligible to receive a loan up to a maximum of $5,000 at a negotiated interest rate. The financing can be structured as a guarantee or as credit enhancement. Each of the five local SEEDS program has a credit committee that reviews the business plan and the financial projections and decides whether to make the loan. Loan proceeds can be used for a variety of capitalization expenses, including licenses and permits.

Providing ongoing technical assistance is essential to SEEDS success. Training participants are assured of a follow-up system of technical assistance for at least one year after startup. The new business owner must meet monthly with the SEEDS coordinator to discuss specific areas of business management and try to avoid possible management problems. An advisory committee of management and professional persons provides expertise to the SEEDS coordinator.

In three years of operation, SEEDS has committed nearly $250,000 in 57 direct loan projects, with the loans bringing in about $106,000 in other capital, including equity, and creating 86 jobs.

Vermont Job Start is a state-funded economic development venture that provides loans up to $10,000 to small, owner-operated enterprises. Entrepreneurs must have a family income less than $14,000 to qualify. The program operates through five local representatives who provide business assistance and loan packaging to applicants. Each loan must be approved by a local board of bankers, business people, and low-income persons. During fiscal year 1988, Vermont Job Start made 48 loans with an average size of $4,800. Because of its technical and financial participation in new businesses, the program is able to approach financial institutions directly for participation in order to leverage its funds. In effect, banks have accepted Vermont Job Start financial participation in a venture as a substitute for equity. (Corporation for Enterprise Development)

Several states recently have begun demonstration programs to help welfare recipients start their own businesses. By mid-1991 there were more than 100 programs providing training and technical assistance to help low-income people start their own businesses. (Guy, Doolittle, and Fink) Recipients in these programs generally take a 3- to 6-month training course, often offered through or managed by a nonprofit organization, covering business practices, accounting, and taxes. Micro-enterprises can help increase personal savings without affecting welfare eligibility if individual access to the funds is restricted. In Illinois' demonstration, 70 percent of participants were able to get off welfare. Although only 15 percent were able to support their families solely from business activities within one-year, income from self-employment helped make an additional 10 percent of the participants self-sufficient. (*SGPB Alert*, 1990) Pennsylvania's program began in early 1989 in three sites. After 15 months, the program had cost state and local government $950,000 had enrolled 189 people, of whom 135 had completed training and 61 had started businesses. (Hinds) In one program, a third of the participants said they had prior self-employment experience, suggesting these programs may help make marginal businesses more profitable, revive failed businesses, or legitimize "underground" businesses. (Guy, Doolittle, and Fink)

A different example of micro-business development is the Women's Self-Employment Project (WSEP) in Chicago which started its Full Circle Fund in late 1988. The fund is a group-based self-employment credit program targeted to low-income neighborhood women, based on the Grameen Bank model. The fund organizes women into groups of borrowers and provides them with noncollateralized individual loans. The fund provides initial loans $100 to $1,500. Once the initial loans are repaid, subsequent loans can reach $5,000. The Fund charges an interest rate of 15 percent, and each borrower must contribute 5 percent of the loan amount to a group emergency savings account. Each borrower must agree to save a small portion of her income annually.

Members of the group, or "borrowing circle," approve the loans after the WSEP loan committee and its fund agent review and comment on the loan requests. The fund makes two loans at a time; after the first two borrowers make three timely payments, two more women become eligible for loans. The key to this model is that although an individual borrower does not assume liability for all the borrowers, each loan and future source of credit depends on all group members being up-to-date on payments.

In addition to "collective responsibility," the fund has two other important characteristics. One is its minimalist approach to training. The fund provides no up-front training or technical assistance other than a brief orientation. Success rates are improved by keeping the businesses as simple as possible. The second important characteristic is the significance attached to developing solidarity, improving motivation, and creating peer support. The circles meet biweekly to discuss loans and review progress of the self-employment initiatives, all designed to help one another.

By spring 1990, the fund was operating five borrowing circles and had lent $15,600. Funds have been used to purchase equipment, such as a surger for a sewing machine, and for supplies and working capital for ventures like clothes making, child care, and catering. Forty percent of the borrowers were working full-time on their ventures, and most had other sources of income. (Cohen)

Several issues confronting the fund illustrate the problems facing self-employed poor people in poor neighborhoods. One problem is the welfare system's penalties for success, particularly the loss of Medicaid. Although they may earn enough to get off welfare, self-employed poor people rarely can afford health insurance. At this point it is not clear how the welfare reform act's transitional provision for Medicaid affects self-employment. Additionally, welfare limits on personal assets, currently $1,500, make it very difficult for people to own meaningful amounts of equity or equipment in their businesses. Finally, self-employment earnings can be irregular. Good months may trigger people off welfare; then, if their earnings drop dramatically, they have no safety net.

On the welfare penalty issue, it is worth quoting from an MDRC evaluation of a micro-enterprise program for welfare recipients: "Most new businesses do not provide their operators with much personal income during the initial start-up phase. Mainstream entrepreneurs typically overcome this barrier by using personal savings to cover living expenses during their start-up period and buying assets on credit. This enables them to reinvest most of the sales revenues in the business. AFDC recipients cannot follow these practices under the usual welfare regulations. Most or all of the business revenue, assets, and loans are treated as personal income under standard AFDC grant calculation and eligibility rules. These amounts are deducted from the client's grant or — in extreme cases — render the client entirely ineligible for welfare. This leaves the AFDC recipient without start-up capital or the money to support herself during the initial months of business operations. Under SEID, the federal government agreed to special AFDC rules for handling business income and assets, and the states and counties had to apply these rules correctly when calculating clients' AFDC eligibility and grant amount." (Guy, Doolittle, and Fink, p. vii)

A second issue relates to the economic context in which self-employment programs for poor people are placed. Informal markets are not well-developed or lucrative in most poor neighborhoods. Where there are small informal markets, it may be counterproductive for a person to "go above the table" with a small venture, because they could sacrifice small but uncounted income from below-the-table informal business activity. (Molina) Further, many self-employment ventures may face overpowering competition from well-financed businesses. Most self-employment ventures are personal services, businesses that typically have very low incomes. These kinds of businesses may also be unstable with little longevity.

The success of programs that support borrowing circles or self-employment ventures may depend on their ability to develop markets for their products, which in turn may depend on creating, enlarging, and sustaining a network of friends and other contacts. Accessing organizations in the community and taking advantage of supplementary services also may contribute to successful self-employment ventures. But neighborhoods that are ethnically or socially diverse and areas with low population densities may pose formidable obstacles to market networking. Such neighborhoods also may impede the development of effective reinforcing groups and economies of scale in administering micro-loan programs.

Third, self-employment ventures by their nature tend to have only one employee. Thus their direct economic impact on the community may be limited to the one person who reaps the benefit, the self-employed person, and possibly the provision of a service of a higher quality or at a lower cost.

Fourth, micro-enterprise programs for poor people cannot "run themselves" — they require dedication, strong commitment, and a flexible approach. The MDRC evaluation points out that the most successful local administrative organizations were those that were independent or very specialized and self-contained parts of other organizations. Staff in these organizations were able to devote much time and energy to make their programs successful. To the extent organizations try to operate a micro-enterprise program for poor people "on the side," they never obtain the staff or resources to do well, either because promises of additional resources are never realized or the workload is much larger than anticipated and these organizations cannot make adjustments. (Guy, Doolittle, and Fink)

Finally, and as implied above, operating a micro-business enterprise program for poor people can be a slow process. The amount of pre-loan loan counseling and technical assistance required may be lengthy and intense, and it may take a great deal of time for them to complete business plans.

The U.S. Department of Labor recently began two self-employment demonstration projects, in the states of Washington and Massachusetts, funded through the unemployment insurance (UI) system. These two demonstration projects are one option among several demonstration projects designed to aid the reemployment of dislocated workers. The self-employment projects are designed to build on the fact that about 8 percent of dislocated workers become reemployed through self-employment.

Both projects provide interested claimants with self-employment assistance including payments and business development services, but the approach in each state is different. In Washington, where the project operates in six sites, UI payments to selected applicants are used as lump sum payments for startup capital for micro-businesses. In Massachusetts, UI payments are made periodically as income support payments while the selected participants plan and establish their own businesses. Both projects have control groups and experimental groups.

The qualifications for participation consist of (1) being unemployed and eligible to receive UI assistance; (2) filing a new claim, i.e, not unemployed in the previous 12 months; (3) having no immediate prospects for employment, and (4) being 18 years of age or older. Eligible people are notified and can voluntarily attend an orientation session on self-employment. People who are still interested after the orientation session must submit an application. The state employment security agency reviews the applications to ensure that the applicants have a clear business idea. Applicants with appropriate applications are then randomly assigned to treatment and control groups. As soon as people are assigned to a treatment group they are no longer required to search for wage employment.

In the Washington program, within two weeks of selection, participants must attend a one-week, self-employment training seminar covering business feasibility, marketing, finance and accounting, and organization and management. A business development counselor works with each participant after completion of the seminar to provide individual business counseling, assistance in developing a business plan, and specific problem-solving assistance. Participants are also organized into an entrepreneurship club that meets monthly.

Participants receive weekly UI benefit payments while attending the training and working on their businesses. Participants who meet a set of milestones receive a lump sum payment equivalent to their remaining UI entitlement, which averages about $4,200 but can be as high as $7,200. This payment must be used for business startup capital or to meet basic living expenses during the startup period. The milestones that must be met include (1) completion of the training seminar, (2) development of an acceptable business plan, (3) establishment of a business banking account, (4) meeting all licensing requirements, (5) obtaining adequate financing for the proposed business. A business development counselor reviews the business operations about two months after the lump sum payment to identify areas where technical assistance may be needed.

The selection process and early stages of participation in the Massachusetts project are similar to those in Washington. The initial seminar, however, last one day, and each participant is then assigned a business development counselor. Participants are required to attend biweekly meetings for additional training and peer support.

Massachusetts handles UI payments quite differently than Washington. Participants in Massachusetts receive biweekly payments equal to their regular UI payments for up to 24 weeks as long as they (1) work full-time at starting their business, (2) attend the enterprise seminar, (3) attend the initial counseling session, and (4) attend the biweekly meetings. Additionally, participants can receive a loan of up to $10,000 from a private bank, with the loan application and the business plan reviewed by a committee established for the project.

By fall 1990, about 750 participants had been selected in Washington. Over 44,000 people received invitation letters; 3,160 attended the orientation session; and 1,936 submitted an application. Of those participating, 91 percent were white, 66 percent were male, the average age was 39 years, and the average education was 13.8 years. Nearly 600 people attended all four business training modules. Nearly 400 received lump sum payments, ranging from $783 to $7,380. Over one-half (54 percent) the businesses started were service businesses, and about 15 percent each were retail trade and manufacturing.

In Massachusetts, over 10,000 people received invitation letters; nearly 400 attended an orientation session; about 260 applied; and 105 were selected. Of these 105, 87 percent were white, 65 percent were male, the average age was about 39 years, and their average education was about 14 years. In both Washington and Massachusetts nearly two-thirds of the participants came from professional, managerial, and technical occupations, and only about 20 percent came from production and labor occupations. (Wander and Messenger)

Business Support Assistance

Helping to start or expand businesses, aiding minority business development, and facilitating self-employment and micro-businesses can help alleviate poverty, partly by creating wealth for poor people and partly by creating earnings. But little is gained if these businesses close after a couple of months or even a couple of years. Earnings and wealth may disappear if businesses terminate. As important is the level of earnings that can be generated over time. The age of business and wage levels are highly correlated. "In new enterprises, only about 8 percent of the workers earn more than $25,000. More than 20 percent of the workers in enterprises five or more years old earn this much. The entire wage distribution shifts upward as new enterprises age." (Leonard and Jacobson, p. 300) That smaller firms tend to pay lower wages is in part an age effect. Consequently, business support services designed to improve the long-term viability of a firm can help sustain and increase earnings and wealth, increasing the possibility that poor persons will achieve self-sufficiency.

Access to reasonably-priced capital is a problem for many startups and small firms, but weak management and business skills also are a problem. Some estimate up to 75 percent of business failures are due to bad management. When hard times come, weak management skills often throw small companies into chaos. Small companies are particularly vulnerable to the adverse consequences of a single mistake, because they have less margin for error. The fact 42 percent of the companies that filed for bankruptcy in 1990 had outstanding liabilities of $5,000 or less suggests business support assistance need not be a major undertaking, especially if it is provided early enough. Unfortunately, many small and inexperienced business owners do not recognize trouble early enough, do not call for help until the money runs out, and then even if they find help, can not afford to pay for it. Nearly all the resources of the "turnaround business" (people who get paid to offer advice on management, marketing, refinancing, or restructuring) are devoted to large corporations. (Rowland)

This section covers four different kinds of business support assistance: training for potential or actual entrepreneurs, especially programs that emphasize entrepreneurial opportunities for poor people; business incubators, which provide fledging businesses with low-cost space and access to support services they may not be able to get on their own; programs that provide management and operating assistance to businesses; and the manufacturing network, a new and promising business assistance tool, through which businesses, especially small manufacturing businesses with similar characteristics, band together to access resources available only through the economies of scale achieved through cooperation. The section ends with a discussion of the importance of developing a policy that can overcome disadvantanges of small businesses.

Entrepreneurial training

Many small and new firms fail because the entrepreneur lacks the basic skills necessary to establish a business. Successful courses have demonstrated entrepreneurial abilities can be improved and failure rates reduced through training and technical assistance. The idea behind these programs is that entrepreneurship is a teachable skill.

Entrepreneurship training often is available through publicly-supported institutions such as entrepreneurship programs at community colleges, vocational education centers, and universities. In the past decade, several training programs specifically for low-income entrepreneurs have evolved. Entrepreneurship programs for disadvantaged persons differ from conventional business training programs in three ways: they help entrepreneurs start "micro" businesses rather than "small" businesses; they are more comprehensive than conventional business assistance programs; and they provide psychological support for low-income entrepreneurs — some even help their clients resolve personal problems that might interfere with the success of the businesses.

The distinction between micro-businesses and small businesses can be somewhat indistinct, but micro-businesses generally: (1) employ five or fewer people; (2) can be started with very small amounts of capital (frequently under $1,500 and nearly always under $10,000); and (3) have very low overhead, often because the entrepreneur runs the business out of his or her home. By initially restricting themselves to micro-businesses, low-income entrepreneurs reduce the amount of gross business income necessary to earn a decent living, and reduce the managerial requirements needed to keep the businesses functioning efficiently.

Most entrepreneur training programs culminate in the writing of a business plan. However, unlike conventional business assistance (where the business plan is often treated as a marketing piece to obtain financing), low-income entrepreneurship programs do not treat the business plan as an end in itself. Rather, the business plan emerges after prospective entrepreneurs learn and are led to think about all aspects of running their own business: producing and marketing the product or service, legal structure (incorporation, licenses, registration of name, etc.), internal management, and capitalization and financial pro formas. The resulting document is actually more of a self-employment action plan listing all the steps the entrepreneur must go through to start and operate the business than a business plan designed to raise funds.

The Hawaii Entrepreneurship Training and Development Institute (HETADI) illustrates the potential success of entrepreneurial training for low-income persons. Since its start in 1977 with U.S. Department of Labor funds, HETADI has assisted over 3,000 people through regular classroom training. During the first class, participants describe their proposed ventures. About 50 percent drop out because their ideas are impractical or because they lack the commitment. Those remaining take a three month course, meeting once a week, while they prepare business plans for their enterprises.

The institute's founder explains the business plan curriculum "makes the course immediately and personally relevant; and it gives each person a concrete project as a goal. Psychologically, it is the litmus test for determining how committed a person is to the training and to getting into business. Intellectually, it is a very demanding task that forces a person to think in a logical manner through the steps that he or she will have to take in order to launch a successful venture. In the process, it also helps the fledgling entrepreneur make as many mistakes as possible but to do so on paper and not when it is too late." One-half of those completing the course have started a business and have had a higher survival rate than comparable micro-businesses set up by the population at large.

Providing support beyond business-specific technical assistance is vital for low-income entrepreneurs. Because of the life experiences of most low-income individuals, they frequently need special support in the areas of self-esteem, effectiveness in interpersonal relations, and managing government assistance and family resources.

The special needs of low-income entrepreneurs also have led to a growing number of support services designed to help those living in a low-income environment, such as aid with government assistance eligibility and payments; assistance with child care, medical benefits, and other special concerns of increasingly female single-parent low-income households; aid in debt and credit management; support in developing confidence and personal skills needed to visualize and "act out" successful entrepreneurial behavior; and support in developing the ability to visualize relatively long-term personal and business goals and to work systematically towards them.

A good example of this type of program is the Women's Self Employment Project in Chicago, which was discussed earlier. WSEP provides a package of assistance that includes business planning, technical assistance, personal development and support, and financing. (Corporation for Enterprise Development) It targets unemployed and underemployed low- and moderate- income women who live in Chicago. The vast majority of their participants have been black women. Eighty-two percent of the participants have incomes under $15,000. Since it was founded in August 1986, over 200 women have gone through entrepreneurship training, and about 50 are now self-employed. Their enterprises include cosmetology, day care, catering, floral supply, story-telling, image consulting, textiles, mail order, and word processing.

The core of WSEP's program is peer group training sessions, consisting of about 15 women each, which meet once weekly for 12 weeks. The training program is designed to: (1) develop the traits and characteristics required to be successfully self-employed, (2) teach the basic skills and knowledge required to start and operate a business, (3) complete a personal plan of action for business startup and operation for each participant, and (4) help the participants secure financing for their self-employment projects.

The curriculum is organized around five themes: (1) energy, (2) talent, (3) time, (4) money, and (5) support. The energy sessions focus on marketing because in starting a business, most of the energy is spent on marketing. Very close attention is paid to market segmentation. In fact, much of the art of developing a successful micro-enterprise is carving out and producing a product or service for that niche.

Talent refers to the ability to produce the product or service. In the training sessions, women are asked to bring in and demonstrate their product or service for the group to critique. WSEP helps each woman to assess what additional skills, or training and equipment she will need to make her product, how her product compare with the competition and what she can do to improve her product.

In the session about time, WSEP also covers time management and the legal aspects of running a business, including incorporation, licenses, and tax requirements. In the sessions on money, participants do cash flow projections and accounting. These topics are not taught in the abstract; each participant goes through the exercises for her particular business. This enables the woman to determine whether her business will provide enough income to fit her financial needs. If it will not, she and the group explore what adjustments would make the business financially successful; for example, price adjustments, reduced production costs, or a different market segmentation.

WSEP takes a fairly passive role in helping women obtain better services, providing referrals but little direct intervention. The psychological support comes primarily from the peer group itself, although how supportive the members of a particular peer group are to each other has varied. WSEP's experience has been that less supportive peer groups occur not because of ethnicity, but because of income differences.

Several JTPA programs have had initial successes in entrepreneurial training for AFDC recipients. An Entrepreneurial Training Project outside the Seattle metropolitan area provides 20 weeks of classroom training on small business management and includes a personal effectiveness track to build self-esteem and confidence. Its graduates are eligible to apply for a loan of up to $5,000 from the PIC's revolving loan fund, which was capitalized by grants from five foundations. By mid-1990, 42 of 45 women successfully completed the training. Twenty-three businesses had been started, and 18 of these businesses have been operating for one year or more and have total sales of nearly $500,000. Eight of these businesses are owned and operated by AFDC recipients, and seven have earned enough to transition from welfare. Four other participants have secured jobs, and two others are attending college. In addition, the owners of these businesses hired 13 people with backgrounds similar to their own. (Duncan)

Incubators

Business development can be encouraged through specialized facilities such as industrial parks and incubators — commercial and industrial space specifically designed to nurture the growth of new, young, or expanding firms. An incubator houses small businesses, usually star-tups, in one facility which is often an abandoned factory or office building. An incubator stimulates job creation and entrepreneurial development by nurturing the successful growth of its tenant businesses through services such as low-cost space, shared support staff, and joint purchasing and use of capital equipment. Although many incubators do not provide this full range of service, well-designed incubators can provide the intensive care needed to increase the successes and accelerate the growth of new firms. Entrepreneurs are able to share problems, exchange information, and raise common concerns. They also can engage in technology sharing and joint venturing. These economies enhance business growth, technical development, and stability.

In the past decade, small-business incubators have become a popular tool for state and local economic development. By early 1991, over 400 incubators existed in the United States and Canada. About 17 percent are linked to a university and focus on high-tech entrepreneurs; nearly 40 percent are sponsored fully or substantially by state or local governments or nonprofit organizations, and are used to develop inner city or depressed rural areas; another 14 percent are for-profit, operating like venture capitalists; and the balance are mixed in their form and purpose. Most incubators are small. The median floor space being 25,000 square feet and the median number of tenants is 13. (Reiff)

Incubators can benefit low-income people by targeting businesses owned and operated by disadvantaged entrepreneurs to be the tenant firms, and by locating in low-income areas so the jobs created by tenant firms may go primarily to low-income residents. In devising an incubator policy, states should first recognize what types of incubators best serve their disadvantaged population. Incubators sponsored by government or nonprofit organizations usually try to stimulate job creation and entrepreneurship in a depressed community or urban neighborhood. Incubators sponsored by universities often foster commercialization of university and faculty research.

Several states provide seed funding for organizations wanting to start incubators; financial assistance for site acquisition, improvement, or con-struction; operating subsidies; coordination with other development programs; and technical assistance to communities and organizations developing an incubator, assisting organizations obtain incubator sites (possibly even contributing some of its own unused properties) and making sure they are eligible for state economic development programs that finance site improvements. Private matching requirements for state grants or loans can help ensure the investment of private resources in an incubator.

The New Haven Science Park shows how difficult it is to use a technology-oriented incubator to assist poor people and distressed areas. Begun in 1983, the park received substantial contributions from a nearby chemical corporation, private developers, and Yale University totaling nearly $40 million. State government contributed nearly $6 million, and the federal government and local government, over $4 million. Although 100 of the 170 business startups had survived by the end of 1989 and created about 1,200 jobs, the incubator had not revitalized the inner city neighborhood where it was located and had not provided jobs for many unemployed workers. Most of the jobs were filled with professionals and skilled technology workers. The incubator was losing about $1 million annually.

Nonetheless, state support for incubators is extremely important, particularly for incubators serving low-income populations. Incubators that have succeeded in low-income communities have relied heavily on public sector support. The higher level of real estate risk combined with the wider variety of incubator services required to nurture tenant firms increase the need for state funding. The Milwaukee Enterprise Center, which houses 53 businesses, is losing $98,000 per year although it receives about $500,000 in grants and $300,000 in rent. But about 40 percent of the 260 jobholders in the incubator were formerly receiving some kind of public assistance. (Reiff)

The Fulton-Carrol Center in Chicago demonstrates some of the ways an incubator can stimulate community economic development. (Corporation for Enterprise Development) Local groups founded the Fulton-Carrol Center to stem the decline of a manufacturing neighborhood. In the previous 25 years, the neighborhood had lost over 320,000 jobs as industry moved to other regions of the city or out of Chicago. The Center served 81 firms (57 of them startups) that have produced over 500 net new jobs. Of the 44 current tenant, firms, 21 are owned by women and minorities. Incubators in Akron, Chicago and the South Bronx have used their construction contracts as an opportunity to provide job training in the construction trades. In some cases, incubators have required tenant firms to use the JTPA job training system as the first source for filling jobs. In these ways, incubators have achieved some synergistic effects between job creation and skills training.

While small business incubators may have an important immediate impact on a community's economic development, the greatest impacts take root more slowly, as successive generations of firms enter, grow, they leave the incubator. Over the medium-term, an incubator can foster net job growth by helping tenant companies grow faster and better and by decreasing their failure rate, thus creating and retaining jobs. Over the long-term, tenant firms in an incubator can foster greater entrepreneurship in a community by serving as role models for potential entrepreneurs and by inspiring future generations of new businesses.

A 1990 study of incubators by Coopers and Lyrand points out that while low rent and other operational services were important, these firms say acces to capital was even more important. However, less than one-third of all businesses that leave an incubator and become successful on their own say the incubator played an important part in their ability to obtain financing. The study also concluded that incubators need to provide more access to accountants, lawyers, and other consultants and that incubator managers need to be better trained. Another possible weakness of incubators is that many businesses relocate far away from the incubator, inhibiting the incubator's ability to create or retain jobs in the community in which it is located. (*NADO News*)

Management and operating assistance

Business success frequently depends on the quality of the judgments made about market opportunities, comparative advantages, product positioning, and venture capitalization. To analyze a business opportunity and to build a sound business plan, the business owner or manager must acquire credible, relevant information about technologies, markets, competitors, and factor markets.

State and other public officials have established or funded organizations that provide information and analytical support to prospective business owners and managers. Business assistance services usually provide information and support in venture feasibility assessment, market analysis and planning, business planning, business organization and staffing, capital or loan packaging, financial planning and control, and business operations management. Access to data about new technologies, demographic data from U.S. Census files, and current information about government procurement or foreign trade opportunities are useful to most businesses.

Most technical assistance programs assume the business owner has sufficient knowledge about the industry and its key technologies to operate effectively within it. But the owner may need assistance in some business analysis and management functions in order to decide if a business idea is a sound one. Additionally, new business owners may need advice on how to develop an effective plan to bring the idea to fruition.

The small business assistance programs that have been developed may not be very helpful to the target groups of an economic opportunity strategy. The SBA's Small Business Development Centers program had 56 centers and 560 subcenters in March 1990, with federal funds of $50 million accounting for 58 percent of the centers' total funding. The Centers tend to serve whites (81 percent) and males (62 percent) with some college education (83 percent) who were already in business (two-thirds — usually the retail or service business) when they apply for SBDC assistance. The assistance is relatively brief (60 percent spent 3 hours or less working with program staff). The centers tend to be best at helping with accounting and bookkeeping and filling out loan applications; they are less successful in helping businesses apply for government funds or in identifying sources of capital. (Ols)

In many instances these programs are not well-known by the clients they are trying to serve and are not well-coordinated. A recent report in Iowa suggests there are so many technical assistance providers "users cannot hope to understand the system; even persons involved in providing services are confused....A recent survey of several thousand Iowa businesses indicates that few of Iowa's business development programs are well-known or extensively used...Services need to be more pro-active and more customer-focused. Service providers need to be knocking on new business' doors and assessing their needs rather than waiting for them to walk in the door." (Iowa Entrepreneurship Task Force, p. 11) The report recommended the use of a voucher system, applicable to both public and private providers, in which greater choice is given to the customers.

Finally, few small- and medium-sized businesses have been able to access technology assistance programs, assistance that may be necessary and is certainly important if manufacturing is going to be globally competitive. The U.S. Office of Technology Assessment found only 2 percent of small- and medium-sized enterprises were being reached by technology extension services. (Rosenfeld) This may reflect a critical weakness in American industrial organization. In Japan, both government and large companies provide small companies with technical help. For example, large Japanese businesses may help transfer technology to their smaller suppliers, but when American firms outsource components to small suppliers, the technology to produce these components often is outdated. The director of one manufacturing technology center suggests the technology used by small suppliers may lag their industrial customers by 30 percent. (Holusha)

Many states already have a network of business information and technical assistance support for businesses, much of it built around the higher education system. While most of these state programs provide business education and counseling to the general public within school's service area, some direct their support to low-income or other targeted communities. The Wisconsin Innovation Service Center is a well-established program based at the University of Wisconsin at Whitewater. (Corporation for Enterprise Development) For a modest fee, the program evaluates inventions or new product ideas using consulting specialists in technology and product marketing, along with a computerized data base of relevant technology information. The center's leadership has actively tried to expand its service to women and other under-served groups. The program provides market planning and access to product-seeking manufacturers for those product ideas that evaluate positively. The center augments fee income with very modest support from Wisconsin's SBDC program, and indirect cost support from the university.

Various publicly-supported agencies funded and/or sponsored by the federal Minority Business Development Agency or by state development agencies also provide business support for this clientele. Programs oriented to low-income community clients are apt to build their business development support program around capital access services (business financial planning, equity capital formation, fundraising, and "loan packaging"), but programs that are most effective in supporting viable ventures devote considerable attention to venture analysis and planning. The stronger programs work to create special opportunities for their clients through procurement setasides, capital subsidies, joint venture opportunities, and work comprehensively with suitable clients to develop sound business enterprises around these opportunities.

Wisconsin's Bureau of Minority Business Development provides a range of services, including directories of minority business resources and certified minority businesses, a market-developing trade fair called "Marketplace," and a newsletter for minority suppliers. It also provides outreach to strong out-of-state minority firms considering expansion as part of the state's "Forward Wisconsin" business recruitment program.

Pennsylvania's Community Conservation and Development Program (CC&D), uses seed capital grants to sponsoring community action agencies and other state based nonprofits to attract these groups into a nine-month business training, venture analysis, and business planning program conducted jointly with a private development assistance and financing firm. CC&D makes several grants to venture subsidiaries of these organizations each year, leveraging two or three additional private dollars for each CSBG dollar. After seven years almost all the CC&D-capitalized firms are still operating, and the opportunity analysis and planning in the state's nonprofit community have improved noticeably.

Oklahoma's Rural Enterprise Inc., a private development agency, concentrates on developing viable businesses by analyzing and introducing inventions or technological innovations with commercial potential. A staff of engineers and marketing specialists systematically reviews technology opportunities, then helps local entrepreneurs prepare a business plan. The agency has explored about 50 oppportunities since 1981, and several have developed into job-producing entities. (Corporation for Enterprise Development)

A growing number of states are initiating programs that help businesses adopt new technologies. Illinois and Georgia provide examples of different approaches to technology adoption or "modernization" as these programs are sometimes called. (Hagey)

In 1960, the Georgia legislature created the Industrial Extension Service (IES), now a network of 12 regional offices within the Economic Development Laboratory, one of 20 laboratories administered by the Georgia Tech Research Institute. IES' mission is to help small and mid-sized manufacturers become more competitive by assisting them in the adoption of new technology and otherwise to improve their productivity. The state funds about 85 percent of IES' $2 million annual budget. IES can provide in-depth, on-site consulting services in such areas as facility planning and layout, production and inventory control, market research, advanced manufacturing technology, and quality control. At times, IES relies heavily on the other laboratories for computer science and information technology, electro-optics, materials science and technology, and communications. In 1990 IES provided more than 900 technical assists, held nearly 50 workshops or short courses, and conducted 11 in-plant training classes.

In 1986, IES and the Georgia Department of Community Affairs began cooperating in the implementation of the department's Economic Improvement Program (EIP). Each year EIP uses about $3 million of the state's small cities Community Development Block Grant Program funds to provide low-interest loans through rural local governments to businesses for job creation or retention purposes. At least 60 percent of the jobs created through this assistance must be provided to low- or moderate-income persons. The funds can be used for a wide variety of purposes, including purchasing and installing equipment, constructing, expanding, or otherwise improving buildings and facilities, land purchase, and working capital. About two-thirds of the businesses served are existing businesses.

The relationship has been mutually rewarding because the department (1) obtains a much more accurate sense of whether the business's proposed use of funds is appropriate and viable in the long run and (2) knows that IES will provide or has provided assistance to improve the competitive position of the firm. At the same time, the firm has access to low-cost, good-term funds to undertake some or all of the improvements IES determines is important to the long-run viability of the firm.

Illinois' modernization initiative began operating in 1990. It consists of two programs, a small grant program and a larger loan program. Small- and mid-sized manufacturing firms that have been operating for at least two years but need financial assistance and are suffering a competitive disadvantage are eligible to apply to the Illinois Department of Commerce and Community Affairs for modernization funds.

The Modernization Assessment Grant Program provides grants for two purposes. Grants of up to $10,000 are provided for a competitive base analysis, a comprehensive assessment of a business's operation done by a consultant who produces three products. The "baseline statistical report" summarizes key measures and benchmarks used to assess the firm's per- formance. The "competitive base analysis report" identifies weaknesses in manufacturing technology, operations management, market and product niches, organizational and human resources, and finances. The "problem resolution report" identifies the problems the business must address and makes short term and long term recommendations. The grant must be matched, and the project must be completed within 6 months.

The second part of the grant program provides funds for Productivity Improvement Service (PIES). PIES is an in-depth analysis of a specific problem accompanied by a thorough implementation plan. Businesses are expected to implement the detailed modernization strategy produced by PIES. A PIES grant covers up to 50 percent of the cost to a maximum of $100,000 for a project lasting no longer than 12 months. A firm does not have to receive a comprehensive assessment grant in order to apply for a PIES grant.

Illinois Modernization Retooling Loan Program provides low-inter- est, long-term (7 to 10 years, or three to five years for working capital) loans of up to $500,000 to cover 25 percent of the cost of a project involving the purchase of advanced machinery or equipment or similar assets or expenses necessary for technological innovation. The project must retain or create jobs, increase productivity, and increase revenue or decrease cost. Owner equity must contribute 15 to 25 percent of the project cost.

The Illinois legislature appropriated $1.5 million for the grant pro- gram and $2.1 million for the loan program in FY 1990 and $1.5 million and $1.9 million, respectively, in FY 1991. By spring 1991, the Illinois Department of Commerce and Community Affairs had awarded 17 PIES grants totaling about $1 million and 49 competitive base analysis grants totaling about $260,000, and made six loans totaling more than $1 million. The average grant recipient employed 117 workers, and 63 percent of the firms receiving grants employed fewer than 100 people. All firms that received loans employed fewer than 150 people.

Market development

States can encourage private sector employment of low-income persons by developing markets for the products of companies which are owned by or employ disadvantaged persons. States can also contribute to the health of targeted businesses by purchasing their goods and services. Government purchasing of goods and services can provide credibility so that other purchasers, borrowers, or suppliers do business with a venture. This can be especially important for businesses operating in low-income communities. The credibility lent by government purchasing may help these businesses reach beyond their traditional networks into the broader business community from which they are usually isolated.

Targeted procurement is usually carried out with a procurement setaside program that requires the government to buy a certain percentage goods and services from businesses owned and operated by minorities, women, the physically handicapped, or other populations. Similarly, procurement preference initiatives are probably the most direct form of state assistance in product market development for businesses. States generally authorize a minority business development arm of the government to certify the firms eligible for such assistance, qualifying them for placement on a list of approved vendors or similar publication. State agencies and advocacy groups representing the interests of such firms typically widely distribute this list of qualified bidders and vendors, increasing the chances of effective market making.[41]

Procurement networks are a more indirect method of strengthening businesses. Several states sponsor or contribute to the funding of informational and educational programs — sometimes called procurement networks — that provide information about federal, state, and local procurement functions. Some states have working relationships with the

---

[41]The 1989 Supreme Court decision, Richmond v. Croson, outlawed the City of Richmond's program that guaranteed a certain percentage of construction contracts to minority firms. The decision requires state and local governments to prove there has been a history of discrimination. By early 1991, 12 to 16 states had re-established setaside programs. (Collins)

state-based subsidiaries of the private Minority Supplier Development Council, sponsoring joint workshops, trade fairs, and education and training forums. (Corporation for Enterprise Development)

In a somewhat different vein, several states actively assist help market locally-made products in "export" markets beyond state borders. For example, Montana's Production Promotion Program works with state-based manufacturers and fabricators to identify and tap such markets and to create a distinctive image for their products.

A few state and local governments provide networking assistance that goes far beyond government procurement. For example, Cleveland's Matchmaker Program organizes the purchasing directors of major businesses to increase the number and dollar value of subcontracting with local minority firms. Created under the umbrella of the area's de facto chamber of commerce, the program essentially reverses the trade fair concept. Instead of inviting minority firms to display their goods and services at an open event, the Matchmaker Program involves one purchasing corporation at a time. The company sponsors a gathering for its own staff and for current and potential minority-owned suppliers. These supplies are introduced to potential purchasers on a one-on-one basis, and are given the opportunity to sell their product or service. (Corporation for Enterprise Development)

States also can assist market development by supporting entities that improve the chances of state-based small, minority, and other targeted business for federal or corporate contracts. Most states can count on at least a few private nonprofit agencies, state and community colleges, or units of the state government to maintain current information about federal contracting and procurement opportunities. Many agencies provide both information about these opportunities and assistance in preparing bids, securing performance bonds, and otherwise meeting federal procurement standards.

One example is the Minority Supplier Development Council (MSDC). A nonprofit member organization of over 3,600 corporations, MSDC brings together corporate buyers and minority business enterprises through the efforts of its 50 regional councils. These councils certify qualifying minority business enterprises (MBEs) as minority-owned and operated, act as a clearinghouse and marketplace for information about needs and capabilities, and provide training and assistance to certified minority firms seeking to strengthen their supplier and marketing capabilities. Over $10 billion of member procurement business was placed with MBEs in 1987. While the MSDC program is funded by member corporations, states can add their support to the work of the regional

councils by jointly sponsoring trade fairs and exhibitions, sharing information about state procurement opportunities, collaborating on MBE cer-
tifications, and otherwise highlighting the market development work of the
MSDC.

Several community-based organizations have helped small businesses
market their products by creating exhibition space for low-income
entrepreneurs. This low-cost method of market development has been
used by MICRO in Arizona and the Women's Self Employment Project in
Chicago. Both have held trade fairs for their micro-enterprise clients to
display their wares and meet other business persons and potential buyers.
Not only do these exhibits enhance sales, but they also enable a low-income
entrepreneurs to network with other businesses, to legitimize their businesses, and to increase their identification with and commitment to their
own businesses.

Business networking

We should not think of small businesses solely as isolated small
establishments. It is more appropriate to think of them as a decentralized
network of companies. In this perspective, creating the "capacity to build
strong production networks constitutes a new kind of competitive advantage." (Howard, p. 89) Unfortunately, this country's relative absence
of "small business networks and the infrastructure to support them goes a
long way toward explaining why, with few exceptions, the small-manufac-
turing sector in the United States lags behind that of other major industrial
nations." (Howard, p. 89)

Small businesses need networking. They do not have the economies
of scale or the resources to engage in workforce education, marketing,
technological modernization, and research and product development, that
major corporations have. A 1988 U.S. Department of Commerce survey
points out manufacturing firms with more than 500 employees are 16 times
more likely to adopt certain technologies than firms with fewer than 100
employees. (Howard) A similar situation exists in Canada according to a
1989 survey done by Statistics Canada. (*Commerce News*, 1991 a) At the
same time, it is inefficient for state government to deal with small businesses one on one. Small business networks can help small business
policies and programs be more effective.

Small businesses that are left to fend for themselves are more likely to
compete on the basis of low wages and poor working conditions than on
the basis of high quality and productivity. Small businesses in this country
pay lower wages (by as much as 30 percent) and offer fewer benefits than

larger companies (as noted earlier, part of this may be an age effect). Yet, this is not the case in all countries. (Howard)

Manufacturing networks can perform three critical tasks: (1) aggregate production to enable small firms to meet the demands of large purchasers, (2) increase value added by helping small firms increase their ability to produce finished goods instead of performing a small, interim task and letting another firm make the final product, and (3) effect cost-sharing and economies of scale. (Hatch, 1990) One business commentator notes: "Small business can help countries compete only if countries create the conditions that make for a dynamic small business sector. In the end, a society gets the kind of small business it wants." (Howard, p. 103)

Several states are beginning to create, or facilitate the creation of, networks for small businesses, generally called flexible manufacturing networks. The network building process starts with identifying a cluster of related firms and ends with the creation of network hubs, or "permanent service centers through which the networked firms manage their affairs." (Hatch, 1988) The network centers can provide a wide array of services, including, subcontracting, procurement, electronic communications, strategic planning, equipment sharing, and loan guarantees. Through the network, such tasks as market research, product design, or transportation are shared. Additionally, network managers or brokers provide ongoing technical assistance to the network members. Manufacturing networks, however, require a balance of scale. On the one hand, they need a minimum number of firms to take advantage of and provide resources to the network. On the other hand, because of the importance of micro-innovation, complementary use of resources, and the need to build trust through communication, the scale has to be small enough to permit regular face-to-face communication. Experience suggests a 60-mile radius may be the maximum geographic scale, although some rural networks run 100 to 200 miles.[42]

The Illinois Department of Commerce and Community Affairs illustrates one state's approach to creating manufacturing networks. Illinois' initial effort is focused on export manufacturing networks, partly because

---

[42]Loveman and Sengenberger conclude that "concentration in a locality may not merely be significant for the pooling of resources and for their exchange, but also for the process of diffusion of innovation and new technology....Density of demand and supply is also an important functional requirement of occupational labor markets that rest on easy substitution and mobility of workers with the same skills across firms....Further, work sites must be close enough geographically to avoid undue mobility costs." (Loveman and Sengenberger, p. 56)

only 18 percent of the state's 20,000 manufacturers export their products, although as many as 75 percent may have the potential to export. In 1990 exports accounted for 14 percent of gross state product and about 6 percent of the state's total private workforce.

The department is trying to create a network through a request for proposal (RFP) process. Its RFP explains why networks can be valuable to small- and mid-sized firms. "Small and medium-sized companies often face barriers which keep them out of international markets. Managers in many of these companies simply lack the experience to assess their potential to compete in international markets. Other companies lack the resources to conduct the necessary market research or to follow up on trade leads. Some companies require assistance in modifying their products to meet foreign standards, and others need assistance in arranging financing or transportation of their finished products. Communication with foreign buyers also presents a barrier as does the need for specialized legal services to do business with other countries. The establishment of Export Manufacturing Networks which will allow these companies to pool resources, coupled with the technical support of knowledgeable network managers and export training assistance, will assist these companies in overcoming these initial barriers." (Illinois Department of Commerce and Community Affairs, p. 2)

Illinois' RFP establishes four goals for the project: (1) establish Export Manufacturing Networks throughout the state; (2) provide training in export-related skills to key personnel in small and mid-sized companies who are members of the network; (3) help network brokers organize and ease access to technical assistance and other resources available from federal, state, and local governments; and (4) recommend changes to state laws, regulations, policies, or programs to improve the state's climate for exporting.

To accomplish these goals, the contractor is expected to (1) refine the network model (roles, responsibilities, tasks, processes), (2) identify target industries, (3) establish coordination objectives, (4) develop curricula, (5) select and train brokers and other key personnel (including state staff), (6) establish networks, (7) provide on-going technical assistance, (8) reiterate the process (in other sectors and other parts of the state); and (9) evaluate network effectiveness.

The RFP requires that at least 65 percent of the costs be provided as a match to the state grant. The state expects to begin the process by the end of 1991 and have a network in operation by the end of 1992.

Economic Opportunity through Supply and Demand: A Summary

State economic development practice no longer emphasizes supply-side activities — incentives designed to lower the factors of production, especially capital or land, to attract firms who are relocating or estabishing branch plants. Now state economic development practice emphasizes demand-side activities — incentives designed to create new or sustain existing businesses to increase aggregate output and demand through activities targeted to specific industries.

The traditional supply-side approach to economic development is not gone and still is relevant, but rarely is it used to provide economic opportunties to poor people or distressed areas. Its core economic opportunity focus, if it has one, is to provide incentives, usually capital incentives, to businesses that move to or expand in distressed areas. Enterprise zones are the most recent and most publicized example. To the extent enterprise zones target specific firms, promote startup businesses, and attempt to increase aggregate economic output and demand, they may be considered among the newer demand side activities. In practice, however, most enterprise zone programs fall within the supply-side approach, and do not help rebuild distressed areas or provide much economic opportunity to poor people.

The supply-side activity now most pertinent to increasing economic opportunity for poor people is workforce education and training, which has never been a core economic development practice. The business community and the economic development community talk about the issue, but little actually happens. Privately financed workforce education and training mostly affects upper level managers, and involves a relatively small number of firms. Publicly assisted workforce education and training greatly has focused on the more disadvantaged portion of the workforce, and has become "owned" by welfare, training, and, more recently, community nonprofit organizations and institutions. The economic development community rarely is a major player. This is unfortunate because economic development practitioners have much better access to the business community. It becomes doubly unfortunate because evidence suggests tying remedial education directly with skills training in a workplace context may be the most effective way of improving the labor force performance and self-sufficiency of poor people, especially welfare mothers.

While demand-side practice is now the focus in economic development, its emphasis on venture capital, high technology, and exports may limit its utility as a major resource for economic opportunity. Some aspects of demand-side activities do provide an opportunity for economic development practice to promote in a significant way economic opportunity for poor people. These aspects include encouraging risktaking, targeting specfic firms, aiding the market, and focusing on working with startup businesses, entrepreneurs and micro-businesses, and small businesses.

Minority business development is one key. Black businesses employ relatively more blacks than white businesses, but minorities, especially blacks, are underrepresented in business ownership and wealth. The increasing importance of self-employment and the major role played by small businesses, especially small manufacturing firms, in net employment growth and economic competitiveness, also make tapping these resources for economic opportunity very important.

At least three dilemmas must be overcome, however. First, creating entrepreneurs or small businesses in personal services or retail trade may be problematic, at least after an initial aura of success. The propensity of these kinds of businesses to fail has a long history, especially if they are unable to expand out of a small, closed set of consumers. Second, these firms often need both financial and business support service assistance. Providing one kind of assistance without the other, or providing only short-term or superficial business support assistance may be ineffective. Third, these firms often have weaknesses, such as low-wage and fringe benefits and lack of workplace training and education, that must be addressed.

Public policies toward small and new businesses may significantly influence the income and asset opportunity small firms are able to provide to poor people and their potential contribution to America's ability to compete globally. Otherwise, Eisinger's conclusion about state demand side activities may be and remain correct: these activities generally "are not geared to the employment and welfare needs of the poor. The unskilled, the uneducated, the geographically and culturally isolated are not likely to benefit in substantial numbers from programs that enlarge the pool of venture capital or help to nurture a new high-technology industry....Economic development remains by and large a world apart from the welfare state...and is a policy domain in which a middle-class vision defines both the nature or the problem and its solutions." (Eisinger, pp. 342-343)

4

Delivering State Economic Opportunity Resources

As the preceding chapter shows, states often implement economic development-related programs by working through local governments, the private sector, and nonprofit organizations, especially community-based organizations. Also, states increasingly are attempting to link various programs and activities, especially job training, education, and welfare. Because of the complexities of implementation and the varied institutional resources required to address poverty, states must pay as much attention to the delivery of resources as to the substance of programs and activities.

This chapter addresses two important facets of resource delivery, local implementation and collaboration among resources. The chapter first reviews the four major sets of institutional resources available for a state antipoverty policy — education, welfare, job training, and economic development — and discusses barriers and incentives to linking them. Next, the chapter looks at the rationale for and some experiences with the local implementation system, then reviews building local capacity. Finally, the chapter reviews approaches to collaboration and describes successful collaborative efforts.

States often do not deliver economic development-related resources directly for two reasons. First, some state constitutions or laws prohibit it. Second, it may be impractical due to a state's geographical size. States are more apt to deliver directly through locally-based state offices welfare and employment service resources than education, job training, or housing resources. On the other hand, local organizations deliver some welfare resources, and some states directly deliver some education, job training, housing resources, and more frequently, economic development resources.

Even if it were legally and practically possible for states to deliver resources directly, there are some arguments against it. One is that states can be much more effective if they cajole, nudge, and leverage other entities and resources, especially those of the private sector. The second argument is that public bureaucracies are paternalistic and provide top-down services with little lasting value.

Proponents of the first argument think the public delivery system must be redesigned. The key elements of this redesign include (1) responding to real demand rather than creating supply, establishing a new program, for example, and hoping demand is high enough to use the program; and (2) leveraging additional resources, especially requiring a commitment of private sector funds before committing public funds, to obtain through wholesaling a scale and breadth of resources large enough to solve the problem or attain the objective. In such a system, programs or resources would be available on a competitive basis — users of resources would have to want them, and compete against one another to get them. Since the resources would have to meet a market test — there would have to be a real demand for them — accountability would occur. Programs or resources would have to show real use and impact. This "market facilitive" delivery system could take many forms, except a public agency directly providing a full and complete resource that has not been market tested or designed.

The second claim argument against direct state delivery of resources charges a public delivery system is more responsive to political pressure or need than to success. Also, a public delivery system does not create, indeed it prevents, a sense of ownership and control among those it is trying to serve. Proponents of this argument advocate an "empowerment" delivery system that reflects community control through a geographical targeting of resources to a very poor community or neighborhood. Journalist David Osborne describes this empowerment delivery system: "I think we can even think about delivering many public services through local development institutions to get that local ownership....The model we use now is sort of the top-down model where the poor are passive clients and public bureaucrats provide services for them — and I think that model fosters dependency. I think we're learning how to empower local communities by investing in local organizations....The focus of our development work should be on building local capacity — building the capacity of local institutions, local leaders, local actors and local communities to work together in new ways to create economic growth....Genuine development will not happen in a poor community unless it comes from within. Government can help, the private sector can help from the outside, but we can't make it happen from the outside."[43]

---

43 Presentation by David Osborne at COSCDA's conference on Expanding Opportunities for Employment and Self-Sufficiency, Cleveland, Ohio, June 21-23, 1988.

The market facilitative delivery model is broader than and can incorporate some aspects of the empowerment delivery model. For example, community-based organizations can play an important, although not dominant, role in the market facilitative model. Local organizations and leadership are important to both models, and both models recognize the importance of integrating a variety of social and the economic resources. The last chapter of this report suggests a competitive delivery system similar to the market facilitative model, but any delivery system developed by a state will need strong local organizations and effective collaboration among resources.

Resource Linkage

To respond effectively to poverty, institutions and agencies, resources and funds, and policies and programs must be linked in mutually complementary and reinforcing ways. Resource linkage is critical to designing and implementing a state antipoverty strategy for two reasons. The nature of poverty requires using multiple resources in a patterned fashion to address the array of poverty problems. Second, addressing poverty is expensive, and the fiscal restraints facing the states and the nation will limit additional funds in the near future. As noted below, a substantial amount of money already is budgeted for poverty-related problems. These funds, and the institutional resources and programs they represent, must be linked to maximize their effect.

The term "linkage" refers to a continuum of multiparty relationships among resource providers. Although such a continuum may be conceptual, it helps clarify the kinds of relationships that must be considered in creating the resource collaboration so important to an effective antipoverty strategy. The continuum moves from communication through coordination, cooperation, and collaboration, to integration.

Four major sets of institutional resources form the basis of a state antipoverty policy: education, job training, welfare, and economic development. All are involved in employment training, especially the first three. States have the most experience in linking welfare and job training, and are beginning to get experience in linking welfare, job training, and education. States have not yet linked economic development in any meaningful way to one or more of the other sets of institutional resources to assist disadvantaged persons and distressed communities.

Buckshot Federalism

To respond to complaints that a certain clientele are not being well-served, or a specific delivery system is not being used, or a certain activity is not being funded, our political system often creates new programs. In 1988 the Congressional Research Service identified 73 "antipoverty" programs funded at $159 billion that were authorized by 18 congressional committees and administered by 12 federal departments. (Levitan, Mangum, and Pines) Medicaid, Title X of the Public Health Service Act, Title XX of the Social Security Act, and the maternal and child health services block grant all fund family planning services. Recently, California had over 80 job-related training programs, and Michigan, over 70. (Grubb et al.) A 1986 study in New York found 42 different employment, training, and remedial education programs administered by eight state agencies with total annual budgets exceeding $380 million. (Mauro and Yago) In fiscal year 1989, the federal government spent $60 billion on programs and services for children, allocated through 340 programs. (National Commission on Children)

Over time, this buckshot approach generates a number of cacophonic programs and leads to complaints about duplication, inefficiency, and ineffectiveness. "Multiple layers of bureaucracy and extensive recordkeeping and reporting requirements — developed in part to guard against misuse of public funds — often cost more than they save," according to the National Commission on Children.

The structure and politics of our federal system of government ensures compromises and complexities in the way programs are financed and managed. Few domestic programs are entirely financed and administered by the federal government. Most involve some financial commitment from and management participation by state or local governments, or other delivery agencies. For example, "most of the 219 new grants authorized between 1963 and 1966 intentionally by-passed state and local government....Both the War on Poverty and the Model Cities programs channeled funds to community-based organizations created to increase the participation of lower income residents and to put these programs beyond the control of local power brokers." (Robertson, p. 253)

The states' financial and administrative roles in welfare policy illustrate this complexity. States manage the AFDC program and pay about one-half the costs. They have substantial discretion in setting need and payment standards and using the "special needs" and "emergency assistance" portions of the AFDC program. States manage the food stamp program, but the federal government pays for it, and state discretion is minimal. States pay for slightly over 40 percent of the costs of Medicaid, administer the program, and have discretion in the kinds of benefits included beyond a mandated core. General assistance is paid for by states (and some local governments) and administered by states (and some local governments). The federal government pays for and administers its other food benefit programs; it pays for nearly all and administers most of its education assistance programs. It pays for nearly all its subsidized housing programs, but delegates administration of most of them to local public housing authorities, which operate largely independently of state and local government. It pays for nearly all the costs of the JTPA program, but delegates administration to the states and "entitlement" private industry councils and local governments. It pays for nearly all its energy assistance programs, but these programs are largely administered by states. It pays for about two-thirds of the costs of various social service programs, but these are largely administered by the states. And it pays for and administers the earned income tax credit program.

Many of these programs have different eligibility requirements and funding cycles. Some of these programs are entitlement, like AFDC, food stamps, and Medicaid, in the sense that those who meet the means test get the benefits. Others are discretionary, like subsidized housing and job training, where those who meet the means test do not necessarily receive the benefits. It is a little wonder why many people consider welfare policy unmanageable and ungovernable.

This buckshot federalism makes developing overarching policy difficult, and makes policy and program collaboration even more difficult. Although the number and importance of federal categorical grant programs diminished in the 1980s, the legacy of buckshot federalism remains, and its existence and impact may never disappear. The primary cause of buckshot federalism may now be the cumbersome and fragmented congressional subcommittees, whose prerogatives and independence are often reinforced by federal bureaucracies. For example, Congress has established three major but separate institutions for employment-related training: vocational education within schools, based on the Carl Perkins Act for vocational education; job training outside the schools involving state and local governments and the private sector, based on the Job Training Partnership Act (JTPA); and the recent job-training program with welfare programs, JOBS.

Unfortunately, concepts like policy collaboration or program coordination excite neither the academic community nor lawmakers. Complaints about the unwieldiness of current policies and programs can result in conclusions that government is part of the problem and not part of the solution, or that new approaches need to bypass existing channels and agencies. Nonetheless, this complexity has to be squarely faced in state approaches to competitiveness and poverty.

Linkage Barriers and Incentives

The complexity of social policy naturally makes linkage very difficult. This section describes some problems that must be overcome to obtain effective linkage. Several factors help promote linkage, however, and these are identified before discussing resource collaboration.

The states' experience in the 1980s with coordinating welfare and work requirements shows that when states had substantial flexibility, they developed different structures and processes of linkage. Many of these differences depended on the degree of involvement of welfare, JTPA, and employment service agencies and whether participation by these agencies was formal or informal. Although organizational arrangements did not appear to affect service quality, the experiences illustrate several linkage issues. (Burbridge and Nightingale) The illustrations below are drawn from this experience.

Fragmentation and turf

Institutional fragmentation is one of the most visible barriers to linking economic development and employment and training activities. For example, few states put JTPA and CDBG responsibilities in the same agency, and many states house community development, employment training, and economic development in three separate organizations. Economic development activities are not always located in a single state agency — tourism promotion, business technical assistance programs, or industrial development loan programs may all be in separate agencies.

Fragmentation is made more complex by the fact that employment and training, education services, and economic development often are delivered by local entities that set their own priorities, hire their own staff, and often function in a web of peculiarly local interests that strongly influence program development. A public agency is usually held accountable, and its success measured, only by the extent to which the agency fulfills its specific mission. The division is exemplified in the JTPA system where local PICs have independent boards, but a mandated source of funding. Although the state can set priorities and performance standards, the local agency chooses which programs to fund. Many vocational technical institutions and community colleges function with even more autonomy, acting as independent entities able to commit to programs and policies of their own accord.

The most common barrier to linkage is simply the issue of "turf." Too often, staff of an agency or program believe, or others think they believe, they should control all activities directly related to their core responsibility; for example, that all job development and placement should be centralized in the employment service agency. This raises fear in others of having their personnel, budgets, and reputation lessened. In the recent past, turf conflict between JTPA and the employment service has often been pointed. Rapid policy and program changes or competition for limited resources tend to heighten turf concerns and inhibit linkage.

Another barrier to linkage is that different programs and program personnel can have different perceptions about services and clients, some of these ideas may be based in perceived or actual program constraints, and some may be based on broad program philosophy. For example, a JTPA-dominated process may yield little day care assistance, because JTPA program staff may want to use scarce supportive service funds for other purposes, or because they do not believe that day care is a real barrier to employment. Welfare personnel may be less interested in invoking sanctions or taking other punitive actions, while non-welfare agencies may not have a good understanding of the barriers and problems facing welfare recipients.

Similarly, job training or placement administrators may have a stricter definition of "job ready" than welfare agencies, and these differences can inhibit coordination as the welfare agency sends referrals to job placement agencies. Welfare agencies might see the reluctance of job placement agencies to work with their clients as a bias against welfare recipients. Also, a JTPA-dominated process is less likely to use extensive case management, in part because JTPA subcontracts most services, leaving management to its various service providers, because JTPA staff do not come from a social work tradition, and because case management generally is considered an administrative cost.

The interests and perceptions of business, the prime client of economic development officials, are often barriers to establishing programs for the disadvantaged. The prime interest of business in employment and training is access to a relatively skilled job-ready population. This contrasts directly with the premise of most employment and training programs: that with the right programming, the disadvantaged (and others) can be "trained" into a job. In fact, as one prominent observer notes: "Business is not really interested in training... You have to show them the need for training at all." The point is supported by a Pennsylvania official: "Training is the lowest thing on the totem pole... companies need someone to run a machine." Most employers use training for existing workers rather than new hires. (Public/Private Ventures, p. 15) Where an expanding economy does mandate new hires, business, particularly large business, still appears to associate some stigma (perhaps as a holdover from CETA days) with the employment and training system and its client population. Officials in a number of states have noted that business sees some employment and training institutions as unresponsive and irrelevant. While no distinct prejudices were described, one state official noted that welfare affiliation was, to some employers, "a problem." (Public/Private Ventures)

Programmatic constraints

The means by which programs and systems operate, the client groups they serve, and the roles and restrictions surrounding program design all offer additional barriers to linkage. The most obvious barrier is that programs are actually different, no matter how similar their objectives, activities, or clientele may be, and these differences are usually consciously chosen. What someone may see as an unimportant program characteristic that is a burdensome barrier to linkage may actually be an essential component of a program in which the "barrier" can be eliminated only by dramatically changing the nature of the program. These very specific programs often are created in response to specific advocacy and interest groups.

The targeted nature of employment and training programs often impedes linkage. Many employment, training and education programs are directed to clients with particular socioeconomic characteristics, such as dislocated workers, ex-offenders, refugees, transitionally needy, pregnant and parenting youth, or AFDC mothers. The narrow nature of this targeting and the restrictions in funding, service and programming tend to inhibit flexibility and the establishment of broadly-based program efforts. JTPA's emphasis on job placements as the key measure of success may influence employment training agencies to focus on more employable participants. The agencies' need to maintain ties to the business community may keep them from dealing with the most disadvantaged persons, a group that would include most AFDC recipients. AFDC recipients often have basic skill levels below the standards set by JTPA training.

Categorical programs abet agency concentration on narrowly defined services, and often discourage consideration of larger, more important issues, or how a particular service fits into a larger problem-solving effort. Because of this specificity and targeting, service providers often operate in different locations, forcing those seeking assistance to wend their way through a maze of application forms and organizations. "...Families frequently are required to travel to different locations, complete lengthy applications, and comply with differing eligibility rules and regulations (including interviews; documentation from employers, landlords, medical providers, or all three; and asset verifications). Some will qualify for all three programs, some for just one or two. Others will encounter daunting procedural and bureaucratic hurdles." (National Commission on Children, p. 317)

More serious from the economic development point of view is the stigma attached to some targeted programs. Targeting has helped lead economic development officials away from programs aimed at the most disadvantaged and toward broader programs open to all. This position is reinforced by a natural inclination to a more employable clientele. Reflecting a strongly perceived business bias toward a skilled, job-ready population, economic development efforts have tended to focus on the recently unemployed and soon-to-be dislocated workers.

The nature and direction of existing economic development programs also tend to work against the development of programs for the disadvantaged. In most states, economic development programs focus on firms with 50 employees or more. Typically, these firms' greatest needs are for skilled entry-level workers and upgrading of the existing workforce, needs that current employment and training programs are least prepared to meet.

Other programmatic barriers reflect questions of training, planning, and efficiency. For example, economic development officials pride themselves on a quick response to business requests, but they often find the employment and training system, particularly in community colleges and vocational schools, has a different mode of operation. As one official described it, "Education institutions generally make their decisions by committee and have a longer time line...many companies are oriented toward short-term results." (Public/Private Ventures, p. 17)

Additional programmatic constraints to linkage include different recordkeeping and reporting requirements. For example, if JTPA has one standard for recordkeeping and reporting on its clients, and the welfare agency has different, more stringent requirements for its clients, then it would be very difficult for JTPA agencies to work with welfare clients because they would have to establish a second, separate set of recordkeeping requirements for the subset of welfare recipients who use JTPA resources. (Regulatory and reporting requirements do differ between JTPA and JOBS. For example, JTPA's reporting requirements do not produce the kind of information required monthly by JOBS.)

Significant barriers to coordination often consist of minor program characteristics, such as different application requirements, cycles, and time frames; and different contracting requirements. For example, it may be illegal for some agencies to enter into a contract if the pay for their services depends on a future performance review.

Incompatible computer systems, a particular problem for tracking clients across programs which adversely affects comprehensive feedback on client progress or outcomes or needs, also adversely affects linkage. The problem is not the paucity of computers, but the lack of integration. Confidentiality is a common difficulty; people have privacy rights that may be difficult to hurdle when agencies begin to collaborate, and this issue must be worked through carefully. Another problem is inconsistent interpretations of federal or state regulations, such as the effect of JTPA Summer Youth program income on an AFDC grant, or whether to advocate child care disregards or child care subsidies for welfare clients.

The absence of effective linkage often raises the specter of duplication and waste, which makes it all the more difficult to gain public and electoral support for antipoverty programs. In the employment training area, duplication often exists in assessment and job placement. (Burbridge and Nightingale) A key reason for this is JTPA programs often contract various employment training-related services to different vendors. A Service Delivery Area (SDA) may undertake recruitment and initial assessment, but contract job readiness training to another agency, basic skills training to a third, and placement to a fourth. Also, most of the job developers in an area probably approach the same firms, with little incentive to share contacts or job leads. These duplication problems are probably much more intense in urban areas because of the greater use of community-based organizations.

Programmatic constraints can be particularly severe when an effort is made to provide a comprehensive array of services. Each funding source mandates its own specific accountability, which can cause fiscal and administrative nightmares to an organization that accesses multiple funding sources to provide a flexible array of services to its clients.

Certainly, political barriers exist: some groups or agencies may be able to put political pressure on institutional leaders or elected officials to get their "fair share" of program resources or to lay claim to resources because they best represent or are the only ones that can represent or provide outreach to certain communities or clientele. In some cases effective linkage may give way to political dispersion.

Incentives

There are several incentives for linkage. The most important is that a very strong economy with very low unemployment rates helps mainstream

AFDC recipients or other poor people through job training, job placement, and related services. Understandably, a "hot" economy places a premium on putting people into the workforce, and the hotter the economy the more the quest for additional workers will focus on those who may be considered marginal in a weaker economy.

Another factor promoting linkage is the degree to which state officials push collaboration. If state leaders provide clear, explicit policies and exhortations for collaboration, local officials do follow-through and engage in activities that address the announced and encouraged policies.

Political initiatives also can foster linkage, but this usually occurs when political leaders highlight their concerns with a particular target group or need, such as adult illiterates or high school dropout rates. Entrepreneurial administrators can promote coordination as a way to increase resources or reputation. For example, JTPA can get high marks in performance standards by working with welfare clients; at the same time, welfare agencies can tap JTPA for training resources for their clients that otherwise would not be available. Also, the importance of personal initiatives and relationships cannot be underestimated; fostering increased personal contacts can lead to improved coordination. (Grubb et al.)

Federal prompts for linkage, such as mandating information sharing, help establish an atmosphere conducive to coordination and increase awareness of programs, but their contribution may be very limited. Both the Carl Perkins Act and JTPA require coordination at the state level, but much of this formal requirement involves formal information exchange and overlapping membership on various committees.[44] While the JTPA statute may suggest using education agencies, most state JTPA programs interpret the requirement expansively to include any agency offering educational services, such as private schools and community-based organizations. It appears that information exchange and formal coordination between JTPA and vocational education has brought about little program

---

[44] JTPA's 8-percent funds are designed to improve coordination with education. Some states divide these monies among secondary and postsecondary schools or require schools to apply to local private industry councils for the funds (Wisconsin, North Carolina). Some states first establish clear priorities and distribute 8-percent funds according to these priorities. The funds may go to education agencies or to correctional facilities (Iowa), welfare to work programs (California), or specific training (Kentucky). But in most states, 8-percent funds are simply another source of job training dollars with slightly different strings attached, and are not used to facilitate system change. Most 8-percent funds are allocated for one year and are disbursed in relatively small amounts, minimizing opportunities for system change. The match requirement is usually met by in-kind contributions and creates administrative problems without enhancing coordination. (Grubb et al.)

integration and little program change. Also, federal funds for coordination are relatively small. The 8-percent JTPA funds are a small percentage of JTPA funds, while Carl Perkins Act funds account for about 2 to 4 percent of vocational education resources spent by postsecondary schools and 5 to 10 percent by secondary schools. (Grubb et al.)

The most powerful incentive for linkage is paying for it. Setting aside or making resources available only for linkage helps produce linkage. If the amount of linkage money is small or short-lived and if linkage is seen as costly or risky, however, even offering to pay may have limited affects. At the same time, the relative scarcity of resources, especially if framed within the context of having to address the same set of related problems, often prompts searches for and the implementation of resource linkage. The examples at the end of this chapter illustrative the potential effectiveness of paying for linkage.

Creating Resource Collaboration

As mentioned earlier, linkage can be viewed as a continuum of multiparty relationships. At the less intense end of the linkage continuum is communication — organizations and agencies simply sharing information. This can be personal and ad hoc, for example, one or two staff people from a couple of organizations occasionally exchanging information; or it can be formal and systemic, for example, regular and sustained meetings among key level staff based on explicit agreements. Communication is absolutely necessary for effective linkage, but communication by itself does not necessarily lead to common undertakings.

A more intense level of linkage is coordination. Coordination is a conscious, explicit effort to ensure that multiple resources and activities not interfere with each other, or that they reinforce and complement one another. Coordination requires a commitment to act, not just to share information, but the action is often unilateral, within a single organization or program, and the adjustments are usually marginal. Examples of coordination include welfare agencies referring job-ready clients directly to employment services; JTPA staff going to other agency locations to do job development and placements; and collocating JTPA and employment service staff.

Cooperation implies much more of a joint undertaking than coordination. Organizations recognize that they have some similar goals and objectives, attempt to share or use one another's resources, and help one another use their resources effectively. Examples of cooperation include setting aside JTPA training slots for work-welfare clients; providing JTPA funds to employment services to do job development and placements for

JTPA clients; and diverting welfare grants to a wage subsidy for JTPA-run on-the-job training.

Collaboration suggests the creation of shared goals, with organizations actively helping one another achieve results that cannot be achieved individually by pooling some of their resources, and jointly planning, implementing, evaluating, and accepting shared responsibility for their performance. (Melaville and Blank) Examples include extensively using JTPA funds for work experience for teen welfare parents, using adult education funds for GED classes for welfare recipients, using welfare funds for child care connected to JTPA training, and funding a large program by pooling funds from JTPA, work-welfare, Title XX social services, and CDBG. (Burbridge and Nightingale)

At the most intense end of the continuum is integration which is an actual merging of resources, organizations, and operations.

Buckshot federalism and the existing plethora of organizations and institutions make linkage difficult. Simple communication is often difficult because of the heavy use of esoteric acronyms and language, the categorical nature of many programs, and the different geographical focus and location of many organizations that are involved in similar activities or problems. Certain kinds of linkage, especially communication, coordination, and cooperation occur and have positive results. But the kind of linkage that is usually necessary for truly effective results is collaboration. Collaboration commits staff and resources to pursue shared goals in a way that usually alters the organizations and programs involved in the collaboration. While integration may also yield highly effective results, the political and administrative reality of creating widespread and comprehensive integration is slim.

Linkage is not easy; collaboration is difficult. Yet, if states are to develop effective antipoverty strategies and use their economic development resources with other sets of institutional resources to address the intertwined issues of poverty and economic competitiveness, states must effect collaborative ventures.

Unfortunately, there is no recipe that can be mechanistically followed to produce collaboration; there is no key that unlocks a secret route through the complicated maze of buckshot federalism. Below, however, are several suggestions for creating the environment necessary for collaboration, developing a structure for collaboration, and establishing the operating guidelines for a state-driven collaboration.

Creating the environment for collaboration

Four elements are necessary to create an environment conducive to collaboration. Collaboration requires commitment and trust. Collaboration can occur more easily when organizations, agencies, and other groups have a history of communication and cooperation. Participants are familiar with one another and their resources and usually have built a level of trust. Where there is no culture of cooperation, it becomes extraordinarily important to initiate and sustain extensive communication among representatives of institutional resources. The role of the governor, and of agency heads and other organizational leaders, becomes particularly important when extensive communication must be established. Direct gubernatorial leadership is often necessary to move bureaucracies and overcome turf protection.

The second element necessary for collaboration is a well-articulated vision. Two kinds of visions facilitate collaboration. One is a broad vision of a desirable and believable scenario. This vision should communicate the need for change and help "rally the troops" around a goal. The second is a more practical vision, one that specifically contains the objectives to be accomplished, the activities to be undertaken, and the resources to be involved. (Melaville and Blank)

Vision-setting provides potential collaborators an understanding of a valuable goal that requires changes in the way people operate and resources are used. It also energizes people to focus on new goals and change old agendas. Vision-setting requires leadership, and is a particularly critical role for a governor. In states with successful collaborative ventures, the governor usually has played a central, visible role in vision setting, encouraging, almost pushing people, into new behavior. A governor's active presence can help dissipate perceptions or philosophical differences that often exist among different program or organizational staff. People in the human services institutions may need to see that "business" and "economic development" are not dirty words. Similarly, people in economic development institutions often need to understand that providing employment and earnings to poor people does not mean business as usual, and that it is a vital objective for the economy and integral to their mission.

Vision-setting and gubernatorial leadership are important also because government often operates with geologic timing, taking forever to make incremental adjustments. The leadership provided by a governor can short-circuit the time it takes government to change. At the same time, vision-setting and gubernatorial leadership can help overcome the other kind of timing problem often faced by government: the tendency to take short-run views and make decisions solely on exigencies of the moment, and not view policy beyond the next election. Embarking on a major collaborative venture, like a state antipoverty strategy, requires attention to the long-term goal and operation of the collaboration. Antipoverty collaborative ventures often take time to work and show their effectiveness. Too often political leadership is impatient.

Third, accountability is important because collaboration involves participants from many different organizations and operates within a complex program context. Collaboration requires clear expectations. Everyone, including the collaborative participants, must be aware of the expected results. Clear expectations not only provide accountability but also guide collaborative participants in performing their roles. Thus, clear objectives; activity and resource allocation benchmarks, or a series of interim standards that can be used to keep the venture on track and show progress; constant monitoring; and the making of mid-course corrections need to be built into the collaboration.

Finally, collaboration requires effective communication and relationships at the staff level. While the key early role needs to be played by the governor and his or her key policy staff, especially in setting the vision for the collaboration, mid-level staff must be involved early and continuously. Sometimes it may be important to select staff participants carefully, so that the early fragile stages of collaboration can be nurtured. Collaboration requires staff with grit and determination. Mid-level and other staff may also have to undergo special training so that they understand the contributions of the various resources and become familiar with delivery techniques and required documentation and recordkeeping.

Structuring collaboration

This report reviews three options for structuring collaboration: rational oversight, the use of an intermediary, and incentive funding.

The most traditional approach to collaboration promotes program and organizational linkage through planning or rational oversight. This approach can increase familiarity among agencies, promote joint planning, allow the packaging of different kinds of funding to accomplish common goals, and facilitate increased flexibility in state or local funding. Potential collaboration participants engage in intense planning to develop a rational, comprehensive scheme for the use of resources, and meet regularly to review progress or provide input into agency decisionmaking. This may lead to formal written agreements to coordinate activities and share client referrals and to formal financial agreements to transfer funds from one agency or program to another.

It is not uncommon, especially in the education and employment training area, to see attempts at rational oversight and financial contracting. A frequent example is that of the local SDA contracting, often on a competitive basis but nonetheless building relationships, with an education agency, usually for classroom training and remedial education, sometimes for assessment. In some cases the SDA buys "slots" for its clients in regular instruction in the education agency, with JTPA paying for tuition, fees and ancillary services, and clients sometimes getting Pell grants. Sometimes a community college receives state revenue for its JTPA students, thereby lowering the cost to the SDA. (Grubb et al.)

A less frequent example occurs when the education agency uses JTPA funds to pay for assessment, counseling, day care, and transportation for its JTPA-eligible students. This model is limited in practice because only 15 percent of local JTPA funds may be used for support services. Another example is an education agency that provides customized training for particular firms and reserves spots for JTPA clients. (Grubb et al.)

States have been able to use JTPA 6-percent incentive funds, which the state can allocate to local employment training programs based on state criteria, to foster local collaboration. States can require education, employment training, and other agencies to review JOBS plans; states can require employment training plans to specify how they will meet the needs of JOBS participants; and states can require employment training councils to include representatives of welfare, education, and other related representatives. (Porter)

If the rational oversight approach involves the relevant sets of resources, it can be effective. But it usually involves only a small number of participants and a limited amount of fund sharing, as some of the illustrations above indicate. When this approach does involve a substantial number of participants, it usually ends up as coordination or cooperation within the linkage continuum.

While many states have adopted some form of consultation, planning, or liaison designed to promote collaboration, few have reached the point of routinely reviewing new projects for the possibility of developing linkages. The result is much more communication, information sharing, and marginal adjustments to programs than pooling resources, substantial financial contracting, and the development and use of shared goals.

Another option is to use a third party to deliver a comprehensive array of services. This approach uses multiple funding and an organization that is not integral to the education, welfare, job training, or economic development institutions. This intermediary can be an existing organization or a new organization created solely to effect collaboration.

Large organizations often have difficulties distributing resources in distressed areas or to specific locales because they lack specific knowledge of local needs, competencies, or opportunities. Intermediary organizations can be well acquainted with the activities of the smaller organizations they serve and be able to channel effectively resources to the local level. Intermediaries can provide a bridge between the large government agency or foundation wishing to fund community economic development and the community-based organization.

Establishing a new institution that combines funds from several different sources creates a separate identity and can integrate funds rather thoroughly. However, these new agencies must also juggle different standards, accountability reports, and funding cycles, and may simply make the existing plethora of related agencies more complex if they simply add to and do not replace other agencies. (Grubb et al.)

The most effective approach to collaboration is to pay for it through incentive funding. Dedicating funds to a collaborative initiative has three clear benefits over other approaches: ease of implementation, effective use of available resources, and opportunities to leverage federal funds. In some cases, it promotes a level of creativity and flexibility seldom found in employment and training programs.

Unlike other forms of interagency collaboration, incentive funding may require only a request for proposal (RFP) open to particular organizations or agencies. A program can be put together relatively quickly, avoiding the need for costly and difficult program development or bureaucratic restructuring. Experience shows an initial setaside of as little as $300,000 can be sufficient stimulus for new programming, and that RFPs can be conceived, developed, and implemented in as little as one year.

New, targeted funding may be the best way to make existing resources, programs, and institutions work together more efficiently. States already have the key components of good program design: resources to stimulate new jobs (based in commerce or economic development programs); a functioning employment and training system (based in the PICs); advanced education and training facilities (community colleges or technical schools); and a system to provide management and support services to the disadvantaged (welfare). Position papers and well-meaning efforts at coordination usually will not make these four separate systems work together; money often will.

The RFP mechanism lends itself to capturing both existing and new federal program dollars. The flexibility of new federal funding mechanisms allows states to take quick and maximum advantage of these resources, building programs that match state funds with a three-to-one or four-to-one federal contribution from these new sources.

Nurturing collaboration

Because collaboration is fragile, the state must nurture it. The state should act as a facilitator or mentor, assisting non-state organizations to form and collaborate. While the state is in a unique position to articulate goals and objectives, the state cannot carry out an antipoverty strategy using only its own resources and agencies in a command and control fashion. Because problems, people, and organizations vary, a state cannot create a single model of collaboration that would work everywhere. The state must try to achieve some sense of local ownership, and must permit substantial local design.

Although the state needs to be flexible, it cannot operate under a philosophy of anything goes. The state must establish guidelines and benchmarks, monitor and evaluate, and communicate its findings and concerns. The state must intervene in the collaboration to make adjustments where warranted, perhaps even changing collaboration participants. If the state, especially through the governor, has articulated a vision, fostered communication, involved high- and mid-level staff, and set clear expectations and standards, it will be able to carry out its nurturing responsibility. This suggests that collaboration funding should be as performance-based as possible. Program outcomes must be defined and measured and linked to funding, and information on outcomes must be obtained and communicated. Yet, performance funding should recognize the need for flexibility. Performance funding should not interfere with the creation of different collaboration structures and processes, and should include multiple definitions of performance. (Hoachlander)

State and local governments must ensure that full and accurate data are collected and analyzed over time. Although this may be frequently impracticable, consideration should be given to establishing control groups, a consideration that this report will not dwell on. The nearly ubiquitous computer makes this more possible now than just a few years ago, if recordkeeping and information systems are compatible. Even though extensive data collection and analysis take time and money, they are worth the cost. One of the reasons there is so little systematic and valid information from which to design and implement policies now is the absence of much good data from past policies and programs. Those who claim "we know what works" may be basing their claims solely on the basis of ideology or anecdotal experience.

Policies should include provisions for individual assessments and mutual obligations for program recipients. As to individual assessments, for example, one cannot assume that all 19-year old mothers on welfare, or all the male, young adult, minority residents of a ghetto poverty area, have the same resources and needs and will respond similarly to the same incentives. Regarding mutual obligations, both the programs offering resources and the clients of the resources should have specific obligations to one another. The resource recipients must understand their obligations.

In summary, collaboration is essential, but fragile. While diverse conditions and circumstances require flexibility in a state's approach to collaboration, the state must nurture collaboration by establishing performance guidelines, monitoring performance and interviewing when necessary. Collaboration also requires a set of mutual obligation between resource providers and their clients. Finally, creating a vision of the process and goals of collaboration is critical, and a major responsibility of governors.

Local Delivery System

Many economic development strategies depend on partnerships between local communities and their indigenous resources and outside resources and institutions. Often these partnerships are unsuccessful because the people they aim to aid are ill-equipped to participate in them. Unless distressed communities and disadvantaged persons are capable of taking advantage of opportunities, incentives, and resources, they will remain competitively disadvantaged. Local individuals and groups should be able to analyze local needs and articulate those needs to government and the private sector. They should possess the skills to undertake successful enterprises and provide the enterprises with ongoing support. Building local capacity must focus on individuals and on organizations.[45]

Leadership Training

No community can sustain successful development without a core of dedicated and skilled leaders, community entrepreneurs equipped to find innovative approaches for community enhancement. Increasing the ability of local officials and residents in low-income and economically-distressed areas to participate in economic development activities enhances their

---

[45]Many of the examples of leadership development and capacity building are taken from MDC, Inc.

ability to communicate with state and local policymakers. At the same time, state and local governments gain invaluable opportunities to learn firsthand about local problems, enabling them to design more effective programs. But efforts to increase the involvement of minority and low-income groups in public affairs seldom are matched with training to help representatives of poor communities meet the challenges of the positions to which they are elected or appointed.

Leadership development is one of the most basic elements of capacity building for communities trying to create jobs and renew themselves economically. Although formal community leadership programs proliferate today, few attempt to train citizens for active roles in development, and even fewer are targeted to distressed communities.

Leadership training programs for low-income communities should be specialized, and comprehensive. First, a leadership development program should teach about economic trends and the strengths and weaknesses of competing development strategies, about the policy process and the operations of key development organizations, and about assets and resources needed for economic improvement.

Second, an effective leadership development program needs to develop a range of skills among citizens in distressed communities. Leaders should develop the ability to analyze issues, develop realistic options for action, and gain personal and process skills, enabling them to work productively with different groups of people, manage conflict, and build consensus. Basic technical skills will enhance local leaders' abilities to develop policy from sound information. These skills include the ability to interpret and use data, analyze the assets and detriments of a local economy, and understand the tenets of strategic planning.

Third, an effective leadership training program should include simulated and actual opportunities in which participants can apply their skills and knowledge to real problems.

Fourth, leadership training should help create networks to provide a mechanism for ongoing change. Leadership ranks need constant replenishing. Training can build networks and develop structures for ongoing training through existing organizations or the creation of new organizations. Networks can link members of an economically-disadvantaged community with valuable contacts outside the community. Periodic follow-up training and other opportunities to reflect on the process of guiding community change can also benefit local leaders.

The following examples of leadership development programs address some of these objectives:

- The Rocky Mountain Institute (RMI), a nonprofit organization in Denver, Colorado, has designed a community assessment and planning approach called the Economic Renewal Project. The project's four main objectives are to plug financial leaks from the community, strengthen existing businesses, encourage new local entrepreneurs, and selectively recruit businesses from outside the community. The process is conducted through community meetings and citizen task forces that identify problems and solutions.
- The Highlander Center in New Market, Tennessee, operates an economic development training program in two community colleges to help low-income people understand basic economic development theory and alternatives. They then apply this knowledge to economic development strategies to improve their communities. The program demonstrates that by understanding local and regional economic issues, analyzing the changes in a local economy, conducting simple cost/benefit analyses of various economic development strategies, and using the basic concepts of development finance, citizens are better able to address priorities at a grassroots level.
- The Heartland Center in Lincoln, Nebraska, helps communities understand the nature of economic growth and change by building a leadership development program around the concrete task of generating a "vision of the future" and a plan of action to meet future goals. Participants are taught to use hard data and their imaginations to select a course for their community's future. Teams are formed as citizens work together toward solutions. The program emphasizes hands-on learning rather than applying leadership skills in a vacuum. Heartland's program provides a straightforward and effective way of boosting a community's ability to apply basic skills to actual problems.
- Since 1965, the Kellogg Foundation has supported state and regional programs to help rural citizens and members of the agricultural community participate in public affairs and advocate for rural issues. The Kellogg programs help individuals understand critical trends by relating local and state issues to national and international development so that community leaders can understand the forces affecting their communities. These programs are often based at land-grant universities and operate as continuing education activities through cooperative extension services. In 1987, more than 20 programs funded by Kellogg or based on the Kellogg model were in place. Programs refine the skills of those already in positions of leadership and

develop new leaders. Most introduce people to the workings of political and economic systems so they can better analyze public policies and solve policy dilemmas.

- The Wilowe Institute in Arkansas is a private, nonprofit organization that identifies, develops, and supports leaders in rural and urban areas. It holds an annual symposium on issues of statewide concern, then shares ideas from the meeting with other organizations in the state. The statewide meetings also help build a statewide network of concerned citizens. A fellows program provides intensive workshops for low-income, grassroots citizens. In addition, the Institute provides "action training" in the field by taking past fellows into a rural community to hold a one-day symposium. The Wilowe Institute is currently working on ways to convene meetings where rural and urban leaders can undergo leadership training and discuss key issues.

Creating Organizational Capacity

Low-income and distressed communities also need to develop the institutional capacity for a long-term approach to expanding economic opportunity. Capacity building refers to activities that enhance the functional competence and versatility of an organization. Technical assistance refers to help that is needed to carry out specific operations or programs. Community-based efforts generally should rely to some extent on outside assistance from experts with particular specialized skills. While capacity-building is more useful over the long-run, it is time-consuming. One approach is to provide ongoing capacity-building activities, while offering one-time technical assistance for complex problems that the organization will rarely face.

Capacity building occurs through identifying and improving the skills of individuals and by building the ability of local public and private institutions to undertake or influence local development. Economically-distressed communities often lack a range of competent organizations that can respond to local concerns and work to see local priorities reflected in public policies. These organizations are needed to amplify and coordinate the efforts of motivated individuals and provide a mechanism for concerted action toward the development of economic opportunity.

Training and technical assistance activities can work against capacity building because they focus on the technical elements of completing a particular project, such as a housing development, which are generally undertaken by outside experts without truly bringing the community into the process and building its inherent capabilities. Technical assistance should accompany efforts to build local leadership and involve local organizations in the development process. Technical assistance is successful from a capacity-building point of view if the experience a local group gains from one project makes each successive project easier.

Capacity building programs for low-income communities should address three types of organizations: (1) competent local government institutions able to execute their responsibilities to meet the needs of a wide range of citizens and interest groups in a given community; (2) strong local or community-based organizations that can complement and supplement the efforts of the public and private sectors to develop new opportunities for disadvantaged citizens, and; (3) effective intermediary/resource organizations that can provide a bridge between the distressed communities and the public and private resources on the state and national levels.

Building local government capacity

States have long recognized their role in building the competencies of local government. Many states have adopted mechanisms to provide this type of training. Universities in some states, such as Virginia, have established Institutes of Government to equip local officials with the skills needed to do their jobs. In South Carolina, the State Development Board uses teleconferences to train local development personnel through its Economic Development Institute.

The Pennsylvania Department of Community Affairs offers an outstanding example of providing technical assistance to general purpose local governments. Its technical assistance services include training, on-site consultation, and peer-to-peer technical assistance.

The department trains over 20,000 people annually, offering over 70 courses. Examples of the training courses the department regularly offers include:

- contracting for municipal services,
- risk management and municipal insurance,
- road and street maintenance,
- downtown revitalization,
- economic development,
- housing rehabilitation,
- neighborhood preservation,
- property tax assessment,
- labor relations,
- organizational development,
- police management,
- small computers,
- time management,
- cash management,

- municipal bookkeeping/accounting,
- municipal budgeting,
- industrial wastes program, and
- sludge management.

The department has a full-time training staff and a video tape library, and works with other state agencies, local government associations, and colleges and universities. It also trains nonprofit organizations in board training, effective public relations, fund raising, grant management, program planning, and other areas.

The department provides on-site consultation in intergovernmental cooperation, general management, financial management, code administration, public works management, police administration, personnel administration, and community development. An intensive peer-to-peer technical assistance program focuses on police administration, municipal finance, downtown revitalization design, and community action agencies. Through the department's circuit rider program, several small localities can share professional staff in municipal management, public works, personnel, recreation, finance, economic development, code enforcement, and public safety. Finally, the department maintains and publishes local government statistical data on revenues, expenditures, taxes, and indebtedness.

A local capacity building program that emphasizes economic development and the manufacturing industry is Michigan's Local Area Modernization Program (LAMP). LAMP is an offshoot of the Michigan Modernization Service, which advises manufacturers on the adoption of programmable production equipment, and offers a manufacturing support services program that provides training plans, labor relations consultation, and market analysis services to manufacturing firms with fewer than 500 employees. LAMP, which is targeted to smaller manufacturing firms, analyzes the manufacturing base of a locality (usually a county) by surveying at least 75 percent of the firms operating in the area to develop a database on firm demographics, products, processes, and uses of technology. Staff from the Industrial Technology Institute at the University of Michigan use the data and other information to analyze supplier-customer linkages and prepare recommendations on how local economic development strategies can improve the competitive capabilities of local manufacturers.

Building the capacity of community organizations

Although small local organizations will always rely on technical assistance for more specialized knowledge, they should develop base levels of expertise to ensure they provide a resource for the community and can competently manage the public and private resources supporting their operations. Budding organizations may need the same types of assistance that new small businesses need, such as assistance with legal structures, personnel management, general administration, financial planning, recordkeeping, public relations, and operations management. Special needs may also exist in an organization such as a community action agency that decides to move into the economic development arena. Organizations intending to run their own ventures will need to become familiar with the organizational development needs of a business venture. States may need to assess the fiscal systems and management capabilities of community organizations and intermediaries where public monies may be expended. Technical assistance can be provided to organizations lacking these basic institutional capacities and can offer mechanisms for boards and staffs to receive training in these areas.

Community Development Corporations (CDCs) are particularly vital organizations because they explicitly promote economic renewal activities. CDCs have evolved a great deal since their pioneering days in the 1960s. While the 1980s brought a swift end to the major sources of federal funding, it did not reduce the number of CDCs; between 1981 and 1986, over 1,000 new CDCs emerged.

In Massachusetts, the Community Development Finance Corporation was formed as an independent, public corporation to provide equity and debt investments in CDC-sponsored enterprises in blighted areas. In addition, Massachusetts provides small grants to CDCs and other community-based organizations as well as general administrative expenses to organizations working in distressed areas through its Community Enterprise Economic Development program. The program has created new CDCs and provided continuing support. The state-established Community Economic Development Assistance Corporation is a quasi-public institution that provides technical assistance in project development, staff development and other areas.

Florida adopted its state Community Conservation Strategy after riots in 1980 in the Liberty City area of Miami. It included a program to provide interest-free loans and grants to CDCs operating in distressed areas. Miami's focus on community-based development took off after the riots in Liberty City made it clear that the city faced the problems of a maturing urban center with a definite underclass, racism and disinvestment in poor neighborhoods. Miami created a network of new and retooled community-based organizations that currently controls nearly $90 million worth of development programs including housing, real estate development and commercial revitalization in Dade County and the Miami area. Efforts to establish new groups were undertaken at the county level, in the Office of Community and Economic Development for Dade County. Florida has provided funding for administrative support supplemented by private sector involvement from the Greater Miami Local Initiatives Support Corporation.

Other examples of CDCs include the Delta Foundation in northwest Mississippi which was founded to help inject investment capital and cultivate entrepreneurship and business expertise in an impoverished rural region with a large minority population; the Hilltown Community Development Corporation in western Massachusetts, which promotes small business development by providing entrepreneurial training and small enterprise loans; the Spanish-Speaking Unity Council in Oakland, California, which provides organizational and program development assistance to other organizations through its Development Resources Consulting Group; and the Mountain Association for Community Economic Development which has designed economic development projects that target business opportunities in key industries in the area, such as the hardwood products industry.

Community-based organizations, especially those in distressed communities, fight a continual battle to secure funding for specific projects and to maintenance operations. Community and local organizations need to reach a level of stability that allows them to devote most of their time to working for economic growth rather than worrying about how they will pay the rent and meet the payroll. The development of stable funding sources is a goal of most CBOs. Even in low-income communities, community and local organizations should draw upon sources of local support, such as personal savings, government transfer payments, social programs, and service contract funds that can fuel economic development. While some states have provided direct funding for community-based organizations, others have established loan funds to provide seed capital to CBO projects or to cover startup expenses. The following three examples illustrates the kind of assistance states can provide to CBOs.

- Ohio has set up an association of CDCs with 57 members funded primarily through private sources, with a small amount of state money. The nonprofit association aims to promote the work of CDCs in the state, build expertise within CDCs, and build public awareness about CDC activities. Ohio's funds are housed in the Department of Development in the form of small grants that are awarded on a competitive basis for particular projects.

- In Massachusetts, the state-funded Community Economic Development Assistance Corporation provides technical assistance in real estate development to nonprofit organizations in economically-distressed areas. It also provides interest-free risk money to cover soft costs, such as architect fees, legal services and application and permit fees. The Community Development Finance Corporation is a state-funded venture capital agency that makes loans to businesses and affordable housing projects in distressed areas. The corporation only makes loans to communities where CDCs are located and CDCs sponsor the projects.
- The New York Division of Housing and Community Renewal operates a program that funds the administrative costs of over 300 nonprofit organizations conducting economic development activities. The state has established an elaborate network that allows the groups to share technologies. The division also provides technical assistance ranging from basic accounting to how to run a board meeting. The state program is designed to foster independence and the ability to develop innovative programs within the local organizations themselves.

States can ensure educational institutions have incentives to work with communities in enterprise development, leadership and other capacity-building ventures. Secondary and post-secondary institutions can play an important part in preparing people to assume leadership roles, or they can get involved in specific economic development projects. Schools, colleges and universities are particularly important in isolated areas where they may house most of the technical resources for an economically-distressed community. Innovative efforts include the School-Based Enterprise Program in Hartwell, Georgia, which provides high school students with hands-on experience managing and running small businesses and makes the school the focus of community renewal activities. The school can elect to retain or spin off these businesses.

Community colleges are another potentially valuable resource because they can offer a range of business training services and specialized services such as literacy education and other forms of human resource development. Community colleges may offer a particularly promising delivery system because most are already experienced at providing practical training and community outreach. In addition, two-year schools such as Hocking Technical College in Ohio have developed revenue-generating businesses that provide on-the-job training and fill demands in the local economy.

Four-year colleges and universities have become more interested in economic renewal activities in their local areas and have proved a valuable source of technical assistance, data collection, and leadership. For example, the Northwest Area Foundation gave Iowa State University a grant to use its expertise to aid community development in the Southern Iowa Development District Project which targets a nine-county rural region.

In Washington, the Department of Community Development and Washington State University formed a community revitalization team that provides technical assistance to distressed areas. The partnership has offered demonstrations and workshops that provide leadership and organizational development training as well as programs designed to help local areas gain access to startup funds for local projects. The team works with economic development organizations, local governments, chambers of commerce, tribal organizations, businesses, and other local groups. These efforts are targeted to counties with high unemployment rates, those that have experienced sudden or severe loss of employment, and areas with a high percentage of individuals with incomes below the county median.

In Ohio, Cleveland State University established the Center for Neighborhood Development as part of its urban center. The nonacademic center is designed to support the efforts of neighborhood organizations in housing and community development activities.

A range of other systems exist which could help build citizen capacity in distressed communities. These include churches, chambers of commerce, agricultural extension agents, and rural electric cooperatives. The question is how they can be retooled to meet the needs of disadvantaged communities.

Yet from a state perspective, relying on community-based organizations can be problematic. CBOs often have many functions, such as financing, owning, or managing property, lobbying city hall and the state house, operating programs, helping shape local development policy, recruiting businesses, and providing technical assistance to neighborhood residents, has no clear notion of what they are about, what they do well, and what they do not do well. Sometimes they are not supported by the citizens they purportedly serve, and they are unaccountable for their performance, relying more on political or moral suasion for their livelihood and funding than on measures of cost-effectiveness. Some people argue that information brokering such as leading local businesses through the maze of regulations, is what CBOs can do best, but few CBOs spend much time doing this unglamorous task. (Buss and Vaugh) From a regional or metropolitan perspective, a multitude of CBOs can result in intra-regional competition and a proliferation of plans. For these and other reasons, intermediary organizations have sprung up, with states increasingly seeing intermediary organizations as a way to clarify and improve the outputs of the plethora of CBOs.

Intermediary organizations

Intermediaries collect resources from larger organizations and distribute them to smaller organizations. Intermediaries do more than funnel resources, however. The mark of a true intermediary is its ability to provide additional services. The intermediary combines the distribution of money or information with some added value, such as technical assistance. Intermediaries can help local organizations develop the capacity to work with other groups on the local and state level and allow local organizations to pool scarce resources and avoid duplication of effort.

Because intermediary organizations bridge the gap between smaller community organizations and larger entities such as state or federal governments or large corporate funders, they may be ideally suited to provide technical assistance. Intermediaries may also be an effective mechanism for states and other large funding entities to channel funds to the local community. Intermediaries could provide ongoing evaluations that may be more attuned to the problems facing a community since they should be aware of the barriers that community or particular minority populations face.

Three intermediaries, the Greater Miami LISC, the Greater Miami Neighborhood Organization, and the Greater Miami United Technical Resource Center, provided technical assistance to community-based organizations that was critical in establishing a network of community organizations in Miami. As one local government official described it, "We were talking about groups that, in 1981, had no track record, no experience, but they were committed to rebuilding their neighborhoods. That commitment, once it was there and once it was demonstrated, wasn't enough to build those shopping centers, to get the housing constructed. It really took technical work with them on putting together business plans."

Chicanos por la Causa (CPLC) in Arizona is a CDC that has grown to become a statewide intermediary organization with a $4.2 million annual budget. It also has a host of affiliate nonprofit and for-profit organizations operating housing and real estate development projects, a credit union, and several loan funds. CPLC has worked extensively to help the state develop a comprehensive economic development approach rather than a set of fragmented programs. CPLC staff have gained skills that have allowed some of them to move into state agencies. According to CPLC's president, "We've used internships, we've used the business colleges and universities, we've brought in interns and used these kinds of people that grew up in our community and then turned them into qualified applicants and qualified people that could be used by the private sector, and more importantly, that could be used as qualified staff for our different· programs."

In some cases, states may create intermediaries. North Carolina funded its Rural Economic Development Center to develop and test initiatives for rural economic development in the state. The center works in partnership with other state government agencies just as, on the local level, municipal and county governments could work in partnership with community development corporations or other community-based organizations.

Examples of Resource Collaboration

This section presents four examples of state-generated resource linkage. The Ohio example shows the initiative taken by a state development agency to engender job-based collaboration set within the context of welfare reform. The New York example shows the beginning of a comprehensive neighborhood-based collaboration driven largely by a state social services agency. The last two examples, Pennsylvania and Maryland, illustrate a state-initiated collaboration reaching across economic development, employment training, and welfare resources.[46] In each of these four cases, collaboration at the state level was designed to produce collaboration at the local level.

Ohio's Demonstration Employment Opportunity Program

In spring 1990, Ohio launched a demonstration program using the RFP incentive process. Although led by the Ohio Department of Development, the Department of Human Services, the Department of Education, the Ohio Bureau of Employment Services, and the Ohio Board of Regents — state agencies already working together to implement the JOBS program — cooperatively planned and helped implement the demonstration program.

---

[46]The information on Maryland and Pennsylvania is taken from Public/Private Ventures.

The state agencies designed the demonstration to be part of the JOBS program, but emphasized providing an adequate and skilled workforce to employers. The state awarded demonstration grants to local governments, through a competitive RFP process, to foster and test better ways of identifying, creating, and retaining job opportunities for job-ready AFDC recipients, placing appropriate persons in those jobs, and supporting them in employment for the time necessary to ensure self-sufficiency.

The state established a very important secondary goal: improving the collaboration of local groups and individuals involved in human services, employment services, job training, education, and economic development, and involving the business community in the collaboration. This goal articulated the state's belief that collaboration was necessary to (1) ensure that JOBS participants are prepared for jobs available in the local job market, (2) get businesses to recognize the JOBS program as a valuable resource to meet their workplace needs, and (3) get economic development professionals to see JOBS and similar programs as integral to their economic development objectives.

Ohio also saw the demonstration as an opportunity to improve its own performance by providing resources, incentives, and technical assistance, removing state-level barriers, and becoming an active partner with localities in efforts to assist disadvantaged persons.

RFP content

The state's department of development and department of human services provided $500,000 in state and federal funds for the demonstration program. Ohio limited demonstration grants to a maximum of $75,000, and encouraged localities to contribute local, nonfederal funds as a match to generate additional federal JOBS money. State customized job training money also was available as a JOBS match if localities undertook eligible customized training activities.

Ohio limited eligible applicants to those in existing JOBS or JOBS demonstration counties (43 counties), but did not limit the project to a single county. Applicants could be a local government, a local office of a state department, or a private nonprofit organization. A broad-based network of local public, private, and nonprofit organizations, businesses, and individuals had to designate the applicant as lead agency for the project and had to provide written statements agreeing to participate in and provide resources to the project if funded by the state. Ohio required the support and involvement of the Private Industry Council, the county department of human services, the local employment service office, and a local economic development or business organization. Consideration was limited to one applicant per county or multi-county consortia.

Because it was a demonstration program, Ohio wanted to fund a variety of projects, including established collaborative networks and those struggling to be born. The state also hoped to fund projects in a variety of areas: areas with labor shortages, areas of high unemployment, urban areas, rural areas, and small and mid-sized cities. Finally, the state wanted to fund different types of lead agencies.

The RFP had five sets of eligible activities. One set was job creation or retention activities, such as targeting job development efforts to certain industries, developing first-source hiring agreements, providing financing subsidies to businesses for job creation, or developing entrepreneurship. The second set of eligible activities focused on identifying and targeting job training, for example, expanding the use of existing training programs, or providing training in industries willing to commit to job placements. The third set focused on marketing: marketing and coordinating various employer incentives, such as OJT and the targeted jobs tax credit, marketing individual incentive programs, such as the earned income tax credit, or improving the selection criteria for referral of JOBS clients. The fourth set of activities dealt with coordination and linkage: collocating existing services, developing collaboration in assessment and other tasks, or cross-training staffs. The fifth set covered retention and long-term employability: supporting JOBS recipients after placement or evaluating long-term success.

Applying was a two-step process. First, applicants submitted a "concept paper" that described the need for the project, the project's connection to the local labor market, the proposed collaborative network, and the proposed project. It also identified the specific performance measures the applicant intended to use to measure the success of the project. After reviewing these concept papers, a state interagency team selected applicants who were asked to prepare a final, more detailed application.

Ohio used eight criteria to select the winning applicants: soundness of local planning and analysis, composition of collaborative network, involvement of economic development agencies and businesses, use made of existing resources and the extent to which the use of these resources by clients and businesses will be simplified, firmness of commitments of resources, characteristics of the lead organization, project feasibility, and the extent to which project selection would result in a good mix of projects statewide.

The concept papers were due in May. The state notified final applicants in June. Final applications were submitted in July, and the state selected 11 grantees in October 1990.

Local projects

Ohio funded a variety of applicants and project types. A county community action agency was the lead agency in two cases, one rural county and one urban county. In another rural county, a private, nonprofit development corporation, working under the auspices of the chamber of commerce, was the lead agency. In Cleveland, the lead agency was a community-based industrial development and job training organization that was organized and supported by other community-based organizations.

The rural projects emphasized job preparation and placement in computers work, and all involved the local school system. In one rural project, the community action agency was to form a nonprofit corporation to employ and provide OJT to 20 AFDC recipients. The local vocational and technical school was to provide on-site training and a business firm agreed to provide technical assistance to the training. The other rural project involved a wide array of agencies active in helping special needs populations, such as the mentally retarded, the physically disabled, or those suffering from drug or alcohol abuse.

The urban county project included comprehensive case management, business marketing (a strong outreach to businesses to prepare for job placement), and advocacy. This project emphasized placement in business service and manufacturing jobs. Two organizations, both oriented to the business community, became partners with the community action agency for the first time. The local urban league and school system also were involved in this project.

The Cleveland project focused on the west side of the city and was committed to helping job-ready AFDC clients find jobs with 400 small manufacturing firms in the same neighborhood. Several service agencies agreed to provide support services in the neighborhood, rather than require clients to go downtown. This project was heavily oriented toward participation by community-based organizations, although it also involved the school board and funds from two local foundations.

Most projects tended to commit to job placement for 20 to 35 people. Total costs ranged from $100,000 to $230,000.

Interim results

An interim progress report produced in September 1991 indicated all projects were well underway with extensive collaboration being sustained at each site. Significant and successful effort were being made to avoid duplication by using existing job clubs, assessment programs, and supportive services. The only negative note sounded was that job placements were fewer than originally projected, due in large part to the impact of the recession that was unforseen in early 1990. By September 1991, the 11 grantees had enrolled 1,817 clients and conducted 1,954 assessments. The grantees had placed 729 people into pre-employment training and 598 people had completed training. Employers had interviewed 241 people and hired 257. An additional 76 people had received on the job training. The average gross weekly wages of those hired was $195.02, or $4.88 per hour; 85 percent of the employment was full time; and 63 percent of the employees had some kind of health insurance. Nearly one-quarter of the employment was in the clerical or sales area; another 26 percent was in the services area, and another 3 percent in machine trades.

New York's Neighborhood Based Initiatives

New York also initiated a locally-based demonstration program in 1990. Unlike the Ohio program, New York's was based in statute, with much more detailed guidance (Ohio's RFP was eight pages long, compared to New York's 39 pages), and was much more comprehensive and long-term.

In 1990, the New York legislature enacted the Neighborhood Based Initiatives (NBI) Act. The law acknowledges that the absence of a unified strategy for service delivery is particularly onerous on communities suffering widespread poverty. The act's goals are to (1) expand and strengthen service delivery and help identify reduce barriers to effective service delivery and (2) provide integrated and coordinated services to selected distressed areas in the short-run, while helping these areas develop long-range plans to address their overall social and economic conditions. In other words, integrated service delivery should be followed by more long-term housing and economic development activities.

The NBI legislation contains three key components relative to providing integrated services. First, the law permits the state's Comptroller to transfer funds from appropriations made to any state agency to support NBI services. Second, the Department of Social Services can enter into a single, unified contract with an NBI project. Third, when approved program costs cannot be funded using existing government or private resources, the special appropriation for NBI "service gap" monies can be used to support these costs.

Thus, state government has three major roles. One is to act as a facilitator — initiating the planning process and assisting neighborhood efforts to develop neighborhood-based services. A second is to act as capacity builder — providing technical assistance and helping neighborhood service providers meet programmatic or administrative requirements. The third role is that of funder — targeting existing sources of public funds and coordinating efforts to identify regulatory or statutory waivers that enhance the neighborhood's ability to implement its NBI project.

The law established an oversight committee of 21 state agencies chaired by the Department of Social Services. The committee is charged with selecting applicants and providing technical assistance. By the end of 1990, the oversight committee had prepared a Request for Applications (RFA) and had preselected 17 high-need communities: seven neighborhoods in New York City, five outstate urban centers, and five upstate rural areas. The preselection was done in accordance with the law's requirement to select urban, suburban, and rural sites, and after a review of detailed "community need" data, such as percent minority, median household income, and poverty, dropout, teenage birth, infant mortality, public assistance, and unemployment rates. The committee also used "readiness" as a preselection criteria — evidence of networks, such as an economic development zone program, community schools, or adolescent pregnancy networks. The committee asked the 17 preselected communities to apply, noting that four to six would be selected initially to share $500,000 in planning grants, with the intent of sharing $2 million annually in follow-up implementation or "service-gap" grants.

The range of eligible applicants is wide. It includes nonprofit, public, or private agencies, a school district, a local government, or any combination. The oversight committee encouraged partnerships.

RFA Content

Each applicant had to complete and update its "community profile." The committee completed an initial community profile for its preselected communities, based on the community needs data. This profile briefly described the target area and demographic characteristics, and identified key issues and resources. The updated profile had to (1) identify the boundaries of the targeted neighborhood (the committee suggested focusing on a single housing project or at least a neighborhood not exceeding 10,000 households so changes could be studied over time), (2) describe the services currently existing in the community, (3) identify the service gaps and barriers, and (4) identify the resources available to implement the project. Applicants had to provide neighborhood resident feedback.

The approach to developing or expanding services to neighborhood residents could vary. Entirely new services could be added, or existing programs expanded; services could be provided through a single multi-service agency or by subcontracts through a lead agency, or several agencies could be funded. But the committee posited services should be offered in a neighborhood setting and highly recommended delivery of services at the same site. Applicants had to show linkages among a variety of service agencies.

Each applicant also had to provide for at least one of two core services: comprehensive case management or 24-hour crisis intervention. Comprehensive case management had to contain at least the following eight components: outreach, intake and screening, assessment and reassessment, service planning, plan implementation, monitoring and follow-up, crisis intervention, and counseling and exit planning. The crisis intervention service had to be located in the neighborhood and had to include at least: a telephone hotline, short-term comprehensive case management, and formal linkages with social service, domestic violence, mental retardation, health, mental health, housing, alcohol and substance abuse agencies. The crisis intervention program also had to provide for training, outreach, intake and screening, assessment and reassessment, case management, and counseling and exit planning.

The application had to include provisions for at least two additional services, such as early intervention services, education, employment and training, intensive home-based services, parenting education, comprehensive prenatal care, or alcohol and substance abuse prevention.

Finally, each application had to include measurable objectives for an overall evaluation of the NBI program. This required monitoring, status reports and regular interviews of participants and providers.

The committee used a five-point set of criteria to select applicants. This included the community profile update, the degree to which the applicant understood and would implement the NBI approach (responsiveness of proposed strategy, quality of services plans, coordination plan, work plan with milestones and time frames, linkages to nonfunded agencies, and readiness to develop an advisory council), organizational capability, adequacy of budget, and responsiveness to evaluation requirements.

Once a community was selected, it had to convene a Neighborhood Advisory Council. These councils had to promote partnerships among all the sectors and resources involved in the program along with neighborhood residents. The community, with the council in the lead, then had to prepare a five-year Strategic Neighborhood Action Plan. This action plan had to focus on economic, business, labor force, and work skills issues, and treat housing and physical infrastructure. The plan had to indicate how economic and physical development strategies would be coordinated with the comprehensive case management, crisis intervention, and other services initially funded through NBI.

The state issued its RFA in January 1991, and responses were due in March 1991. In September, the state announced its selection of six sites among the 17 that applied. These sites include two neighborhoods in New York City, three upstate urban-suburban localities, and one rural county. Community-based nonprofits are the lead agency in four sites, while county government agencies are the lead in the other two. The programs are scheduled to start in the six sites in January or February 1992.

Evaluation

An important part of the NBI program is an evaluation to determine the following:

- How state agencies collaborated in planning, providing technical assistance, funding, and monitoring of NBI and the extent to which this collaboration helped local communities reduce barriers and make more resources available for serving neighborhood residents.
- Ways that local community groups and local government collaborated in developing the service plan and delivering services to the targeted neighborhood, and the effects of this collaboration on the quality of the NBI proposal, the five-year plan, and the delivery of services to residents under the plan.
- The procedures for delivering services more efficiently to targeted residents in or at-risk of crises and the extent to which these procedures removed barriers to participation in programs and improved the quality of service.
- The extent to which the service delivery programs produced specified outcomes for program participants and improved the quality of life for neighborhood recipients.
- The differences among NBI sites and the factors that affected any differential attainment of NBI goals at each site.

Maryland's Industrial Jobs Opportunity Program

The Industrial Jobs Opportunity Program (IJO) began in Maryland's Department of Human Resources (DHR) when an additional $2 million in federal funds became available. The department wanted to make the demonstration work and the welfare programs it was already operating more effective. DHR officials realized that while they were doing well in providing support services to clients, they had done little to develop links to the private sector. Ties to the two most logical links to business — the Private Industry Councils (PICs) and county economic development agencies (EDAs) — were most obviously deficient. Recognizing that "money talks," DHR sought to use its funding to make the connection. After tapping the president of the Baltimore PIC as its ambassador to business, DHR began to make the case that private sector involvement was needed to move clients from welfare to work. Thanks to energetic lobbying by private sector leaders and the hook of a relatively large sum of money, a preliminary planning process was devised and fairly widely accepted.

Under this plan, the $2 million was distributed to all 10 Maryland SDAs. SDA was given the responsibility of devising a program that would involve the local welfare office, the PIC, and the EDAs in a collaboration leading to employment for welfare recipients. A wide variety of projects were considered, including many with an economic development orientation, such as loans to firms, funds to develop business incubators, and funds for job development. Other monies went to support services, additional JTPA training slots, and to develop pre-employment programs. In all cases, program guidelines were deliberately kept flexible; the only proviso was that funding directly or indirectly must increase the employment potential of welfare recipients.

In 1987, the Maryland legislature appropriated $5 million for IJO to replace the federal funding and expand program operations. In 1988, an additional $2.5 million was appropriated.

Performance
IJO has met most of its initial goals. It has served 4,873 AFDC recipients, of whom 2,129 were placed in unsubsidized jobs with 1,860 still in pre-employment and education programs. Eight of 10 program sites obtained an average hourly wage for participants at or above the adult minimum living standard for that region. A recent study by Abt Associates showed that in each program site a new program, new service, or an increase in existing services for AFDC recipients occurred due to IJO funding. Other findings included: (1) each site made a particular effort to supply needed support services for clients; (2) all 10 sites were able to obtain formal agreements from participating economic development agencies; and (3) economic development agencies generally have used IJO

funds to supplement existing activities, including job development, business loans and subsidy activities.

Principles and guidelines

Three principles govern the IJO program. The first is the need to use new, targeted funding to build integrated programming. Initial development, planning, and implementation have all succeeded in this program because IJO funds provided an incentive to all players. As one state official noted, "Basically what we've said is, here's a pile of money. Now you work it out."

The second principle is the primacy of the private sector in promoting employment opportunities for welfare clients. DHR officials realized early that they could not credibly operate an employment program themselves, that the logical operator was the PIC, and that the cooperation of economic development officials was vital to success in providing jobs for clients. IJO money was dedicated to buying access to the private sector in order to develop these opportunities.

The third principle is the need for flexibility in program development. One of the most diverse states in the nation, Maryland has poor, rural regions with serious unemployment, transportation and economic development problems, as well as two major metropolitan areas and America's richest county. State officials realized for IJO to work, it had to be responsive to all these conditions. One official explained, "The counties have different problems. We asked them for plans that addressed those problems using AFDC recipients as part of the solution. We got some very innovative responses — some of these people would never get served otherwise."

To support its three general principles, IJO developed specific operating guidelines:

- Broad discretion in funding economic development activities. Under current guidelines, acceptable uses include gap financing, low-interest loans, bonuses to employers, capital improvements, technical assistance, and marketing.
- Commitment to comprehensive support services. Funded programs are required to include some support services, such as quality child care, transportation, health benefits, and case management.
- Use of the existing delivery system. IJO programs are designed to take full advantage of existing work/welfare and JTPA programming as part of the comprehensive package offered to clients and employers.

- Performance guidelines. IJO staff have developed guidelines to evaluate service to the neediest clients, the number of placements in unsubsidized employment, the entered employment rate, and average hourly wage. Programs meeting some or all of these guidelines receive performance awards.

Programming

IJO currently funds programs in 10 regions of the state. All programs require the cooperation of DHR, the Private Industry Council, and the economic development agency, and all must be approved by state DHR officials. The following illustrate the kinds of local programs that have been initiated.

- Frederick County: IJO funds pay companies for customized training; financial bonuses for hiring and retraining AFDC recipients; employee support for day care, transportation, and health care; and 75 to 100 percent on-the-job training reimbursement.
- Western Maryland: IJO provides incentive payments to participating businesses by writing down $1,500 of the loans of companies that employ welfare recipients.
- Baltimore County: Building on existing on-the-job training programs, Baltimore County uses IJO funds to allow local business the opportunity to borrow funds at below market rates for upgrading or expanding facilities.
- Susquehanna Region: IJO funds pay for low-interest loans to small businesses for expansion, direct payments to employers for hiring and retraining IJO participants, and targeting private businesses to open and operate day care centers.
- Lower Shore: This rural area uses IJO funds to help develop daily public bus transportation to jobs. Other economic development activities include marketing, gap financing, technical assistance, and a research study to determine existing and future industry needs.
- Montgomery County: In this economically booming region, county officials are undertaking a major marketing effort to inform area employers of the services and benefits available under IJO.

Pennsylvania's Ben Franklin Partnership Program

Pennsylvania has developed a program based on many of the same principles used in Maryland. Like IJO, the new Pennsylvania program is built around new targeted funding, requires a private sector match, and tries to promote economic growth. The Pennsylvania proposal departs from IJO in a direction that may be of national interest. Where Maryland based its initiative in the PICs with economic development agencies as cooperating partners, Pennsylvania will use existing economic development programs directly to channel jobs to the disadvantaged.

The Pennsylvania program is built on the success of the state's Ben Franklin Partnership, widely viewed as one of the most successful economic development programs in the country. Designed to promote job creation in Pennsylvania companies through science and technology, the partnership has channeled more than $100 million in state funds to new and developing companies since the early 1980s.

Four regional Advanced Technology Centers (ATCs) closely tied to area universities operate the program based on the following goals and objectives:

- improve and create jobs in new advanced technology enterprises, including both new and existing firms;
- improve productivity, particularly among Pennsylvania's existing firms;
- diversify Pennsylvania's economy, with special emphasis on increasing Pennsylvania's share of advanced technology firms and/or product markets that are among the national growth leaders;
- establish effective consortium efforts involving the private sector, colleges and universities, and government;
- encourage and strengthen joint private sector/college and university and development programs;
- establish and improve education and training programs to meet the needs of the workforce now and in the future, and manage the impact of technology on the current and future workforce to enable it to adjust rapidly to changing technology;
- provide entrepreneurial development assistance to advanced technology firms that will result in new businesses and jobs in Pennsylvania; and
- encourage the creation and expansion of new technology enterprise in Pennsylvania.

Examples of existing projects funded by the Ben Franklin Partnership Program include:

- A $90,000 grant matched by $300,000 in additional funding to provide comprehensive services and training to companies along Philadelphia's Route 202 corridor;
- A $75,000 grant matched by $500,000 in other funding to provide a comprehensive network of institutional, industrial, and labor services for worker training and education; and

- A $34,000 grant matched by $91,000 in other funding to provide RN and LPN training to skilled and semiskilled health care workers.

Operation of the program has made the ATCs key brokers in regional economic policy, enabling them to establish close contacts with the private sector, to promote linkages between businesses and universities, and to define and develop employment and training initiatives. Now the ATCs are ideally placed to serve as intermediaries between economic development and employment and training programs.

Recognizing the ATCs' advantages, Pennsylvania officials have proposed a model using the centers as placement agents for the state's work/welfare and dislocated workers programs. State officials feel ATCs, operating in conjunction with existing programs, will be able to develop better job placements at lower cost. Again, this is an example of a state using funding to get access to jobs and training that was formerly out of the reach of a disadvantaged population.

Operation

The new program, operating very much like IJO, is based on a statewide funding pool available to the ATCs for creation of employment and training programs for the disadvantaged.

ATCs are the fiscal agents and managers for the new effort, contracting with private firms, universities, and training providers to develop a program model. The ATC program will complement existing state work/welfare and dislocated worker programs, serving as an advanced training and placement component for participants who have already received some preliminary training and remediation. The link to existing programs will also allow the ATCs to incorporate the support services such programs already provide, including day care, medical benefits and regular monthly welfare support.

The new program's goal is to place participants in jobs paying at least $6.50 per hour with benefits and the possibility of advancement. State officials foresee ATCs using their private sector connections to place participants in fast-growing fields, such as financial services, information processing, and health-related services, a mix similar to current ATC programming. Projects are designed with the regional economy in mind, so that participants from inner city Philadelphia, for example, could be trained for job openings in fast-growing suburbs. Funded programs pursuing this strategy will be expected to work with the private sector in promoting alternative transportation arrangements. The initiative is structured to make maximum use of community colleges and universities as training providers, with the hope that links to higher education can also be established. An additional advantage in using ATCs as program managers is their ability to develop programming with colleges and universities, a tie that has been difficult for some PICs to establish.

The initial funding for the new initiative was $1.1 million, including $500,000 in state economic development funds, $500,000 in federal welfare funds, and some dislocated worker money. Additionally, participating private sector companies will contribute a local match of resources. In its first year of operation, the program served about 250 clients statewide. State officials view the new initiative as part of a multi-year program effort and appear willing to devote additional resources to expansion if the initiative is successful.

Principles

The Pennsylvania design is notable in that it does not create a wholly new program model, as in Maryland, but uses flexible funding to tie together existing systems. Pennsylvania's incorporation of work/welfare programs into models of this kind provides a number of advantages in addition to the personal support base — welfare benefits and medical and day care payments — associated with the welfare system. Linkage to an existing program offers the opportunity to ensure clients have received some training prior to entry into the new employment initiative. This preliminary training may remove some of the barriers traditionally associated with welfare clients and may offer an additional incentive to prospective employers.

Comments on State Collaboration

The examples illustrate that the creative and collaborative use of four sets of institutional resources — economic development, welfare, education and employment training — can produce a whole that is more comprehensive, flexible, and effective than any of its parts. In such a system, welfare funding can pay for JTPA training and education, which in turn can purchase the private sector access enjoyed by economic development agencies. Through collaboration, the disadvantages of each system — welfare's "image," JTPA's and education's tight program restrictions, and economic development's low funding base — are minimized in favor of the contributions each makes to a comprehensive program. A collaborative initiative of this kind avoids the creation of new bureaucracies in favor of building on the existing strengths of the current system.

The following guidelines can help states launch a successful collaboration.

1) Use a moderate level of funds dedicated to creating collaborative programs. Sources for these funds might include JTPA 8-percent funding, economic development funds, CDBG funds, federal welfare, employment resources, or Carl Perkins dollars.

2) Designate one of four institutions — education, economic development, welfare, or JTPA — to take the lead in managing a comprehensive program.

3) Establish clear incentives for private sector participation, such as subsidized wages, recruitment and training of qualified workers, loans, grants, and/or development/tax incentive packages.

4) Establish clear financial or program incentives for participation of the other three agencies. Incentives might include placements, matched funding, training and/or support services.

5) Develop a workable program model for job development and placement that includes flexible local implementation and maximum use of existing resources.

6) Establish and use performance guidelines with measurable goals.

7) Evaluate the collaboration's effectiveness with clients or customers and the costs of operating new collaborative programs.

In a nutshell, states must increase the appeal of collaborative ventures, facilitate local action, establish common definitions, advocate changes in national law and administrative practices where appropriate, create joint data bases, introduce management innovations, make funding contingent on collaboration and performance, create models and demonstrations, offer oversight and evaluation support, and provide flexible but not loose guidelines.

5

A State Economic Opportunity Strategy

State Antipoverty Policy Framework

This chapter begins by outlining several policy approaches to addressing poverty and by setting a framework for a state economic opportunity strategy. Antipoverty strategies differ depending on how they deal with three major components: theme, target, and delivery system. This report suggests states consider an antipoverty strategy that uses the themes of self-sufficiency and assets, focuses on a regional target that emphasizes the family whenever appropriate, and operates through a competitive delivery system.

Antipoverty Policies

There are probably as many observations on antipoverty policies as there are observers. This report characterizes an antipoverty policy by the way it treats three components. One component, the theme, identifies the central substantive programmatic thrust for fighting poverty. Another component, the target, addresses the consumers or recipients of the policy and the context, if any, in which they are targeted. The third component, the delivery mechanism, describes the way of delivering antipoverty resources.

None of the components are mutually exclusive (or fully inclusive), but antipoverty policies tend to pay more attention to certain themes, targets, and delivery systems. Each reflects a particular set of values and beliefs about the causes of and "cures" for poverty. Many antipoverty policies are based either on narrow dogmatic stances or on an unthinking amalgam of approaches. Consequently, the value of other approaches, the weaknesses of the chosen approaches, and the chaotic mixing of components are often ignored.

Antipoverty Themes

Incomes: A basic antipoverty theme, which was more popular 25 years ago than today, is that people are poor because they have little income. The most direct way to address this problem is to provide the poor with enough income to lift them out of poverty. The most notable proposal with this theme was the negative income tax. For people who believe a country as rich as ours should not tolerate poverty and who value a progressive tax system, using the tax system to provide poor people with a relatively high threshold level of income is an easy and just solution to poverty.

This theme places a high value on letting poor people spend their money the way they want to, implying most poor people are no different than the nonpoor. It treats all poor alike, which is often considered a positive aspect the of policy. This theme also has the additional benefit, to some people, of eliminating or downsizing the welfare bureaucracy so often criticized as siphoning off resources that otherwise would go directly to fighting poverty. Finally, this theme is favored because it does not impose an onerous or degrading application process on the poor. Unfortunately, the income theme has a substantial disincentive to work.

Maintenance: Another approach to fighting poverty is based on the belief that poor people differ from the nonpoor in that they do not have sufficient skills to function adequately in our society. Programs with this theme provide the poor with the assistance they need to function minimally like the nonpoor. These supportive services include family and budget counseling, job search and job readiness help, substance abuse assistance, and literacy and self-assertiveness training. In practice, many different kinds of services are provided, often by many different service providers. Sometimes accepting these services is a precondition for receiving or maintaining income assistance. In many instances, these services are available only through a means test.

These services might be considered maintenance services because their primary intent is not to make poor people nonpoor, but to permit poor people to function at least at a minimally adequate level in society. In this strategy, poor people eventually become nonpoor because of their own capabilities or because of the consequences of other policies in conjunction with the basic level of support provided by the maintenance services.

Self-sufficiency: The self-sufficiency theme is based on the premise that poor people who are mentally and physically able should move from welfare dependency by becoming self-sufficient, primarily by earning an income that would immediately or eventually remove them from poverty. This approach also may view an effort to earn income as a quid pro quo of receiving income assistance. If this approach includes services, they are structured, goal-oriented, and focused on directly leading to earnings and employment.

This theme differs from the maintenance theme in that self-sufficiency is the overriding objective and becoming nonpoor is not left solely up to abilities of poor persons or the consequences of other policies. It is based on the belief that poor people want to work and earn enough to get off welfare and should be obligated to apply themselves and respond appropriately to self-sufficiency resources and opportunities.

Rhetorically, self-sufficiency is now the dominant anti-poverty theme. But much of the current welfare policy debate is about how much welfare recipients should work, and this discussion has "conservative" and a "liberal" poles. "Liberal" self-sufficiency advocates argue the nature of labor markets, racial discrimination, lack of child care, and lack of education make it nearly impossible to force welfare recipients to work because the quality of their employment and earnings would be unrewarding and insubstantial, especially when contrasted with the level of welfare income and support. Consequently, government-sponsored jobs, day care, and other support services must accompany a work requirement.

"Conservatives" argue that most welfare recipients do not work because they do not want to, and they will work only if forced. They argue that even low-wage jobs will eventually benefit both the person and society and help achieve social integration. Consequently, as this argument proceeds, the work requirement in welfare should be increased substantially. Although increased work requirements may decrease average job quality among welfare recipients, total employment, earnings, and welfare savings would increase, and strides would be made toward social integration. According to this view, work participation will remain low to the extent welfare administrators dislike to enforce work requirements and want to protect recipients from having to take "dirty jobs." (Mead, 1988)

Assets: A fourth antipoverty theme focuses on creating, obtaining, or nurturing assets for poor people. The assets theme is based on the belief that in a capitalist economy the way to become nonpoor and stay out of poverty is to build assets that can provide a continuous regeneration of wealth and income. These assets include home ownership, business ownership, and increasing personal savings that can be used for economic or human investment. The assets approach is probably the newest approach to poverty. While its ultimate goal may be economic self-sufficiency, it short-circuits a skills-education-earnings approach by directly and quickly bringing poor people into asset ownership and economic production. Once poor people have a minimum level of assets, they can obtain a better education, improve their skills, and sustain their participation in the social and economic mainstream.

Community development: The fifth theme is more geographically and politically oriented than the other four approaches. The community development theme emphasizes the need to organize politically, institutionally, and economically poor people and the resources of a poor community, and the need to improve the physical and socioeconomic attributes of a relatively small geographical area populated by poor people.

The community development approach has three premises: (1) poor people must have an organizational capability and a political presence if antipoverty efforts are to be successful, (2) antipoverty efforts must be multifaceted, not limited to one or two major activities, and (3) antipoverty resources must be funneled or used in a geographically bound area so resources do not leak away and are not drawn off for other purposes or targets. This approach builds on finding, nurturing, and creating grass-roots skills and resources within poor communities. These skills and resources are the raw materials needed to develop community-wide organizational and political strengths that, in turn, can foster long-term socioeconomic benefits for the community's residents.

Targets

Of course, all antipoverty policies are targeted to poor people, but policies tend to have a dominant target. Targeting has two dimensions. One concerns the extent to which poor people are covered, the other with the extent to which resources are focused on a geographic place. For example, AFDC focuses only on poor people, but only on a relatively small number of poor people, about one-third. On the other hand, social security focuses on poor as well as non-poor people. Antipoverty policies also differ in the emphasis they put on devoting resources to poor people within a geographic area and the extent to which these resources should be geographically targeted to revitalize a poor community. For example, food stamps are place irrelevant. AFDC has more of a place focus because benefit levels and other program characteristics vary by state, but it predominantly emphasizes family (largely single-parent families until the FSA). On the other hand, the Community Development Block Grant Program, especially the entitlement program, emphasizes place, partly because it is administered by local governments and usually focuses on a limited number of small places within each locality, and partly because there is no means-testing for its recipients.

Tension exists among these targets. It may be impossible, for example, for a policy to serve two different targets well or pursuing one target maybe counterproductive to pursuing another target. Individual and family targets tend to emphasize people, while a community target tends to emphasize place.

Individuals: Most antipoverty policies consist of services targeted to individuals. Eligibility criteria for many programs are based on individual characteristics, and the services that are provided are usually oriented solely to the individual. Whether the service is budget counseling, skills training, or health, the "patient" is the individual. Little attention is given to the people with whom the patient lives and the relationships she or he has with them. Even when a family attribute, such as income, triggers assistance, the assistance is often provided to an individual in the family not to the family as a unit.

Families: A second approach is less common in this country. This approach focuses on working with the entire family. It is based on the premise that a well-functioning family is essential for both the poor and nonpoor, and one cannot ignore people and their relationships within a family. It makes little sense to provide solely occupational skills training to a young mother if her child has health problems and the alcoholic father of her child abuses her. This approach tries to provide appropriate services to all family members and encourage long-term relationships among them.

Although food stamps and AFDC programs are based on household eligibility standards, they are not family targeted. For example, before the FSA mandated the unemployed parent program, in many states, the family had to separate before members could receive AFDC assistance.

Further, our antipoverty policies may be inhospitable to families. A much higher percentage of poor single-parent families with children receive assistance than poor married families with children. AFDC serves 59 percent of all poor single-parent families compared to 12 percent of all poor married-couple families; Medicaid, 66 percent to 23 percent; food stamps, 65 percent to 32 percent; and public or subsidized housing, 24 percent to 10 percent. While 19 percent of all single parent families with children received the multiple benefits of AFDC, Medicaid, food stamps, and housing, only 3 percent of poor married families with children received these multiple benefits. In 1986, the only major antipoverty programs that served a higher percentage of poor married-couple families than poor single-parent families were unemployment insurance and Medicare. (Levitan, Mangum, and Pines) Clearly, on the average poor single-parent families with children are less well off than poor married families with children. But these figures do reflect a policy tilt, which has been exacerbated by the increasing ineffectiveness of unemployment insurance.

Community: It would be inappropriate to suggest that targeting geographical neighborhoods or communities is the family approach on a much larger scale. Yet, just as the family approach nurtures the family not just the individual, the communities approach works with all or most of the people and institutions in a neighborhood or geographic area. But the communities approach is much more organizational and social-political process-oriented than the family approach. Instead of identifying a family or an individual that should be the target of antipoverty efforts, this approach identifies communities and neighborhoods.

Region: The best known regional target was the Appalachian region during the 1960s. The region is a common target in rural antipoverty policy because of the large geographic area encompassed by much rural poverty, and because of the small populations and lack of economic resources in most poor rural areas. Urban antipoverty policy rarely targets a region, which is unfortunate for two reasons.[47] First, it offers a particularly unique role for state government as just about the only existing governmental institution with authority over an entire urban area. Second, the concentration of nearly all very poor urban residents in a small number of geographic areas in the inner city may make it increasingly difficult to solve urban poverty problems without a regional target.

There are many reasons for the absence of a regional target in antipoverty policy. The residents and elected officials of suburban jurisdictions usually do not want to open their doors. Perhaps many "escaped" from the city and do not want "it" to follow; others may be more willing, but feel that if they make the first move, and if there is no "fair share," they will be overwhelmed. Big city officials often back away from a regional approach because it dilutes their own power and prestige. In national politics, large cities want to get their funds directly from Congress, they do not want to be part of a multijurisdictional approach. A major objective of most cities is to secure their own "entitlement" of funds from the federal government. State governments are usually timid about interfering in local affairs, particularly in sensitive issues like race or poverty. Often there is little benefit in it for state governments, because suburban areas may dominate the legislature and statewide voting, and because the large cities may not welcome such intervention. Finally, the community target and the community development theme often are implicit barriers to a regional approach.

---

[47]A good example of this rural (region) - urban (city or county) split is in the JTPA Program. Although labor markets generally are multi-county, especially in large metropolitan areas, JTPA Service Delivery Areas are county or city based in 33 states. They are town-based in Connecticut and Massachusetts and county - large city based in the following states, which have large number of urban poor people: California, Florida, Georgia, Illinois, Louisiana, Michigan, Missouri, New Jersey, New York, Ohio, Pennsylvania, Texas, and Virginia. The District of Columbia is its own SDA. Only one small urban state, Delaware, has a statewide SDA. (Redman)

Delivery systems

Individual choice: One delivery system emphasizes giving poor people the right and ability to select freely both the source and type of assistance they receive. Advocates for this delivery system argue that it offers a way out of poverty because consumer choice acknowledges the value of the person and the person's freedom to control his or her own affairs, putting the poor person in an equal relationship with sources of assistance, as is often the case with nonpoor people. Proposals for education vouchers and for service credit cards are attempts to move toward an individual choice delivery system. Food stamps and rental assistance vouchers are examples of programs based partially on an individual choice delivery system because recipients can largely choose what food to buy and at what stores, or where to rent. Direct and unencumbered income transfer payments can arguably be placed in this category.

At an extreme, the argument for consumer sovereignty is an argument for individual choice. Many economists criticize in-kind assistance because it is an inefficient way of providing assistance compared to simple cash transfers. Medicaid illustrates this point. The average Medicaid assistance costs taxpayers about $2,000. An average AFDC recipient might receive $9,000 in welfare and food stamp payments and $2,000 in Medicaid. One could easily argue many welfare recipients would rather have $2,000 in cash, than over 20 percent of their benefits in-kind medical insurance. (Burtless)

Government: Federal, state, and local public agencies play the dominant role in delivering antipoverty resources. Most of the resources that can be lumped under the label "human services" are delivered by public agencies: AFDC, food stamps, SSI, Social Security, and many education and job training services. Many "physical development" resources are also delivered by public agencies, such as public housing authorities or local governments, but public agencies do not have the dominance here that they do in human services. Disagreements about which level of government should deliver which kinds of antipoverty resources have been the focus of much attention during the last couple of decades.

Community-based organizations: The use of community-based organizations (CBOs) as a delivery system first became popular in the 1960s, and then nearly became invisible before being resurrected several years ago. Advocates of CBOs point out two characteristics that make them a unique and preferred delivery system. One is their ownership by poor people or poor communities. Because CBOs are usually locally-based, their service areas mostly include the people and neighborhoods they are trying to serve, hence there is a congruence between a CBO's organization and staff and its consumers. Because of this congruence and because many CBOs have members of the community, their consumers, on their governing boards, CBOs are said to be controlled by or at least strongly influenced and motivated by poor people or poor communities, or their direct representatives. This not only suggests CBOs have the direct interests of poor people or poor communities in mind as they make decisions and operate, but also that CBOs have a long-term commitment to their service areas, the neighborhoods and communities within which they operate. As political conservative Stuart Butler said: "when the people delivering a service are the same people who receive its benefits, they have every incentive to serve the poor efficiently." (Butler, p. 28)

A second valuable characteristic of CBOs is their nonbureaucratic nature. CBOs often have fewer legal and administrative constraints than do public agencies. Their charters for action are often broad, and they are less constrained than public agencies are by legal inhibitions on eligible activities or financing mechanisms. Because CBOs are usually small and unencumbered by civil service or traditional bureaucratic behavior, they may be able to act more quickly and efficiently than many public agencies. Finally, CBOs do not have the formal political accountability to a broad electorate that public agencies have; therefore, CBOs can often take controversial action and survive.

Competition: Competition is a hybrid delivery system, in which the original resource provider selects the delivery organization that most effectively use its resources to meet its goals given circumstances of time and place. The delivery provider can be a public agency (even the original resource provider), a CBO, a for-profit firm, a charitable or religious organization, an "intermediary," or any other kind of organization that seems capable of effectively delivering the resource. The delivery organization can change over time, vary among different geographical or political areas, and vary according to the kind of resource being delivered. In theory, this delivery system prevents a long-term monopoly, although some organizations may develop short-term delivery niches. Also, competition may sharpen the effectiveness of all delivery organizations vying for a resource. To an extent, public agencies act as wholesalers, competitively selecting service retailers who actually deliver the resources.

Current antipoverty approaches

Various antipoverty strategies can be formed by combining various themes, targets, and delivery systems. Two strategies dominate today's antipoverty policies. The most traditional strategy combines the maintenance theme with a target of individuals and a government delivery system. This traditional strategy, the welfare strategy, has evolved since the 1930s. It is the single largest strategy, in terms of overall resources, especially if welfare-related resources, like Unemployment Insurance and Social Security, are included. The Family Support Act alters this strategy to an extent by moving its theme from maintenance to self-sufficiency and to a lesser extent by changing its target from individuals to families. For the moment, however, and perhaps even longer depending on how the FSA and related legislation, such as daycare, are implemented, the essence of the welfare strategy remains much as it has for the past couple of generations. The welfare strategy has the power of size, inertia, and tradition, but many attack it as inefficient and ineffective.

The second dominant antipoverty strategy is the community action strategy, which combines a community development theme with a community target and a community-based organization delivery system. This strategy is more wide-ranging than the traditional welfare strategy because it usually includes a substantial amount of physical development and economic development resources. In the aggregate it contains fewer resources than the welfare strategy, although these resources come from many more and a wider variety of programs compared to the welfare strategy. Unlike the welfare strategy, the community action strategy enjoys political and rhetorical support. Anti-bureaucrats from the political left and right often support the community action approach as the only viable alternative to a moribund government bureaucracy. Those who criticize the welfare strategy for its paternalism and top-down approach often applaud the community action approach because of its local (poor people or poor community) control.

Currently, two other antipoverty strategies are struggling to be developed. One of these targets the family and calls for the creation of a national policy that recognizes and nurtures the importance of the family unit. It supports such activities as providing day care, achieving family literacy, and including ghetto males in intervention efforts (from supportive services to AFDC) formerly directed solely at welfare mothers. Some advocates of a family strategy emphasize creating family independence centers as an organizational vehicle for delivering resources.[48] Because

---

[48]One proposal for a family-centered policy calls for the establishment of family investment centers that would provide a common source of intake, eligibility determination, and assessment for all income maintenance, education, training, health, and housing services to those with low incomes; develop a social contract for each family; commit resources to fill the public side of the contract; and oversee and monitor the delivery of services and fulfillment of commitments. (Levitan, Mangum, and Pines)

the family strategy is still in preliminary stages, it is difficult to discern its themes and delivery system, although many of its proponents come from a support service or self-sufficiency and public agency background.

Another antipoverty strategy at an awkward beginning stage focus on the asset theme with an individual delivery system, a strategy some call "empowerment," although this is a slippery term. Perhaps because of its newness, the asset or empowerment strategy lacks detail and consistency. Education vouchers, housing vouchers, enterprise zones and other approaches to deregulation and de-taxation, along with such initiatives on the sale of public housing to its tenants, tenant management of public housing, and a micro-enterprise capitalism, make up the current bulk of this strategy. Its major internal tension resides in its conceptual emphasis on the individual delivery system, such as daycare tax credits, education vouchers, and a pure form of housing vouchers, on the one hand, and its actual heavy reliance on community-based organizations and small geographical place in much of its actual housing and economic development activities. Because of its initial use of CBOs and its anti-bureaucratic attitude, this strategy garners support from both conservative free-market advocates and liberal community advocates. Quoting Stuart Butler: "Empowering the poor means taking power away from the welfare industry. Just like any other cartel, those who benefit from the current power structure understandably resist any loss of control." (Butler, p. 29)

Designing a State Antipoverty Strategy

No single antipoverty strategy is inherently and universally superior to another. A state should design its antipoverty strategy based on careful examination of the magnitude, nature, and trends of its poverty-related problems, its own goals and values, and the strengths and weaknesses of the relevant institutions and organizations in the state. This report recommends states look closely at creating an antipoverty strategy that relies heavily on the region, the family where appropriate, and a competitive delivery system. Further, the strategy should strive for resource collaboration, promote mutual obligations, and make monitoring and evaluation integral to the development and implementation of policy.

Region

States should consider targeting the region for two reasons. First, the analysis of poverty and related issues suggests changes in economic structure, especially a shift away from low-skill, high-wage jobs that once were plentiful in central cities and to increased employment in suburban areas, are strong and perhaps irreversible. The problems of social isolation and the lack of employment opportunities in the central cities and in persistently poor rural areas can be best addressed by emphasizing mobility within a large region. Second, states are in the best, probably the only position, to deal with mobility and poverty across large areas. The United States does not have the institutional structure to work across multiple cities and counties, and attempts to create such a structure have been torturously slow or unsuccessful.

The concentration of poor people in urban areas may overwhelm governments and other institutions to the point where local antipoverty efforts become fruitless, and the locality enters a never-ending downward spiral. For example, 32,798 people received welfare in December 1990 in the 9-town capital region around Hartford, Connecticut, but nearly 95 percent of these recipients lived in Hartford. About 22 percent of the city's population is on welfare, but the welfare population is less than 1 percent of the population of the nine-town area outside Hartford. Further, 70 percent of the 3,346 public housing units in Hartford County are in the city of Hartford, and most of these are in the North End. It is little wonder why Hartford's deputy mayor said, "We cannot survive as a city." (Johnson)

Cities like Hartford, and East St. Louis, Illinois, where about one-half the city's population is poor and 75 percent receive public assistance, are the kinds of central cities that may find it impossible to save themselves. Increasing taxes to pay for becomes counterproductive if it forces higher income residents to move: cities with higher per capita spending and taxing tended to experience outmigration in the 1970s. (Koven and Shelley)

The city of Bridgeport, Connecticut, which filed for bankruptcy in June 1991, has a tax roll of $2.302 billion, a population of 141,800, and a per capita income of $10,543. Contrast these figures for one of the city's neighbors, Fairfield, where the figures, respectively, are $2.34 billion; 53,400; and $20,954. Bridgeport's property tax rate is the highest in the state, twice as high as Fairfield's, yet 15 percent of Bridgeport's residents are on public welfare. (Judson) Although Bridgeport's population did not decline much between 1980 and 1990, it lost over 20,000 white residents, dropping the city's white population from 59 percent to 46 percent. More people would have left if they could have sold their homes. Since 1988, the city has lost 14,180 jobs.[49]

49A recent New York Times article asked the question "How long can New York City redistribute wealth before the wealthy leave?" About a third of the city's budget is spent for things that redistribute wealth. The head of the city's commission on tax policy said, "The

PUT UP OR GIVE WAY

Our current policies expect cities to save themselves. There are at least four reasons a regional approach is neglected. First, the connection between regionalism and antipoverty strategies is rarely made. Second, in some central city politics, it often is more honorable to be in command of a sinking ship than to be involved in negotiations, possibly as an unequal partner, to reach shore safely. Rarely do local central city officials, especially elected officials, advocate a regional approach to poverty. Just the opposite usually happens. Representatives of poor cities in a downward spiral still appeal for direct funds from the federal government, and want no part in extra-local solutions that may dull their own visibility and constrain their own decision-making. Often, with justification, central city officials believe no one except people in their own cities are concerned about their plight, so they do not even consider regional approaches. Responding to the Administration's 1991 block grant proposal, Hartford's city manager said, "The state has no idea what the problems of the urban communities are. We'll get more of the doughnut syndrome, with the cities being the hole and all of the resources going to the suburbs." (Taylor)

A third reason for the lack of a regional target is the embracing of the nonprofit, community-based target and delivery system by both liberals and conservatives. As mentioned before, CBOs are attractive to many people, whether from an attitude of empowerment (of the poor, by the poor, for the poor) or from a belief public bureaucracies are incompetent. Congress creates programs in which CBOs are the only eligible applicants, and it sets aside fund reservations solely for CBOs. The major foundations have supported CBOs as *the* antipoverty delivery system for decades, both rhetorically and financially. Unfortunately, nearly all CBOs, as the name implies, encompass, work in, and respond to very small geographical areas. Their own measures of success relate to the number of people they serve and their success in building their neighborhoods both physically and socially. In different economic times, CBOs as a delivery system and communities as a target might be more effective in fighting poverty. In the 1990s they carry an impossible load and they may impose severe oppor-

---

perception that New York City taxes its residents excessively derives in good measure from the fact that a significant portion of the taxpayer's dollar is spent on income transference from those who are better off to those in need, rather than for the delivery of such services as paved roads, clean streets, and police protection, services that taxpayers have traditionally expected from municipalities." "It's not even the middle class subsidizing the poor any more, it's the poor paying for the poorest." (Roberts)

tunity costs by making it very difficult to look at other targets and delivery systems.[50]

Finally, suburban representatives are often at best unwilling or at worst antagonistic toward regional approaches. For example, suburban Chicago JTPA agencies would not permit Chicago residents to enroll in their programs although the agencies had difficulty finding enough low-income trainees. (Orfield) Perhaps some of this is rooted in a "we take care of our own" attitude, but often it is caused by racial and class fears, anxiety over property values, and concern about the local fisc.

Cards are stacked against a regional approach to poverty. Powerful forces support the community-CBO approach and work against using resources at the regional level. But gaining support for the regional approach is not impossible. The potential payoff of a regional target warrants the leadership and policy innovations necessary to make it work.

Family

A family target, when possible, is recommended because it can solve a current problem with the way many antipoverty resources are used. Services are usually provided to address very specific problems by person-nel who work in an organization (or part of an organization) designed solely to administer that specific service. If several members in a family need two or more services, these services usually are not provided in a connected way. Service providers concentrate on the services they ad-minister, not the comprehensive needs of a family. (Melaville and Blank)

Focusing on the family, not on the service or the individual, can help ensure future self-sufficiency. Given the kinds of jobs and earnings avail-able to people with various kinds of education and skills and given the nature of poor persons and households, usually fragmented and with multiple needs or problems, a cohesive and reinforcing family may be the most effective way to achieve self-sufficiency. A fragmented family "per-petuates a vicious cycle of moral and economic troubles that feed on and create more impaired families. Poverty, drug and alcohol dependency, out of wedlock births, child and spouse abuse, juvenile delinquency and crime

---

[50]One commentator, not unfriendly to CBOs, said, "...many supporters of community economic development engage in apologia [for the failure of efforts and the persistence of poverty] by citing inadequate funding for such local efforts. In point of fact, those local efforts, acting alone, never had a chance of ending poverty for an entire community because the causes of a given community's poverty and the potential for its elimination lie outside that community." (McDonald, p. 18)

are all related in large measure to cracks and breaks in the family framework. Each of these social ills, in turn, breaks down families further." (Levitan, Mangum, and Pines, p. 1)

While other means of service assistance are viable within a family target, providing multiple services within a family context suggests the desirability of "case management." This old-fashioned term has gained new meaning and vitality. This term now means one person or a single team of persons is responsible for helping family members receive all the appropriate services in a systematic process that involves both the service providers and the family. This process includes needs assessment and goal setting; service delivery, perhaps including the authority to commit resources; and monitoring, follow-up, evaluation, and service adjustment.[51]

Competitive delivery system

This report recommends using a competitive delivery system for two reasons. First, there are no areawide agencies or institutions appropriate to a regional approach to targeting. With few exceptions, there are no metropolitan-wide or regional general purpose governments and there are few areawide special districts or authorities that can play key roles in an antipoverty strategy. Second is the premise that the priority in an antipoverty strategy should be the effectiveness of the resource's impact on poor people. This implies there is no inherently superior resource delivery organization or institution. This is especially true from a statewide perspective, where at different locations, different kinds of organizations may be more effective than others. As noted earlier, over time this may be true within one region or area as well.

The absence of a regional delivery system is a critical justification for a strong state antipoverty role. State governments have the geographical breadth, the constitutional authority, the legal power, and the political accountability necessary to orchestrate a regional antipoverty strategy. To orchestrate this regional approach, states must overcome conflicting agendas and skepticism, if not cynicism and hostility. States must develop a vision that can be shared by several different organizations and institutions, establish a collaboration with delineated roles and responsibilities, provide technical assistance and otherwise facilitate the formation of the collaboration and the delivery of resources, monitor and assess the per-

---

[51]See the discussion of case management in Melaville and Blank, and Levitan, Mangum, and Pines.

formance of the collaboration and the impact of resources, and help make adjustments or changes in collaboration participants or activities as necessary.

This is a tough set of assignments, but several positive conditions or circumstances make them doable. One is that most metropolitan areas and regions, except some persistently poor rural regions, have many potential collaboration participants. Voluntary, charitable, and other nonprofit organizations, local governments, special districts or authorities, and private sector organizations, such as chambers of commerce and for-profit businesses, abound in most regions. Second, state government can influence the institutions that provide job training, education, and welfare. Third, state governments continue to strengthen and expand their roles in economic development. Finally, a state's governor has the ability to add the prestige, leadership, and motivation that is central to the required collaboration and that cannot be found elsewhere.

Components of a State Economic Opportunity Strategy

What should a state antipoverty strategy look like, given the workforce and economic competitiveness context raised in the first chapter, the poverty-related problems analyzed in the second chapter, the state of current economic development practice reviewed in the third chapter, and the implementation issues discussed in the fourth chapter?

The remaining portion of this chapter attempts to answer this question from a certain set of perspectives. First, the antipoverty strategy is framed from the perspective of state government. National policies and resources clearly are of paramount importance, but the strategy will focus on state policy and practice, referencing federal policy primarily in the context of state administration of federal programs. So while the strategy recognizes the importance and necessity of state actions, it also recognizes that the effect of these actions are secondary to a coherent and effective national policy.

Second, the strategy is framed from the perspective of economic development. Rather than discussing a comprehensive antipoverty strategy, special attention is paid to the role of economic development policy and practice. This "state economic opportunity strategy" stresses the contribution state economic development practice can make to antipoverty goals and how it fits within a broader antipoverty strategy. An economic opportunity strategy is defined as a set of public policies and activities designed to include poor people in the process of economic development.[52] No specific definition of poor or low income is included because it may need to vary by location or specific activity; however, it generally refers to people with incomes below the poverty standard.

Having an economic development perspective has two important consequences. One, it eliminates from direct consideration concern about people who are not in the potential workforce, such as children, the elderly, or people who have mental or physical incapacities that prevent them from being employed. This eliminates from consideration many if not most educational, health care, and childcare issues, which are important in a comprehensive approach to poverty. It also raises the issue of whether lack of economic opportunity or personal incompetency is the critical constraint preventing employment or economic self-sufficiency. For example, if workforce-eligible persons are poor because they refuse to work steadily, and they refuse to work steadily not because jobs are unavailable but because they have no motivation to work and are incompetent to manage their own lives, then providing economic opportunity may make no dent in unemployment or poverty.

The second consequence of an economic development approach to fighting poverty is the need to play to the strengths and goals of economic development practice. Most economic development practice, or at least its most visible and popular aspects, centers on financial assistance to firms, such as public debt or equity capital, tax incentives, infrastructure assistance, or wage subsidies. This is what economic development practitioners are good at, and what most like to do. The goals of economic development are job creation and business development, increasingly within the context of strengthening the economic competitiveness of American businesses.

A footing for a state antipoverty strategy that is oriented to economic development must be based on a unique advantage of state government: its geographic scale. By the 1970s, major cities were no longer the mechanism that allowed poor and unskilled persons the opportunity for easily earning their way out of poverty, and to become, over a generation or two, members of the working or middle class. The significant structural change in the American economy that began in earnest in the 1970s has made it much more difficult for the poor and unskilled labor force in the

---

[52]The American Economic Development Council defines economic development as the process of "creating wealth through the mobilization of human, financial, capital, physical and natural resources to generate marketable goods and services." (Swager, p. 3)

cities to obtain well-paying jobs. As noted in Chapter 2, manufacturing employment has become increasingly decentralized in suburban and metropolitan fringe areas, and any central city job growth that is occurring is predominantly in the service sector.

The Milwaukee metropolitan area illustrates this point. From 1979 through 1987, the Milwaukee metropolitan area lost over 51,000 manufacturing jobs. Over 32,000 of this loss occurred in the central city, reducing central city manufacturing employment by a one-third. The only parts of the metropolitan area to gain manufacturing jobs were the outer-ring suburbs, which gained nearly 7,000 jobs, increasing their manufacturing employment by 18 percent. Although the metropolitan area gained nearly 60,000 service jobs in the same period, the central city gained only 6,000 service jobs, increasing its service employment by only 3 percent. The outer-ring suburbs gained nearly 26,000 service jobs, nearly one-half the metropolitan area's entire service job growth, increasing their service employment by 45 percent.[53] (White and Osterman)

Laying the Foundation: Linking Place of Work and Place of Residence

The example above illustrates the important linkage between place of work and place of residence. The economic and demographic dynamics described in Chapter 2 are unlikely to change in the foreseeable future. Any economic opportunity strategy that substantially tries to move contrary to these trends has little probability of success.[54] States, therefore,

---

[53] The inner-ring suburbs lost about 20,000 manufacturing jobs (37 percent) and the exurbs lost about 7,000 (22 percent). The inner-ring suburbs increased their service employment by over 19,000 (33 percent) and the exurbs increased their service employment by nearly 9,000 (25 percent).

[54] This parochialism probably is most evident in economic development, where localities (and states) often compete with their neighbors. In October 1991 officials from New York, New Jersey, Connecticut, and New York City signed a "nonaggression" pact which committed them to work together toward keeping companies in the region and attracting new ones rather than seeking each other's businesses. Less than 24 hours after the pact was signed, the Public Service Electric and Gas Company of New Jersey was expected to start a new advertising campaign to promote the advantages of doing business in New Jersey aimed primarily at businesses in the New York City area. Nonetheless, the pact recognizes what should be done, although moving from intent to reality may be very difficult. (Bartlett) Although many individual local governments have created local economic development organizations and avidly pursue local economic development objectives, one study of the consequences of local economic development policies in 212 large cities concludes these

need to ensure that suburban local governments do not use their powers to exclude affordable housing.

There are two complementary and sometimes intertwined approaches to encouraging a linkage between workplace and place of residence. One approach focuses on the market, eliminating public sector constraints on the market or private behavior that interferes with the market. The second approach is a structural approach to providing low-income housing in the suburbs.[55]

Letting the market respond

States can help the market respond to various housing needs by ensuring local land use and regulatory powers do not prevent the production of affordable housing and by helping to reduce discrimination in the sale and rental of housing.

There are at least three complementary approaches states can use to help the market respond to areawide housing needs. The most significant involves greater state policy oversight of and responsibility for local land development practices. Many local governments use two major regulatory practices to exclude affordable housing. The primary practice is to minimize the amount of vacant land zoned multifamily residential; higher density housing, especially multifamily housing, tends to be much less expensive than lower density housing. The other major practice is to increase the cost of development by increasing space requirements, for example, requiring all or most single-family homes to have one or more acres of land or 1,800 square feet or more of floor space; and by increasing site costs through high subdivision standards, for example requiring very wide streets, high pavement depth, curbs, and sidewalks. Lately, some

---

policies "have a significant effect on capital investment but little effect on employment growth... this finding is troublesome in that the rational for local economic development is typically based upon its anticipated effect on employment and income and not on capital alone." (Feiock, p. 653) Conclusions like this reinforce the notion that government can do little to steer geographically private sector employment growth.

[55]The term "suburbs" is used to mean metropolitan political jurisdictions outside the central city that have economic and demographic characteristics substantially different than the central city.

local government have been using very high impact fees to keep out affordable housing.[56]

One way states can exercise oversight of local land development practices is through comprehensive planning requirements that contain specific state goals addressing affordable housing and give state government the ability to approve or disapprove a local plan, with a disapproval having some consequence. The most successful example is Oregon's comprehensive planning policy. Oregon law requires all local governments to adopt comprehensive plans and land development regulations that conform to state goals, one of which is a housing goal.[57] In its housing-related oversight of local plans and development regulations, Oregon has relied on three fundamental principles: fair share housing, least-cost housing, and clear standards.

The state commission charged with administering and enforcing the state's comprehensive planning law, the Land Conservation and Development Commission (LCDC), stated clearly that the state's housing goal "speaks to the need of Oregon households and not the housing needs of [a particular city]. Its meaning is clear: planning for housing must not be parochial. Planning jurisdictions must consider the needs of the relevant

---

[56]For example, one New Hampshire locality prior to 1986 excluded multifamily housing from all zoning districts and permitted the construction of single-family homes and duplexes only if they were on two-acre and three-acre lots, respectively. A 1986 amendment permitted multifamily housing as part of a planned residential development if the development had at least 20 acres. When various geographical limits were considered, only 1.73 percent of the land in the locality would be available for planned residential development.

Zoning also has affected low-cost housing in the suburbs of Washington, D.C. Only 2.5 percent of the residentially-zoned land available for development is zoned for apartments in Fairfax County, Virginia, and builders suggest only 1 percent is usable. In Prince George's County, Maryland, less than 1 percent of the developable land is zoned for apartments; and in Montgomery County, Maryland, about 2 percent of the developable land is zoned for multifamily development. (Downey, 1991 a)

[57]Oregon's housing goal is "To provide for the housing needs of the citizens of the state. Buildable lands for residential use shall be inventoried and plans shall encourage the availability of adequate numbers of housing units at price ranges and rent levels which are commensurate with the financial capabilities of Oregon households and allow for flexibility of housing location, type, and density."

region in arriving at a fair allocation of housing types" and must "satisfy the needs of the region and the city itself for low-cost housing."[58] The LCDC ensures that "strictly local interests of a city or a county must yield if in conflict with overall state interests."

The least-cost housing principle requires every locality to "do its part towards solving the housing needs of the area's residents at all income levels, as far as is reasonably possible given the constraints of land, materials, and similar costs." Based on this principle, the LCDC refused to approve a locality's plan because its "zoning ordinances did not permit either multifamily or mobile homes, and apartments were subject to discretionary approval requirements and strict design standards," although "single family housing was permitted outright in all zones."

The clear standards principle states "approval standards, special standards, and the procedures applicable to both must be clear and objective and must not have the effect, either of themselves or cumulatively, of discouraging, such as through unreasonable cost or delay, the needed housing type." For example, a locality can specify it will approve mobile home parks located on either a collector or arterial street paved to city standards and served by the full range of services defined in the plan, as long as these standards are explicitly contained in the plan. On the other hand, a locality could not require a proposed use to be in harmony with the surrounding neighborhood or demand that it not unduly impair traffic flow or safety in the neighborhood because these standards are too ambiguous and subject to capricious interpretation.

As a result of Oregon's comprehensive planning law, housing goal, and the three housing principles, local land use plans and land development ordinances must be clear and specific and must allow for the construction of various types of low-cost housing, considering regional housing needs.[59]

---

[58]The three principles are expressed in Seaman et al. v. City of Durham, 1 LCDC 283 (1978); 1000 Friends v. Lake Oswego, 2 LCDC 138 (1981); "LCDC Acknowledge of Compliance: City of St. Helens, August 11, 1978; and "LCDC Acknowledgement of Compliance: City of Happy Valley," January 28, 1981. For more information on Oregon and Massachusetts, see Sidor (1984).

[59]Due to state intervention, one analysis concluded the following changes occurred in the Portland metropolitan area: "although local plans designated 3,354 fewer acres for single-family housing, they allow 34,000 more homes because the average undeveloped lot size was reduced from 13,000 square feet to 8,300 square feet; the land available for

While Oregon is the foremost example, Florida, Vermont, Maine, and Washington have comprehensive planning requirements that eventually may be amenable to similar oversight. Other states on the Pacific or Atlantic coasts may develop this potential in the next few years.

A second way states can influence local regulatory powers is through a project-based appeals intervention process. Massachusetts pioneered this intervention in 1969 through its comprehensive permit process. Also known as the housing appeals law, the legislation establishes a comprehensive permit process at the local level as an alternative to a permit-by-permit process and allows appeals from a locality's decision to a state administrative board. The state appeals board can overturn a local decision only if the local decision is demonstratively inconsistent with local needs. The key standard in this determination is the extent to which the locality has helped meet regional lower-cost housing needs. Although the appeals board hears only five to 10 appeals a year, its presence often helps developers of lower-cost housing negotiate with local officials.

Connecticut recently enacted an appeals process, the Affordable Housing Appeals Law, that differs from Massachusetts in that the appeal is to the courts as part of the state's normal adjudicatory system. Any person whose application for an affordable housing development, defined as housing that is assisted housing or housing in which not less than 20 percent of the units will be conveyed with restrictions requiring that the units will be affordable for 20 years after initial occupancy, may appeal directly to the state superior court. Appeals can be made only if a locality has made no commitment to affordable housing or when more than a year has lapsed following completion of an affordable housing project in the locality. In the appeals process, the burden of proof is on the locality, and if the locality cannot meet the burden of proof, the court will wholly or partly reverse or remand the locality's decision.[60]

---

multifamily housing nearly quadrupled, from 2,219 to 8,795 net buildable acres, meaning that as many as 178,337 multi-family units could be built, 139,667 more than before; and regionwide, lands designated as residential now allow 301,482 units, an increase from 129,321 units, and overall densities increased from 4.43 to 9.36 units per net acre." (Sidor, 1984, p. 78)

[60]The first case under Connecticut's appeals law is scheduled for November 1991. The locality is Trumbull, a town of 32,000, and a suburb of Bridgeport. Ninety-five percent of the town's population is white and 93 percent of the homes are traditional single-family houses; there is not a single apartment building and no land is zoned to allow apartments.

A less systemic approach is the bundling of incentives and disincentives. Again, Massachusetts initiated this approach through the disincentive of Executive Order 215 and the incentive of state subsidies for housing for the elderly. The executive order permits the state housing and development agency to recommend and effect the withholding of several different kinds of state grants and loans, such as for open space or water or sewer facilities, if the applicant locality has made little or no commitment to affordable housing. Connecticut has a much newer and more incentive-oriented "housing partnership" program that encourages localities to effect voluntarily affordable housing programs by offering additional state grants in such areas as recreation and transportation.

In some states, the judiciary has spearheaded state intervention into local development regulation practice. The Mt. Laurel decisions of the New Jersey Supreme Court are the most famous example.[61] Recently, the New Hampshire Supreme Court moved in a similar direction. In *Britton v. Town of Chester*, decided on July 24, 1991, the court found the town's zoning ordinance placed an unreasonable barrier on housing for low- and moderate-income families. The court affirmed that the adoption of a zoning ordinance for the purpose of promoting the health, safety, or the general welfare of the community had to encompass the broader region where the town is located. In other words, the town had an obligation to provide regional fair share housing for low- and moderate-income families: "...towns may not refuse to confront the future by building a moat around themselves and pulling up the drawbridge." (*Housing and Development Reporter*, p. 255)

The purpose of this residence-workplace linkage foundation is not necessarily to force suburbs to construct subsidized housing for low-in-

---

A developer has proposed building a 600-unit apartment complex on a 38-acre site near the Bridgeport border which is zoned for a future office park. Because of the area's very high median income (the "affordable" monthly rent for a 3-bedroom unit ranges from $640 to $1,960), the point at issue is not low-income housing but multifamily housing. (Judson)

[61]Mt. Laurel I (Southern Burlington County NAACP v. Township of Mt. Laurel, 67 N.J. 151,336 A. 2d 713, 1975), which focused on the effect, regardless of the intent or purpose of local land use regulation and of excluding lower-income persons, clearly required local zoning to meet local as well as regional general welfare. Mt Laurel II (Southern Burlington County NAACP v. The Township of Mt. Laurel, 92 N.J. 138, 456 A. 2d 390, 1983) sharpened the concepts used in Mt. Laurel I and moved to performance standards to determine whether localities were meeting their housing obligations. Mt. Laurel II particularly highlighted the importance of regional fair share housing " without a fair share allocation no standard exists by which to judge local response, and there is no measure of accountability consequently.

come persons. Rather, it is to let the market respond to regional demand for various housing types and prices without artificially thwarting its ability to do so or unnecessarily increasing the cost of housing. Exclusionary zoning and similar local initiatives have always been problems, but overcoming these local initiatives becomes absolutely vital when large cities no longer have jobs for less skilled and less educated workers. Usually an outside force, such as state government, must intervene because localities have few, if any, incentives to take such action by themselves. Individual localities, especially smaller ones dominated by home owners, may have a strong rational self-interest in lowering local congestion costs and increasing local housing prices. Because local regulations generally reflect the wishes of current residents, not the needs of prospective residents, changing regulations in such localities usually will not come from within. (See Ellickson.)[62]

State intervention in local land development policies is not easy. Having the courts take the lead, as in New Jersey and New Hampshire, can give the executive and legislative branches effective cover. Integrating this intervention in comprehensive planning requirements and oversight may make it easier because it becomes part of a total development and conservation policy. Providing incentives for local action and gradually nurturing a bundling of incentives and disincentives, including an appeals process, probably is the most effective approach. Even this, however, requires some courage.

As initially designed, the recently-enacted national HOME housing program had an incentive setaside that was to be used to encourage states to take these kinds of action by rewarding them with bonus housing funds. But both Congress and the administration, beset with budget difficulties, agreed to eliminate the incentive the portion from the program before enactment. Federal government policy should encourage states and localities to take actions to eliminate regulatory barriers in the suburbs by providing incentives for them to do so. This makes sense not only because of its importance to economic opportunity, but it also makes budget sense:

---

[62]A recent report on housing in the Washington, D.C. suburbs pointed out that the fundamental obstacle to providing lower cost housing in the suburbs is vocal neighborhood opposition. "Around the region, civic leaders have permitted office towers to be built that employ thousands of workers while opposing efforts to build housing for the people who will work in them. Opposing new housing development, even when it is clearly needed, is good politics or simply the path of least resistance." (Downey, 1991 b)

if local regulatory barriers increase the cost of housing generally, federal housing subsidy dollars will increasingly buy less house per dollar.

Housing discrimination

Discrimination in the sale or rental of housing plays a role in inhibiting geographic dispersion to the suburbs. A recent study of 25 metropolitan areas by the Urban Institute concludes blacks and Hispanics "experience some form of discrimination more than one-half the times they visit a rental or sales agent in response to an advertisement in a major metropolitan newspaper." (Turner, Struyk, and Yinger, p. 37) Discrimination appears most frequently and most severely in housing availability (the number of units shown and recommended) and housing transactions (sales effort, terms and conditions, and financing assistance). Most people who experience discrimination in the housing availability phase also experience it in the housing transaction phase.

The study found neighborhood steering (offering minorities houses in systematically different neighborhoods) to be relatively much less severe, probably because most houses shown or recommended to either minorities or whites are located in primarily white neighborhoods. In the 25 metropolitan areas, over 50 percent of the units advertised or shown were located in neighborhoods that were less than 2.5 percent black; less than 20 percent of the units advertised or shown were in areas with a black population of more than 10 percent. Relatively more units not advertised in the major newspapers could have been in neighborhoods with a black population of more than 10 percent, but advertised housing was much more available in white areas. The report notes that even after controlling for neighborhood affluence and the size of the owner-occupied housing, minority neighborhoods are less likely to have houses advertised, shown, or recommended. Thus, housing opportunities are more likely available in predominantly white areas.

Discrimination in the sale and rental of housing inhibits the geographic dispersion of housing for minorities and also makes it more difficult for minorities to access good housing. The incidence of discrimination is probably higher than what the study finds, because although discrimination did not vary with most household characteristics discrimination tends to be lower for higher-priced housing. Discrimination is highest for low-cost housing and for low-rent units. (Turner, Struyk, Yinger)

A substantial bias in mortgage lending comes as no surprise. As analysis of 5.3 million mortgage applications received by 9,300 lenders in 1990 shows that in every city and income group, in black neighborhoods or white, in rich localities or poor, whites were more often approved for mortgages than blacks or Hispanics. White borrowers in the lowest income category (family income more than 20 percent below the locality median income) were approved for mortgages — 69 percent — more often than black borrowers — 65.7 percent — in the highest income group (family income more than 20 percent above the locality's median income). The study, released by the Federal Reserve Board, does not prove discrimination fully causes this bias because the study does not take into account the financial resources and credit history of each applicant. Nonetheless, minority homebuyers are turned down for mortgages two to three times more often than white homebuyers. (Knight)

Part of the bias could be caused by the use of standardized loan criteria and standards. Some lenders have programs that adjust approval criteria in ways that help minorities. For example, many low-income people are use to spending a larger portion of their income on housing. Although many criteria limit debt payment to no more than 38 percent of gross income, about two-thirds of low-income renter households spend at least 50 percent of their income on shelter. (Quint)

Structuring housing opportunity

The HOME program allocates housing funds targeted to house low-income persons to states and large local governments. Beginning in 1992, states will have the opportunity to use housing subsidies to help finance low-income housing in suburbs. To effect such housing, a state needs to make this a conscious objective of its HOME program and must have willing developers and local permitting of the building and site. If not, states may have to make extra efforts, including filing lawsuits.

At the local level, the HOME program may entice a few relatively prosperous suburbs to build housing for very low-income persons. Unlike the Community Development Block Grant Program which many suburban jurisdictions use for public works and other "areawide benefit" activities, HOME funds must be used only for housing low-income persons.

The HOME program is small compared to the federal government's major low-income housing program, rental assistance certificates or vouchers, which supplements the rents low-income tenants pay to landlords. The program is considered successful and cost-effective partly because it is market-oriented. A low-income person finds a place to rent at a fairly reasonable cost (more or less the median market rent for existing housing), and the administering agency, usually a local public housing authority (LHA), pays the landlord the difference between the rent paid by the tenant with the rental assistance certificate, which is generally about 30 percent of the household income, and the "fair market rent."

The rental assistance program may appear to be a program that can foster residence-workplace linkage; in practice this is not so. The jurisdictions of most LHAs are the same as the political jurisdiction of the local government where they are located and whose residents they serve. With the exception of several state LHAs, few LHAs are multijurisdictional, and there are very few multi-county LHAs. Each year LHAs receive substantial funds to administer the rental assistance vouchers and certificates; the more certificates or vouchers they administer, the more funds they receive. This is a disincentive to giving up these certificates and their accompanying administrative revenue to LHAs in other jurisdictions. In addition to this administrative disincentive, many suburban jurisdictions do not have LHAs or they are not administratively covered by another LHA.[63]

Several other federal housing programs do not facilitate, and even impede, residence-workplace linkage. HUD allocates funds to LHAs for the construction of public housing units. Most of these funds go to central cities, which build low-income housing in areas occupied by very low-income persons or already containing a significant amount of publicly-subsidized housing. HUD's new HOPE program may be used partly to provide tenants of inner city public housing the opportunity to own the public housing where they currently live. While the goal of ownership is laudable, many may be drowned by their newfound ownership of inner city assets if these are deteriorated or outmoded or are located in distressed areas. One of the federal government's major low-income housing construction programs is a tax subsidy, the Low Income Housing Tax Credit. The credit generally is used to build apartments in which all the occupants have incomes of 60 percent or less of the median income.[64] While these

---

[63]There are other problems even if rental assistance portability were not administratively constrained. Many suburban jurisdictions do not have rental housing. If they do, it may be too expensive for low-income people even with rent certificates or vouchers. Inner city residents with rent certificates are often not aware of affordable suburban housing, they may be too anxious to move to a new nonminority or nonpoor community, or they may not be able to move to a new location.

[64]A 1990 study of the use of tax credits in 1986 and 1987 shows that nine of every 10 had 100 percent low-income units. The average income of tenants in these units was about 35 percent of the area median income. About one-half the units were located in central cities, and over one-third in the suburbs. (ICF, Incorporated)

apartments are built in rural and urban areas, apartment complexes with only very low-income residents have not been a successful long-term approach to housing low-income people. It probably is safe to say federal housing policy discourages residence-workplace linkage and is inimical to the economic opportunity strategy recommended in this report.

Building new housing for lower-income persons in suburban areas may be critical to housing desegregation. Most suburbs contain very few blacks. In 1980 there were three times as many blacks in the 143 suburbs that were 20 percent or more black than there were in 1,112 suburbs with black populations less than 7.2 percent. The majority of black suburbanization in the 1970s occurred in suburbs with black populations of 20 percent or more. Suburbs with large black populations have the same problems as central cities. They have slow growth, high unemployment and poverty, and fiscal distress. Suburbs where black population growth in the 1970s was more than 3.5 percent were suburbs with new housing stock and a higher percentage of multifamily housing. (Stahura)

One recent study suggests that two factors explain the extent of decline in residential segregation in metropolitan areas. The most important factor is the relative number of blacks. A high relative number of blacks requires a high degree of segregation to keep the probability of white-black contact low. The other factor is newly-constructed housing. Minorities have a greater opportunity to occupy housing built after 1970 in suburbs than housing built before 1970, in part because of the enactment of fair housing laws. (Massey and Gross) The relative number of blacks in a metropolitan area may be a public policy given, but public policy can encourage the development of new housing, especially multifamily housing, in the suburbs.

Intergrating low-income people, especially minorities, in suburbs through public policy usually is neither easy nor uneventful − either for the new or long-standing residents. Although it is not done frequently, it can be done. One of the most effective, and relatively quiet, examples is the Gautreaux Program, mentioned in Chapter 2. Gautreaux is a 1976 Supreme Court decision that addressed racial discrimination in public housing in the city of Chicago; the decision called for a metropolitan-wide remedy for discrimination in the city's public housing.

The Leadership Council for Metropolitan Open Communities administers the program, locating apartments and arranging for participants to receive a federal rental assistance certificate or voucher. Gautreaux participants are either former residents of or on the waiting list for public housing. More than 3,800 families have been relocated since the program began, about half in suburbs and about half within Chicago. Key characteristics of suburban participants, which are very similar to city participants, include: 11.9 years of schooling (pre-move), 45 percent never-married, 60 percent received welfare for 5 years or more, and 51 percent were second-genertion welfare recipients. Studies of the Gautreaux participants have produced the following findings. (Rosenbaum and Popkin)

First, suburban movers were more satisfied than city movers (those who received rental assistance and moved, but stayed within Chicago) with their children's schools and with police services. There was little difference in social integration between suburban and city movers, and suburban movers were more likely to have white friends. Although about one-half of the suburban movers experienced some form of social rejection by their neighbors, most of these problems were minor and nearly all vanished over time.

Second, while the school children of suburban parents initially suffered a decline in their grades (suburban schools had higher standards than their city schools), their grades eventually equaled those of their city counterparts. Suburban school children had the same number of friends overall as their city counterparts. Suburban mothers were more satisfied with their children's schools — especially with their teachers and the safer environment — than city mothers were with theirs. Although children who moved to the suburbs encountered some early racial problems, these disappeared over time.

Third, as pointed out in Chapter 2, suburban movers had employment gains: they were about 13 percent move likely than city movers to have a job post-move after accounting for the effects of individual attributes. Among participants who had never been employed before moving, 46 percent of suburban movers had a job versus 30 percent of city movers. Suburban participants gave these reasons why their employment improved: there were more jobs available in the suburbs (this was the reason most frequently cited by suburban participants), the safer environment allowed them to work because they were less worried about their own safety in getting to work or because they felt comfortable leaving their children alone, and they were motivated to work because their neighbors worked or because their better living conditions increased their own self-confidence. (Second-generation welfare recipients were no less successful in the labor market.) However, some suburban participants identified barriers to obtaining jobs in the suburbs, particularly inadequate transportation and childcare, racial discrimination, and their own lack of skills.

The Gautreaux studies suggest low-income blacks — even long-term welfare dependent mothers and their children — can be reasonably well integrated in suburbs and find employment opportunities. They suggest, further, that transportation assistance, childcare assistance, and skills training assistance could further help the relatively successful integration and employment that occurred solely through subsidized housing assistance.[65] Other studies of racial integration in the suburbs suggest it works best in communities with high education levels, while fricition is more likely to occur in communities where working class whites are displaced or feel threatered. (Shipp)

Structuring Economic Opportunity

Facilitating workplace-place of residence linkage provides a foundation for economic opportunity because it helps remove geographic barriers that may prohibit matching labor supply and demand. Although this report argues that it is a necessary foundation, it also is indirect. A direct approach to economic opportunity, and one integral to economic development practice, relies on credit assistance to businesses.[66] Four sets of credit assistance activities are essential to economic opportunity: minority business development, tying credit assistance with employing poor people, nurturing startups and small businesses through business support services, and workplace-based education and training. Although these four topics are discussed separately at first, they are related and should be seen as a complementary set of overlapping activities that form the core of a state economic opportunity strategy. However, before discussing these four central components of a state economic opportunity strategy, three other points are made briefly.

First, a secondary activity within a state economic opportunity strategy is the provision of technical assistance and credit assistance to help

---

[65]The Gautreaux studies also find suburban participants' primary dissatisfaction is with medical care, namely the refusal of suburban hospitals and clinics to accept Medicaid, probably because state government is often delinquent in reimbursing them.

[66]It is very difficult to estimate even very roughly what states spend each year on providing credit assistance to businesses. A conservative estimate is that in the mid- to late-1980s the 50 states spent annually about $5.8 billion on tax-exempt or taxable bond funds (shallow subsidies) and about $1.2 billion in state funded loans and grants. This figure exclude state loan guarantee programs, credit assistance provided by state-chartered or state capitalized private entities, state administration of federal credit assistance funds, state assistance to local governments that is used for credit assistance, state tax incentives, job training programs, or state-authorized local tax incentives or local bonds used for credit assistance. (See NASDA)

low-income people become self-employed or start or expand microbusinesses. This report recommends such an activity as a secondary activity for three reasons. One, it may be applicable to only a relatively small percentage of poor people. Two, because the focus is on self-employment or the creation of just two or three jobs, the employment and earnings impact can be very minimal. Third, a self-employment or micro-business program for poor people is complex and very time-consuming. However, it can be important and successful for a number of people — especially in some rural areas where there are no practical alternatives — and should be part, albeit a secondary, supplemental component, of a state economic opportunity strategy.

Second, the economic opportunity strategy outlined here differs explicitly from a neighborhood revitalization strategy. The primary purpose of an economic opportunity strategy is to provide employment, earnings, and assets to poor people. The primary purpose of a neighborhood revitalization strategy is to ameliorate the socioeconomic and physical condition of poor neighborhoods. Although both strategies have laudable goals, this report suggests a pre-occupation with neighborhood revitalization may be counterproductive to the goals of economic opportunity. Individual localities clearly may want to pursue neighborhood revitalization strategies. It may be more appropriate for state government, however, to give priority attention to economic opportunity.

A contextual activity related to an economic opportunity strategy that is only briefly mentioned here is equal employment opportunity. States must do what they can to prevent discrimination in hiring, especially in entry-level positions. One of the few scientific studies of hiring discrimination in entry-level positions found that blacks experienced it in 20 percent of the job searches compared to 7 percent for whites. The type of job a black applies for is the most important predictor of discrimination: blacks experienced higher discrimination in white-collar clerical, sales, and service jobs than in blue-collar positions. Discrimination also was higher in jobs offering the highest wages and income potential. Discrimination was about the same in central cities and suburbs.[67] (Urban Institute)

---

[67]The study used the audit methodology, which is used extensively to test for housing discrimination, and included 476 hiring audits in the summer of 1990 in the Washington, D.C. and Chicago metropolitan areas. A 1989 study found hiring discrimination against Hispanics even higher, at 31 percent.

COSCDA

Minority business development

States should give much more assistance to creating and sustaining minority businesses. As noted in Chapter 3, minority businesses tend to employ largely minority workforces even when the businesses are located in predominantly nonminority areas. On the other hand, most white businesses in heavily minority areas do not employ largely minority workforces. Helping create and expand minority businesses can increase the assets of minorities, and it can be a very cost-effective way to increase minority employment.

Private businesses dominate the U.S. market economy. Blacks are substantially underepresented in this market-private business dominated economy, perhaps partly because of an historical reliance on politics and government as a source of and means to employment and income. Until recently, retail and personal services dominated the minuscule minority business sector, but now there are signs that minority businesses, including black businesses, are becoming more numerous and more involved in mainstream economic activity. Yet, there is a long way to go, with black business initiatives facing both racial discrimination and lack of access to capital, even more so than small businesses generally.

State government support for minority business development has been minimal and incidental. It has been minimal in the sense that the commitment of resources to minority business development pales in comparison to other business development activity. It has been incidental in the sense that it has not been mainstream. When state support for minority business development has been delivered through community-based organizations, too often it has focused on the types of businesses with little probability of long-term success and profit — personal and retail services serving a largely minority clientele. The challenge to state governments is to begin assisting more mainstream businesses, such as manufacturing and business services, even if this means bypassing CBOs and a neighborhood revitalization approach to economic development.

Maryland's Equity Participation and Investment Program illustrates one effective approach to mainstreaming minority business. As white business owners retire or otherwise end their business ventures this program provides an opportunity for minorities to purchase the businesses. The advantage of this approach is the ability to gauge the viability of the business since most have a track record.

Assisting minority business startups can be successful as well. Small businesses, especially startup enterprises, have a very difficult time accessing capital, and when they do they pay more for it than larger firms.

A minority business development program should include the following guidelines. First, because of the employment record of black businesses, states should not necessarily require hiring lower-income persons in return for credit assistance. This report recommends that states tie credit assistance as much as possible to the hiring of lower-income persons, but assisting minority businesses especially black businesses, can be an exception to this principle.

Second, states should give priority to funding firms in manufacturing; wholesaling; finance, insurance, and real estate; business and professional services, and businesses that do not serve a fully minority clientele in a minority area. Minority firms in the retail and personal services areas and firms located in minority areas with minority clientele generally are not viable business candidates. This may require states to withstand political pressures to fund minority firms in minority areas regardless of business viability, especially from advocates who simply want to see a fair share of funding go to minority firms or from advocates who are much more interested in responding to neighborhood constituents than in building viable minority businesses.

Third, credit assistance is very important to creating and sustaining minority, especially black businesses. For firms formed from 1976 through 1982, the average total financial capital at the time of startup was $44,552 for nonminority male firms, but only $21,399 for black male firms. (Bates, 1989) This degree of discrepancy existed for both debt and equity capital. In fact, people starting a business who put more equity capital into their business also tend to put in more debt capital. Blacks put less startup capital into their businesses because they have less equity than nonminorities and because fewer blacks who start businesses are college graduates compared to nonminorities. Nonetheless, blacks get smaller loans than nonminorities with the same education, age, and equity capital characteristics.

Clearly, blacks need greater access to capital to start businesses than do nonminorities; however, the need for access to capital also is related to firm viability. The greater the financial input at time of startup, the larger and more viable the businesses tend to be. Also, firms started with borrowed capital are more viable than firms started without borrowed capital. For example, firms started between 1976 and 1982 by nonminority males who borrowed no startup capital had an average sales volume only 61 percent of and an average employment only 58 percent of the average sales volume and employment of firms started with borrowed capital. (Bates, 1989)

States should develop a minority business program that provides blacks with a greater opportunity to access startup capital. The risk associated with providing this capital can be minimized if black business startups serve more than just a minority clientele and are not located in a predominantly minority areas and are in the manufacturing, business or professional services, or wholesaling industries, and if the entrepreneur has some college education and some equity capital. Unfortunately, firms and entrepreneurs with these kinds of characteristics are not the usual targets of minority business programs.

Tying credit assistance to employment of poor people

Too often, state credit assistance programs do not pursue a worthwhile quid pro quo with businesses. Enticing a business to move into the state; preventing a business from leaving the state, closing, or substantially reducing employment; increasing exports; promoting high technology; or helping a firm expand employment too frequently becomes the sole objective of credit assistance programs. The few credit assistance programs that are targeted to distressed areas are generally ineffective.

One of the few credit assistance programs clearly oriented to helping lower-income people is the Community Development Block Grant (CDBG) Program. In the state-administered CDBG program (about 800 large cities and counties receive funds directly from HUD), 20 to 25 percent of the funds are used for business credit assistance for job creation or retention. At least 51 percent of the jobs created or retained must be held by or made available to lower-income persons, and studies suggest a lower-income employment rate of 60 to 70 percent. (Sidor, 1990 a; Siegel and Kwass, 1990; Sidor, 1990 b) Thus, in return for credit assistance that might not be available elsewhere or for favorable terms and conditions, firms must hire a substantial portion of lower-income people among the additional workers hired as a result of the assistance.

The firms that received state CDBG assistance from 1982 through 1986 were largely manufacturing firms (68 percent), very small businesses at the time of receiving assistance (69 percent of the firms had fewer than 29 employees), either startups (25 percent) or expansions of existing firms (45 percent), and rural (about 70 percent of the loans were in nonmetro areas). While the state CDBG experience shows it is possible to condition the provision of credit assistance on employing lower-income persons, about 40 percent of the jobs created or retained through the program paid annual wages less than the poverty level for a family of four. Many of the manufacturing firms assisted were in routine, bottom of cycle, mature industries.[68]

Several conclusions may be drawn from the state CDBG experience. First, it may be ineffective to play a simple "numbers" game with employing lower-income people. The CDBG statute requires that 51 percent of the persons employed be lower income, and other statutory requirements lead many states to impose a 60 percent standard. If a firm can create 40 new jobs with CDBG assistance, but 24 of the 40 must be filled by people from households with incomes of 80 percent or less of the median, then firms that employ largely low-wage, low-skilled workers may be the predominant types of firms willing to receive the CDBG subsidy. These newly-employed, lower-income workers may gain little if they are employed in low quality, dead-end or short-term jobs. On the other hand, if only 12 or 14 of the new employees had to be lower-income, then more firms with higher quality jobs could seek access to the funds and offer better quality jobs to lower-income people. Fewer lower-income persons might be employed, but the present and future rewards to those who are hired could more than make up for the smaller number hired. A more effective approach would be to use the current mix of a firm's employees to develop a hiring standard appropriate to firms on a case-by-case basis.

Second, complex or burdensome administrative requirements can be self-defeating. Very small businesses, especially startups, need access to reasonably priced capital, which they find difficult to obtain from the private market.[69] Especially in nonmetropolitan areas, state CDBG funds infrequently substituted for private capital. (Siegel and Kwass) Yet, anecdotal evidence suggests that since 1987, as federal requirements placed on the CDBG program have increased, its ability to help small businesses and

---

[68]Routine manufacturing industries have a relatively low percentage of managerial, technical, and professional jobs and have lower value added than complex manufacturing industries. Routine industries tend to be at the bottom of their production cycle — their products are in their mature stage of development and production is standardized and not dependent on technically skilled labor. Employment in routine manufacturing industries is expected to decrease 3 percent between 1984 and 1995, while employment in complex manufacturing industries is expected to increase by nearly 18 percent in the same period. (Sidor, 1990 a)

[69]Even the popular Small Business Administration Loan Guarantee Program, which guaranteed over 14,000 loans between October 1, 1990 and June 30, 1991, is not very helpful to startup businesses: "One myth [about the SBA loan guarantee program] is that struggling startups can qualify for the loan guarantee. Not so. In most cases, your business must be stable and profitable to qualify for SBA approval." (Applegate)

increase employment opportunities for lower-income people has decreased because the program has become less popular with businesses. Businesses will put up with only so much red tape. This is especially true for small businesses that do not have the capacity to handle complex requirements and recordkeeping. Complex requirements even affect program operation. States make very few CDBG loans under $50,000 (the 1982-1986 average was about $200,000 and the median $180,000) because the administrative requirements, or cost, per loan are the same regardless of loan size. Smaller loans are too burdensome for states to handle administratively, although many small businesses and startups need loans of less than $50,000.

Third, providing credit assistance without providing other services, especially to startups and very small businesses, may not be the most appropriate technique to aid these business. Two years to four years after receiving CDBG assistance, about 17 percent of the businesses were no longer in business, and another 11 percent were more than 60 days delinquent in their loan payments. Forty-four percent of the business terminations were startups.

Fourth, providing credit assistance alone, especially to startups and very small businesses, may not be the most effective technique to aid the business's employees. In the state CDBG program, 70 percent of the jobs created or retained from 1984 through 1986 paid less than $300 per week, compared to a national median weekly pay of $373. The annual quit rate was about 30 percent. Branch plants and subsidiaries paid substantially higher wages than independent and locally-owned firms, manufacturing firms paid higher wages than service firms, and larger businesses (firms with more than 100 employees) paid higher wages than smaller firms.

Tying credit assistance and business support services
As pointed out in Chapter 3, the predominant cause of small business failure is poor management. Part of the need for management assistance is business management and finance — business and financial planning, marketing, budgeting, cash flow management, accounting practices, and business recordkeeping. Over the past decade, many business management-assistance resources have been established, often with federal or state funding, and often connected with a university or college, but most of these resources offer limited, short-term assistance. Also, the delivery system is chaotic. Many businesses are not aware of these services, many of these services are not easily available to rural or inner city businesses, and the initiative usually is on the business to find and seek help. Unfortunately, many businesses seek help only when it is too late.

Part of the need for management assistance is operational and technological — learning about plant layout and operations and inventory, systems and quality controls, and using new equipment. Over the past several years, a growing "infrastructure" to address these needs has started to develop. While these technology assistance resources overlap business management resources (about 20 to 40 percent of their services may be business management services), a recent study identified over 200 providers annually funded at about $620 million, with about one-half the money coming from state government. (Clarke and Dobson) While the state-supported providers do assist very small businesses (60 percent of the assisted firms have 50 or fewer employees), these providers give high priority to promoting advanced state-of-the-art technology rather than to helping businesses use off-the-shelf technology. Most resources are used to develop and test products and to engage in prototype development, often through research parks and technology research centers. Yet, small and mid-sized businesses require access primarily to existing, proven technologies.[70] Also, these resources tend to be located in suburban areas and small cities, not in central cities or rural areas. Only 13 states have technology extension programs, which tend to do a better job of helping firms adopt existing technologies, and these extension programs account for only 4 percent of the funds spent on technology assistance.

Successful technology assistance programs to small and mid-sized firms have several common characteristics. They pay close attention to the client's problems, rather than to promoting a particular technology. They combine technology assistance and business management assistance, because it often is very difficult to separate the two. They provide on-site service, trading off serving many firms superficially for providing intense assistance to fewer firms. Finally, they provide training to employees.

One problem with the current provision of business support services is that few offer all the above services. Another problem is that few programs tie providing credit assistance to small firms and startups for purposes of job creation with providing business support services, although there are exceptions (see Hagey). This absence of integration of

---

[70]The managers of these resources indicate that one-half to two-thirds of the businesses they assisted sought access to existing technologies, and not to new, advanced technologies. The program managers of Maryland's, Pennsylvania's, and Ohio's industrial extension programs reported that 90 percent, 75 percent, and 91 percent of the firms they assisted, respectively, required access to established technologies, not new technologies. (Clarke and Dobson)

credit assistance and business support assistance may have three overlapping consequences. Weakly-managed firms and firms using outdated and inefficient technology may go out of business, making job creation through credit assistance a Pyrrhic victory. Second, firms with outdated technologies and inefficient operations may lose an opportunity to become and remain globally competitive. Chapter 3 pointed out the importance of small manufacturing firms to America's ability to remain competitive (manufacturing firms with under 500 employees contribute nearly one-half the value added) and to net job growth. Finally, because startups and very small firms often pay low wages or provide jobs with other negative characteristics, providing business support assistance may be able to increase cash flow, or otherwise improve profitability. Economic development practioners can use the linked provision of credit assistance and business support assistance to negotiate for better wages, fringe benefits, or working conditions for employees.[71]

The provision of credit assistance is a good point at which to intervene with the provision of business support assistance, because expanded operations, the acquisition of new equipment, the adoption of new technologies, or the advent of new products often trigger the need for credit assistance. While it may be impossible, and do little good, to force a firm to accept business support assistance, providing credit assistance is an effective way to inform firms about the value of such services and to introduce these services before it is too late to save the loan, the business, and the jobs. Certainly, the provision of subsidized credit assistance provides an inducement for a firm to become knowledgeable about and use business support services.

Tying credit assistance with workplace education

The provision of credit assistance should be seen as an opportunity to invest directly in human capital. As discussed above, credit assistance providers, especially when they can connect the credit assistance to business support services, should attempt to negotiate for improved job quality.

---

[71]This negotiation need not depend entirely on combining credit assistance and business support assistance. For example, New Hampshire in its state CDBG program measures the public subsidy in a CDBG loan and tries to get the business to pay for part of this subsidy by providing day care or making education or training opportunities available to employees. To the extent that business support services can help produce a more viable or profitable firm, the room for such negotiation increases.

If 80 percent or more of the workforce of the year 2000 is in the workforce today and if global competition requires a constant updating of technology, a technology that places more demands on workers' educational and skill levels, then a premium needs to be placed on the education and skills development of the workforce. If nearly all net job growth is occurring in small and mid-size firms, especially firms under 100 employees, then workforce education is especially important to the employees of small firms.[72] Additionally, two of every three new workers start in small firms. (Vencill et al.) Yet as shown in Chapter 3, most workplace education occurs in very large firms and is for upper- and mid-level employees.

Workplace education in small businesses is in its infancy. For example, less than 10 percent of firms with fewer than 500 employees provide remedial education for their employees, compared to over 30 percent for firms with 10,000 or more employees. A 1991 study of 18 small business workplace education programs showed 14 had been operating one year or less, and only three of the programs were offered at businesses employing 100 or fewer people. (Vencill et al.) Using credit assistance to entice small businesses to provide workplace education and skills training may be the most productive approach to furthering what may be a most significant human investment program, especially for lower income and less educated workers. While employees of small companies may need workplace education the most, small companies are least able to afford the loss of time employees may need to take for education, and are least likely to have the administrative resources to invest in education.

The phrase workplace education is defined here as (1) education and training linked to the workplace, such as locating classes on-site, using telecommunications or distance education to the workplace, the business providing materials, meeting space, or release time; (2) including or targeted to production and entry-level workers; and (3) active management support or involvement. At its most effective — and as proposed by this report — workplace education is much more than simply teaching

---

[72]Another example of the employment importance of small firms comes from the Milwaukee metropolitan study mentioned earlier. Although this study uses establishment size rather than firm size, the findings illustrate the overall point. The study shows that manufacturing plants from 1 to 49 in size gained nearly 4,500 employees (3,000 in plants 1 to 19 in size) between 1979 and 1987, while manufacturing plants with over 500 employees lost over 50,000 jobs. In service employment, plants 1 to 49 employees gained over 16,000 jobs, while plants with 500 employees or more gained less than 13,000 jobs. (White and Osterman)

English as a Second Language or teaching basic skills, necessary as these are. Rather, workplace education is not a one-time, short-term event, but a process that over time teaches basic skills, but also behavior and process skills — thinking skills such as problem-solving — and technical skills — skills necessary for achieving specialized functional job skills.

Employers have several motivations to provide workplace education: responding to technological change (e.g., preparing for the possible advent of statistical process control); responding to competitive pressures (e.g., using self-managing work teams); improving employee skills and education, possibly to increase productivity. But most small businesses do not start workplace education because of strong motivation; they start workplace education because someone makes it easy for them to start.

Most small business employers are unfamiliar with workplace education programs and do not have the money or knowledge to start a program. Initial program development can be time consuming and expensive — $3,000 to $30,000 — compared to operating costs. According to a small business study of workplace education, "Almost all the firms indicated they would not have been likely to implement programs without the technical and financial start-up assistance that was made available to them." (Vencill et al., p. 43)

Successful workplace education requires careful planning, support from top management, and a clear communication of program goals, including understanding workers' motivation to participate in the education. Employees must believe the program benefits them, not only the firm; and special attention needs to be paid to employees with lower levels of education, such as making the education available to all production or entry-level employees and not just those with very poor skills and low levels of education. Paid time and release time can be very important.

Despite the above barriers and potential difficulties, small business employers who offer workplace education expect it to have positive effect on the quantity and quality of work produced and on employee morale, self-esteem, and promotability. All the firms participating in the Vencill small business study "plan to continue their programs. Many expressed a willingness to absorb an increased proportion of out of pocket expenses associated with program implementation." (Vencill et al., p. 65)

Through a demonstration program started in 1990, Illinois offers workplace literacy grants to businesses. The Secretary of State's office made competitive grants totaling $118,000 to 16 business in 1990, with businesses matching these funds with a total of $240,700. For 12 of the businesses, this was their first venture into workplace education. The grants ranged from $2,103 to $10,000. A total of 1,100 employees participated in the education, ranging from a low of 4 to a high of 200. Eight of the 16 firms had fewer than 500 employees, although only one had fewer than 100.

Pre-tests and post-test of students are required. The workplace education must be provided only to employees who read, write, or comprehend at less than the sixth-grade level. Six businesses used the grants for both English as a Second Language (ESL) and adult basic education, while five of the businesses used the funds for either adult basic education and basic skills or ESL. The curricula were tailored to the individual businesses. The education in one firm consisted of four parts: (1) basic math training that concentrated on fractions and decimals to ensure more accurate measurements, (2) job safety programming to reduce lost-time accidents, (3) product education, marketing philosophy, and student visits to job sites to see the products in place, and (4) reading assistance focusing on documents used daily in the workplace. Another firm developed a customized assessment instrument and competency-based ESL curriculum.

Nearly all the firms reported increased communication and morale among the workforce as a result of the workplace education, and four or more businesses reported improved efficiency, safety awareness, or productivity or decreased accident rates and rework. In several firms, the employees who participated in the education could help their children with homework for the first time, and many companies found workplace education made implementing changes easier. All the companies participating in the initial program planned to continue their workplace education programs after the end of the grant period.

The program was so successful that Illinois extended it for two years. In 1991, 19 businesses received grants totaling $134,800, and they matched this amount with a total of $636,154, with about 1,600 employees participating. In 1992, 32 businesses will share $252,025 in grants and contribute an additional $626,031 to serve about 2,000 employees.[73]

The advent of credit assistance is a good entry point for workplace education. Because a loan (or another form of financial assistance) is usually made to purchase new or additional equipment, to expand or

---

[73]While several states have workplace education loan or grant programs, Mississippi offers a tax credit to businesses that provide basic skills education to their employees. An amount up to 25 percent of qualified training-related expenses can be credited against state income taxes.

upgrade other fixed assets, often connected with adding new employees, it marks a break in normal business operations and provides a context for beginning education. Economic development practioners can facilitate workplace education by providing full or matching grants to employers and by indicating loan commitments would be more easily or more assuredly made (if not made contingent on) if the employer made at least an initial commitment to workplace education. Given the startup barriers facing small businesses and their unfamiliarity with workplace education, grants probably would have to be made initially to start the education. If planned properly, it is likely that many businesses would be interested in continuing to offer workplace education.

In summary, a state economic opportunity strategy should significantly expand minority business development activities; promote business startups and the expansion and modernization of small and mid-sized businesses, especially manufacturing and business service firms, through the provision of credit assistance; link this credit assistance with business support services, including management assistance and technology assistance; seek commitments from small and mid-sized businesses to employ a significant number (even if it is much less than 50 percent) of lower-income people in return for favorable credit assistance; and help small and mid-sized businesses, especially business with fewer than 100 employees, undertake workplace education for production and entry-level workers. A secondary, supplemental component is the provision of credit assistance and technical assistance to help low-income people become self-employed or start micro-businesses. This economic opportunity strategy must be supported by a state housing opportunity strategy committed to reducing local and other land use and regulatory barriers to the production of affordable housing in the suburbs, and aggressively overcoming racial, income, and large family discrimination in the sale and rental of housing.

This economic opportunity strategy leaves some important questions unanswered. How are the resources of this strategy delivered? Who implements or operates the activities that constitute the strategy? How and to what extent are these economic development resources connected to other resources? To what extent do these economic development activities actually reach very poor people?

Delivering Resources

This discussion of delivering resources is divided into two sections, although the issues discussed in each section cannot be fully separated. The first section, on implementation, focuses on delivering the resources that are core components of a state economic opportunity strategy. The second section, on collaboration, discusses linking economic opportunity resources with other related resources.

Implementation

As mentioned in Chapter 4, states infrequently implement and operate economic development-related programs directly. But this probably is less true of credit assistance activities than employment training, education, housing, and perhaps many kinds of social or human services. Most of the "automatic" credit assistance programs, such as most tax incentives, are implemented relatively simply through the state's revenue administration system. In some instances, local governments or nonprofits are important in "delivering" state tax incentives. While states sometimes give key administrative and even policy responsibilities to local organizations in using state loans, loan guarantees, and grants, many, if not most, of these credit assistance activities are directly administered by states. While most non-tax incentive credit assistance programs are administered directly by states, nearly all these programs leverage private sector funds by requiring participation by financial institutions or owner equity. When states delegate substantial administration, they usually require adherence to an explicit set of standards for the provision of credit assistance to a specific business, such as in the state-administered CDBG program. The most visible instances of states delegating most policy and operational decisions to others occurs when states capitalize local or regional revolving loan funds or provide program funds to CBOs, especially CDCs, for use in projects largely determined by the CBOs.

State administration: The centralized nature of state credit assistance delivery has advantages and disadvantages. Two important advantages are that the state is able to set specific objectives and priorities for the use of its resources, and the state does not have to rely on the good will, interest, or competency of local administrative actors to seek its resources. There also are two important disadvantages. Since many of the other development-related resources are decentralized, collaboration with these other resources can be more difficult, and CBOs often can make little use of the state's economic development resources.

Because it is important for a state economic opportunity strategy to have a regional orientation, the advantages can outweigh the disadvantages. For credit assistance, this means the state must establish policies and resources that give priority to providing credit assistance to minority businesses and packaging credit assistance to startups and small and mid-sized businesses. Also, the state must provide an organized, significant level of outreach and information dissemination, and state administration must be competent.

The state's economic opportunity strategy should also foster the creation of business networks for existing small and mid-sized businesses. As seen in the Chapter 3, a business network can be a very important capacity-building resource to small and mid-sized firms, allowing firms to adopt new technologies, access markets, and share costly expenses. At the same time, a business network can be an intermediary, advising states on the kinds of assistance needed and what firms to assist, adding value in the same way that housing and community development intermediaries add value. This value-added may be most important in helping to orchestrate the participation of other important, but decentralized actors such as PICs, community colleges, vocational-technical schools, business support service organizations, local governments, locally-based state offices, and nonprofit organizations.

When a business network intermediary is absent, state economic development practioners must develop and sustain face-to-face communication among possible resource providers in its economic opportunity strategy, so that economic development-related organizations know about the state's strategy and their possible participation in it, and the state economic development practioners know how various organizations can contribute to implementation of its strategy. The importance of a governor creating and nurturing a vision of an economic opportunity strategy that articulates key goals and motivates participation, as discussed in Chapter 4, can form the basis for sustaining a communications network.

A state can use two major kinds of delivery mechanisms in delivering economic opportunity resources, assuming that the provision of credit assistance generally is centralized in the absence of an effective intermediary. A state can give businesses the option to choose resource providers themselves or a state can partner with one or more vendors in packaging its credit assistance activities, for example by contracting or informally partnering with a university-based industrial extension program to provide business support services to firms receiving credit assistance.

There are several advantages of a state partnering with selected vendors. The state has control over whether to work or how to work with an organization based on the organization's capacity and competency. Second, as each partner develops an understanding of the other's strengths, weaknesses, and objectives, the effectiveness of the partnership can increase. Finally, the economies of scale of such a relationship can make the service very cost effective.

State partnering also has disadvantages. A business could have a bias against the state's partner and not want to work with the organization. Also, if a business thinks the state's partner performs poorly, it could be damaging to the state's future efforts. An alternative is to give the business the freedom to select the resource provider. For workplace education, the business can use its state workplace education funds to contract, for example, with the adult basic education program of the local school system, hire a community college teacher, or contract with a nonprofit organization.

The strengths and weaknesses of state-partnering versus business-option delivery will depend on many specific circumstances. Whichever delivery system it uses, the state needs to monitor performance, and intervene or otherwise make adjustments if performance falls short.

The most problematic area when a state directly administers credit assistance activities occurs when a state places substantial attention on self-employment and micro-business development. Even if a state gives priority to manufacturing and business services instead of the more usual (for self-employment and micro-enterprise practice) retail and personal services, the size of the loans or other forms of credit assistance are likely to be small, in the $5,000 to $25,000 range. If the state places substantial resources behind this priority or if it is able to leverage other funds substantially, this can soon cause an administrative overload. Also, the ability to find qualified would-be entrepreneurs or for would-be entrepreneurs to find state resources can be a substantial barrier. Finally, ensuring that the many would-be entrepreneurs can easily access business support services can be another difficulty.

Local Participation: As mentioned in Chapter 4, CBOs can be a very effective outreach and information source, so they should play an important role in helping entrepreneurs access funds. Some CBOs may be able to provide business support services to micro-enterprises, especially those located in areas inaccessible to the existing network of business support assistance providers.

States may be able to capitalize a revolving loan fund at a CBO with a demonstrated capacity, as long as specific state standards and objectives are pursued. Two considerations need to be reviewed before proceeding in this direction. One is that many CBOs are as much political organizations as they are administrative organizations. Consequently, it may be politically awkward to defund some CBOs even on the basis of demonstrated poor performance. Second, just as a state-administered, micro-enterprise loan fund may burden the state with diseconomies of scale, so the overhead burden of a micro-enterprise loan fund at a CBO level may be spread over too few loans, resulting in substantial inefficiencies. A CBO service area may be too small, and its service area may provide too few opportunities for self-employment or micro-enterprise development that may be important to a state economic opportunity strategy.

City and county governments can be used to administer state-capitalized loan funds for self-employment and micro-enterprise development. Smaller cities, however, may face problems similar to those of CBOs described above, and while some cities and counties may not want to use state funds to pursue state economic opportunity objectives. If the unemployment insurance demonstration programs described in Chapter 3 become widespread, local offices of the employment service could be another available delivery mechanism. The best delivery mechanism may be an independent, regional, or metropolitan-wide nonprofit intermediary committed to working throughout the region or area and to orchestrating the other services necessary for an effective self-employment and micro-enterprise development program. Although none may exist now, the creation of a state economic opportunity strategy along with direct state encouragement may help create such regional intermediaries. Not too long ago, there were no housing or neighborhood development intermediaries.

There are several reasons the economic opportunity strategy described in this report does not rely heavily on CBOs. One is that a state economic opportunity strategy should be regional, encompassing the central city and outlying suburbs. There should be a clear distinction between a neighborhood revitalization goal and a goal of providing earned income and assets to poor people within an economic competitiveness context. Pursuit of a state economic opportunity strategy, however, need not preclude state investment in neighborhood revitalization.

There are several other CBO issues. Resource deliverers should be held accountable for performance. Some resources must be delivered by specialized resource providers which are unlikely to be CBOs. The state should not commit continually to a single resource provider; some competition among resource providers is very positive. Also, there needs to be some balance when the for-profit business sector plays a major role in economic opportunity and is the point of entry for many resources. Finally, the rhetoric and long-term political agenda of many CBOs may not fit well in this context.

Nonetheless, CBOs can play a role in a state economic opportunity strategy. Their biggest asset is their access to and support of poor people and poor communities, thus outreach and information dissemination is an important activity for CBOs, especially informing people about and helping them obtain housing and job opportunities in suburbs. CBOs can be involved in self-employment and micro-enterprise development, and, indirectly, in providing education and other personal resources and skills to poor people. The specific nature of CBO participation will depend largely on the circumstances and dynamics of individual states and areas.

The delivery system for the state's housing opportunity strategy is more clearly defined. There are apt to be few regional institutions the state can use to effect a housing opportunity strategy. The state examples given in the section on housing opportunity provide a range of delivery illustrations. The state needs a communications network for this strategy as well. The state cannot monitor land use and other regulatory and housing practices everywhere, and must rely on local organizations or persons to initiate review or action.

Collaboration

Every public or publicly-supported resource system has a modal point of entry, or intervention point, to its clients or the constituency it serves. The modal intervention point is the most well known or used or most central or popular way in which the resource system assists its clients. For example, in human services the modal intervention point is the intervention of the case worker or income specialist who approves, monitors, and counsels AFDC recipients, although there are many other contact points between the human resources systems and its clients. In education, it is the teacher or other school worker who teaches or works with the student in the school. In the human resources area, the various modal points of entry have been or are being used to expand the resources provided to the client or in some cases, to expand the population served. Thus, the current move toward comprehensive case management depends on the expansion or development of the point of entry of AFDC case workers, or similar service providers. The notion of a comprehensive community school providing a variety of services, like child care, rests on the expansion of the intervention point of primary and secondary education. Providing multiple support services to residents of public housing depends on the interface between the managers of public housing and its tenants.

In state economic development, the modal intervention point occurs through credit assistance to a business. There has been little expansion of the modal intervention point of economic development for several reasons. The broad human resources area serves primarily poor people or serves a significant number of poor people, except perhaps for services to the elderly. Economic development serves businesses and usually has little direct involvement with employees or poor people. Credit assistance is seen almost as an end in itself. It adds to or sustains employment, income, and related economic activity, especially when aggregated and viewed from a statewide perspective. There is little momentum to expand this modal intervention point to add other services to a specific business. For the most part, when states do provide credit assistance, technology assistance, management assistance, workplace education assistance, or other assistance to business, they usually provide these services separately from one another, in terms of programs and staff (or agencies) and serve businesses in a separate, ad hoc, deal-making fashion.

Fragmentation in the human resources area receives much notoriety. A similar fragmentation exists in economic development. Economic development does not serve a significant number of businesses; only a very small percentage of businesses in a state receive credit assistance from state government. Since each economic development program or activity serves a small number of businesses, instances of duplication or thoughts of fragmentation rarely occur.

The modal intervention point for economic development is very different from the modal intervention points for the broad human resources area. A plausible conclusion is that the modal intervention points in economic development and human resources cannot be merged, as they may be within human resources. Effecting collaboration between economic development and human resources requires two steps. The first step is to expand the modal intervention point for economic development — credit assistance to a business — so the practice of economic development can better serve economic opportunity goals. The recommendations made so far attempt to accomplish this objective: providing credit assistance to help develop minority businesses; using credit assistance to startups and small and mid-sized businesses to negotiate the employment of lower-income people; and tying credit assistance with business support services (technology assistance and management assistance) and with workplace education for production and entry-level workers.

The second step is to use this expanded modal intervention point to develop a bridge to the human resources area. Helping poor people is not the main goal of state economic development policy. If economic development practice is pushed too far in this direction, the results and consequences may be counterproductive. The trick is to strike a balance that keeps economic development important and relevant to a business's bottom line and useful for broad economic development goals, such as employment and income, and still permit it to be effectively used to help poor people. This is not easy because many businesses view unemployed poor people, especially if they are young and minorities, as very poor employee risks.

One way to try to achieve this balance is to give a business maximum hiring choice and keep reporting and other paperwork requirements to a minimum. For example, it would be more effective as a quid pro quo for credit assistance to permit a business to select and hire a certain number of employees from a potential pool of JOBS participants, JTPA graduates, employment service referrals, TJTC-eligibles, and job applicants who otherwise document their low-income status than to condition receipt of credit assistance on a business hiring a percentage of JOBS recipients or residents of a specific inner city census tract. It also would probably be more effective to require the business to keep the low-income documentation in its files, subject to possible field audit, than to require specialized and continual reporting to a public agency.

A second way to keep this balance is to try to create a win-win situation for a business. For small and mid-sized businesses couching an economic opportunity objective in terms of a more relevant (to the business) economic competitiveness and workforce education framework may be good strategy. This is most effective if credit assistance can be packaged with management assistance, technology assistance, and workplace education. In this way, the assistance, including the resultant hiring of lower-income persons, can be viewed as an attempt to help the business become more competitive, not as an attempt to turn the business into a social welfare instrument.

Finally, state policymakers and business leaders need to try to change the terms of the rhetoric about economic opportunity. If people with little education and skills, especially minorities, are equated with poverty, and if poverty is equated with dependency and issues of conduct, businesses will be much less likely to become involved in issues of poverty. If the issue is presented as one of improving the education and skill levels of the present workforce and increasing business competitiveness, businesses may be more likely to deal with poverty-related problems.

Targeting

The economic opportunity strategy described so far advocates that states seek a tradeoff with small and mid-sized businesses, who would receive credit assistance and possibly business support assistance and workplace education assistance in return for hiring poor people. But it does not recommend tough targeting standards for either the number or kinds of lower-income persons hired. Depending on a variety of circumstances, this may not lead to the hiring of the very poor, and could result in charges of "creaming."

There are some targeted approaches to economic opportunity that may be worthwhile to explore. These examples are given not as recommendations that they become an inherent part of every economic opportunity strategy, but as suggestions that may be tried on a demonstration basis. In targeting, one of the key factors is which resource system's modal intervention point takes precedence.

An economic opportunity strategy could require specific low-income targeting, for example, requiring that a business that receives credit assistance ensure that a specified percent of its new hires be persons with incomes below 80 percent of the poverty standard. These very low-income hires could be referred to a human resources agency, which would be responsible for assessing the extent to which a new very low-income employee and his or her family needs assistance. If assistance were needed, for example, alcohol abuse, housing assistance, parenting, or medical assistance, the human resources agency would be responsible for packaging and monitoring the assistance.

In this example, the economic development assistance is the lead intervention point, with assessment and comprehensive services provided to the employee and his or her family after the hiring decision has been made. Certainly, other types of targeting could be used, for example, JOBS recipients, poor people living in inner city areas, or JTPA participants. The point of this example is that the hiring of an employee triggers the packaging of family support services. The value of this approach is two-fold. One is that the employer makes the hiring decision, albeit from a relatively narrow range eligible applicants. Second, the employer receives not only credit assistance and the opportunity for business support services and workplace education, but also is assured that his or her new "risky" employees and their families will be receiving other kinds of assistance that could contribute to stable and productive work.

This approach has some disadvantages. Most of the businesses are apt to be located outside the inner city or the central city away from where most "eligible" job applicants live. Transportation and finding out about job opportunities may be big obstacles. The state economic development agency must inform human services agencies and others about possible job openings, so this information can be communicated to their clients. It also may be possible to provide transportation assistance, either directly to the employees or to the employer. Housing assistance, such as a short-term rental assistance voucher, could be part of the services package, and help accomplish two objectives. It could provide a transition period in which the employee could afford decent housing, while wages would increase over time to permit the gradual withdrawal of the subsidy. Also, it could help the employee afford housing near the workplace, (however, it is now difficult to use federal rental assistance in such a flexible way).

Another targeted approach focuses initially on the potential employee, perhaps using a particular human resource agency or program to identify potential employees, undertake assessment, and commit tó provide comprehensive services assistance. This is the usual approach connecting human resource agencies and their clientele to jobs. Once these clientele are identified, say participants in a JOBS program, efforts are made to place them in private sector employment. Unfortunately, the placement process is frequently ad hoc, depending on the personal outreach and contacts made by human resource agency workers or the luck of the hiring process. Unless the human resource agency has a good reputation and track record with business, its efforts may even be counterproductive.

Jointly targeting industries may be one way to improve this ad hoc and often difficult approach. The human resource agencies could identify firms that are likely to hire their clientele, and the economic development agency could identify firms with growth potential or the potential for long-term sustainability. Where there is a joint matching, the economic development agency could approach the firms with an offer of packaged credit assistance if the firm were willing to hire a certain number of the human resource agency's clients. For example, a recent study identified 12 primary and eight secondary "urban industry targets," industries that have performed best in inner city areas during the past decade, and where there appear to be good prospects for employment, upward mobility, and earnings potential for area residents. (NCI Research) Firms in these industries, or in industries identified through analyses of particular areas or in other ways, could be targeted for both packaged credit assistance and hiring of poor people.

Trying to initiate connections between human resource and economic development from the human services side does have a significant disadvantage. It is difficult to bring packaged credit assistance belatedly to firms that have responded to a human service agency initiative to hire poor people because the firms may not need or be appropriate for credit assistance. Economic development agencies want to provide credit assistance to firms that need it and could make good use of it — for real property acquisition or reconstruction, for equipment and other fixed assets, or for working capital that leads to job creation or retention and increased output and wealth, especially for export or export-related firms. There should be no unnecessary or wasteful economic development payoffs or rewards to firms that simply hire lower-income people. Also, firms that need and could use credit assistance, especially startups and small businesses, are likely to be much more concerned about and interested in access to capital at a reasonable cost and obtaining business support services than in hiring poor people.

From an economic development perspective, and from the perspective of most firms, it makes more sense to lead with packaged credit assistance linked with the hiring of poor persons, tying packaged human support services to the employee and his or her family. This is not to deny the important role of human services in making the potential employees attractive workforce candidates.

Economic Opportunity and the Very Poor

How relevant is a state economic opportunity strategy to the very poor — to people with substantial dependency on welfare, to members of the urban underclass, to those who have longed dropped out of the workforce?

An economic development orientation to antipoverty is based on the premise that economic opportunity is relevant. However, perhaps because of the extraordinary visibility of the conditions and behavior of homeless people and the underclass, an increasingly popular perspective of poverty today focuses on conduct and dependency. In the words of Lawrence Mead, today many people may believe the main challenge of antipoverty policy may be not to expand economic opportunity, but to "overcome social weaknesses that stems from the "post-marital" family and the inability of many people to get through school. The inequalities of the workplace are now trivial in comparison of those stemming from family structure. What matters for success is less whether your father was rich or poor than whether you knew your father at all." (Mead, 1991, p. 10) Mead suggests the country's major focus now seems to be on dependency and dysfunction, not on opportunity; policies and programs now concentrate, almost exclusively, on welfare, education, and criminal justice, designed primarily to "direct the lives of those dependent on government"; and we now pay more attention to youth than to workers.

The presence of conduct and dependency as a major perspective on poverty makes initiating an economic opportunity approach to poverty all the more difficult, especially when assumptions are made that most poor people are dysfunctional and cannot or will not take advantage of economic opportunity without long-term or extensive social intervention. The lack of involvement of economic development institutions in today's antipoverty activities may be due partly to the perception of economic development practitioners and the business community that most poor people have neither the interest nor personal competency to work. If actual experiences and practice reinforce this view, it is more difficult to involve economic development resources in antipoverty strategies. But an economic opportunity strategy may be effective if many poor people are not dysfunctional or if they simply need requirements to work placed on them if they do not possess a personal initiative to do so.

The issue of conduct and competency versus economic opportunity is legitimate, but it is an issue of perception as much as reality. Several examples in Chapter 1 point out that much of the current production, entry level, or blue collar workforce has little education, perhaps even a low level of skills. In the popular Illinois workplace education program described earlier, the education is limited to workers who function below a 6th grade literacy level. Two other examples from the Vencill small business workplace education show that there may be many members of the current workforce who are good workers but who have very low levels of education or skills. "The owner [of a small construction company] had been initially "shocked" into awareness of his own company's need for workplace education when he accidentally discovered that one of his best workers [who he was going to promote into a supervisory position] had never learned to read." (Vencill et al., p. 89) In another case, a plant manager of a mid-sized manufacturing company asked his personnel director if many of the plant's workers had less than a high school education, and found out "the number was alarmingly high." (Vencill et al., p. 90) The point of these examples is that an economic opportunity strategy could serve many poor people.

The goal of an economic opportunity strategy should be to provide employment to poor people. Tying the hiring of poor people with credit assistance, business support assistance, and workplace education attempts simultaneously to increase the competitiveness and profitability of small and mid-sized businesses and provide employees with the skills and education they will need to sustain productive employment and increase their earnings so that they can become fully self-sufficient and stay out of poverty.

Businesses often may feel that they are left alone to deal with the problems of having poor people as employees. As noted in Chapter 3, many businesses often perceive many government-run training and education programs as ineffective. While part of this perception may be caused by the clientele of these programs, it also may be caused by experience, either direct or word-of-mouth, about the lack of value or ineffectiveness of these programs. Thus, many businesses may believe that once they hire graduates of these programs, or similar people, they, and they alone, are stuck with dealing with their problems.

The economic opportunity strategy advocated in this report tries to allay this concern by packaging business support services and workplace education assistance with credit assistance and the hiring of low-income people. This may give businesses the sense that their managers, their firm, and the firm's employees all can be helped, and helped in a way that they can control to some extent. Part of this strategy coincides with two notions discussed in Chapter 3. One, workplace education, even in a very broad sense, may be more effective than the traditional U.S. approach of clearly separating education and work. Two, some evidence suggests that employer-based skills training produces better results, higher wages, and more satisfied management, than government or educational programs; federal policy should more effectively encourage and support workplace education and training.

However, most poor people work, and many employed poor people work nearly full time. Many individuals work at jobs that pay less than the poverty standard, but their households are not poor simply because more than one worker in the household work at jobs earning less than the poverty standard. Given the current structure of our economy and its present dynamic, an increasing share of jobs will be in small firms or will be part time or nontraditional. These jobs, at least in the near term or for entry level employees, are likely not to pay high wages or provide substantial fringe benefits. It is wistful to assume that the relationship between family structure and poverty will go away or become less important.

To suggest simply that unemployed poor people should stay unemployed and receive government subsidies because they would not earn enough to leave poverty makes little sense when more people work at poverty-level wages and do not receive government subsidies. To suggest simply and further that adults who chose to have children and not form or attempt to form two-parent families should not work but should receive government subsidies while many others with children struggle to keep a family intact and work hard at earning low wages and do not receive government subsidies is not only unfair but builds a political base on quicksand for antipoverty assistance.

The issues of teenage child birth and family structure are not addressed directly by an economic opportunity strategy. However, addressing these issues, through education, counseling, and a bundling of incentives and disincentives is critical for a successful, broad, and long-term solution to poverty. These issues, and issues related to crime, will be much more difficult to address successfully as long as very poor people are concentrated in large cities or other areas with little access to employment opportunities, especially decent employment opportunities for relatively low-skilled workers.

The economic opportunity strategy advocated in this report places initial priority on employment, but it also argues government and business have the responsibility to ensure that entry-level or low-income workers are provided the opportunity and resources to improve their productivity, skills, and education and become valuable and productive workers in successfully competitive businesses. Unfortunately, earnings in the short-run, and may be even in the long-run, will not allow many people easily to work their way out of poverty. Government, particularly the federal government, also must do a much better job — one might reasonably say, start doing a job — of helping the employed poor.[74] If not, there is no political or policy magic that can be used to provide deep subsidies, such as AFDC, food stamps, Medicaid, day care, education, skills training, transportation, counseling and other personal services to unemployed poor people so that they can be employed in work with earnings high enough to pay for their exit from welfare-related subsidies. Not only will there be no political or policy magic, but there also will be a set of perverse incentives that will sustain if not increase the problems the magic is trying to make disappear.

---

[74]David T. Ellwood among others argues that welfare reform will not work unless nonwelfare reforms, such as expanding the Earned Income Tax Credit, refundable child care tax credits, expanding child support collection, wage subsidies, or national health insurance are implemented. (Ellwood)

6

A Brief Reprise

Anecdotal comments and systematic studies about employer difficulties in hiring even minimally skilled workers abound. Stories and studies about increased poverty, welfare dependency, income inequality, and the urban underclass reinforce the stories and studies of workforce deficiencies. Because over 80 percent of the workforce of the year 2000 is in the workforce today, our ability to deal successfully with poverty-related issues is intertwined with our ability to compete in the global market. Because state governments are major players in economic development, they have a major responsibility to address the challenge presented by the related problems of competitiveness and poverty. Unfortunately, state economic development policy and practice are just beginning to wrestle with this challenge.

This report recommends that states adopt an economic opportunity strategy, and suggests the basic components of such a strategy. A state economic opportunity strategy is neither a comprehensive antipoverty strategy nor a state economic development policy. Rather, it uses state economic development practice to provide earnings, assets, and employment to poor people. A state economic development policy has the broad goals of increasing income, wealth, and employment statewide. This report suggests a significant portion of state economic development practice should be oriented to economic opportunity which should strive to achieve the goals of economic development. That is, a state economic opportunity strategy must be justified primarily on an economic development basis; it is not simply an income redistribution or social welfare policy.

The basic components of a state economic opportunity strategy build on state economic development practice, reflect the realities of the structure and dynamics of our economy, and recognize the nature of poverty-related problems. The core activity of an economic opportunity strategy is the provision of credit assistance to businesses. Every state does this, using: subsidized loans, guarantees, or grants; assistance in improving infrastructure; or tax incentives. This report views credit assistance as the "modal intervention point" in economic development policy. It is the prevailing way in which the state economic development system interacts with its client group. Each public resource system (human services, education, public health) has a modal intervention point.

Some credit assistance to business has been criticized as unnecessary, ineffective, or inefficient. While some of this criticism may be true, credit assistance as an economic development activity is not about to be eliminated or become unimportant. It is necessary, therefore, to use credit assistance to its maximum advantage. Unfortunately, states have not used credit assistance effectively to extract an appropriate quid pro quo from business. Most state credit assistance should be used to increase the hiring of poor people. The provision of credit assistance usually is associated with a major expansion or change of operations of a business, a change that usually leads to the hiring of additional employees. If used as part of an economic opportunity strategy, credit assistance would be available only when a firm agrees to hire a negotiated percentage of poor people, a percentage much larger than its current, relevant proportion of low-wage employees, but not so high that only low-wage, low-skill businesses would be interested in obtaining credit assistance. Given the increasing dominance of minorities and low-skill, less-educated persons in the workforce, this requirement is less onerous than it appears.

In an economic opportunity strategy, credit assistance should be provided primarily to small (fewer than 100 employees) firms and to a lesser extent mid-sized (100 to 499 employees) firms. These firms are the net producers of jobs in our economy and are the firms most likely to need access to credit assistance, even subsidized credit assistance. These firms should be primarily in the manufacturing and business service industries, because these are basic economic activities that create wealth and are important to our ability to compete globally. By and large, providing credit assistance to personal services and retail trade businesses should be avoided. Using credit assistance to help poor people become self-employed or start micro-businesses should be only a small part of an economic opportunity strategy. These activities usually have a narrow impact and are resource demanding and time-consuming. Self-employment and micro-business development aimed at poor people may be a more important economic opportunity component in parts of the country, such as rural areas, with no practical alternative.

Tying the hiring of poor people to the provision of credit assistance to small and mid-sized firms outside the retail trade and personal services industries is only the starting point of an economic opportunity strategy. As in other public resource systems, the modal point of intervention in economic development must be expanded so it includes an integrated set of resources that has substantial impact. Specifically, when state government intervenes with businesses to provide credit assistance in an economic opportunity strategy, it should use the intervention to bring workplace education and business support assistance to the firm. To be effective, an economic opportunity strategy cannot scatter its resources among the business community. The provision of business support assistance and workplace education assistance helps sustain the profitability and competitive ability of small firms and in doing so provides a context for improved and sustained compensation for the workforce of small businesses.

Workplace education is in its infancy, especially in small firms and for production and entry-level workers. Yet, there is a mismatch between worker skills and education and the skill levels demanded by today's jobs, a mismatch likely to increase over time. To be competitive, businesses must improve the skill levels of their production and entry-level workforce. It is unlikely that workers will go back to school or to a stand-alone classroom setting to increase their education and skill levels. Several evaluations of welfare-to-work programs highlight the success of those programs that combine basic education and skills development for poor people in a job setting. This workplace learning context approaches that of other countries, such as Japan and West Germany, where education and workplace skills development are much more integrated than in the U.S. Providing businesses with control or influence over workplace education and training overcomes some of the problems public employment training programs face when businesses believe the programs are weak or ineffective. Finally, studies show that employees who undergo workplace training earn more money than employees who do not.

While several states have programs that finance workplace education and skills development, these programs would benefit from certain changes. First, these programs are often short-term and very limited, offering only English as a Second Language or simple basic skills directly related to employment. The content of workplace education should be expanded to include basic education, process skills, and occupational skills and continued over time. Second, these programs tend not to serve small businesses, the businesses that most need and can least afford workplace education. Finally, these programs are provided ad hoc, unconnected with the provision of credit assistance for purposes of job expansion or retention.

Business support assistance, which includes business management assistance and technology assistance, is the third component of an economic opportunity strategy. It too should be tied to both the provision of credit assistance and workplace education assistance. Most small businesses fail because of management weaknesses. Many small business owners do not seek help until it is too late, although the cost of saving the business, or the mistakes the business made, might have been minimal. At the same time, small businesses tend to use lagging technology and have out-of-date operations. These small businesses rarely need advanced, cutting-edge technologies; they need current off-the-shelf technologies.

Again, while many states have established or help fund management assistance and technology assistance programs, many of these programs should be altered. Management assistance programs tend to have two major problems: their delivery systems are chaotic and not very accessible to businesses, especially small businesses, and the time they spend with businesses is too short and often on topics of marginal importance. Although technology assistance programs often help small businesses, most are geared to developing and providing assistance on state-of-the-art technologies that are not very useful to many small businesses.

In the fourth component of an economic opportunity strategy, economic development agencies should collaborate with human service agencies to make appropriate support services available to the families of poor persons hired through the strategy. Hiring poor people would trigger the delivery of integrated family support services; this is the reverse of the usual human service policy where the poor are targeted to receive support services and then are "marketed" to firms in an effort to get them hired.

A final component of a state economic opportunity strategy should be a much stronger minority business development activity. Minority businesses, especially black-owned businesses and startups, need access to capital even more than most other small businesses. This minority business activity should target potentially successful entrepreneurs and businesses, and should avoid providing credit assistance to personal service and retail trade businesses or businesses that serve a largely minority clientele. Credit assistance should be provided to minority firms regardless of their employment of poor people, for two reasons. First, minority firms, even when located in nonminority areas, tend to employ a predominantly minority workforce. In contrast, nonminority firms, even in largely minority areas, tend to employ a largely nonminority workforce. Second, an objective of a minority business development activity is to help minorities, especially blacks, develop and nurture assets.

A state economic opportunity strategy cannot stand by itself. States must provide a strong affordable housing superstructure for it. Today, job growth is generally occurring in the suburbs, especially in the outer suburbs. States must try to link place of residence and place of work by implementing three policies. First, states must ensure that the private market can build affordable housing where it is needed, and that localities do not use their regulatory power, especially in land development, to exclude this housing. Second, states must facilitate the construction of scattered site low-income housing in the suburbs. Third, states must help eliminate racial and other discrimination in the sale, rental, and financing of housing.

A state economic opportunity strategy differs from, and to some extent is contrary to, a neighborhood revitalization strategy. Because its goal is to provide employment, earnings, and assets to poor people, an economic opportunity strategy must have a regional or metropolitan-wide focus and delivery system. Otherwise, the structure and dynamics of our economy will overpower it, turning it into useless rhetoric. To this end, states should encourage the creation and sustaining of regional business networks that would help small businesses overcome their diseconomies of scale. The networks also would help the state implement an economic opportunity strategy, through collaborations between state economic development resources and related resources in education, employment training, and human services.

An economic opportunity strategy is based on the premise that economic opportunity is relevant to many poor people, and that issues of conduct and dependency do not overwhelm them. Even a successful economic opportunity strategy, however, cannot deliver earnings that pull all individuals out of poverty immediately, or in the short-run. Many poor people work full-time, year-round and they struggle successfully against many adverse circumstances to hold their families together. Most people who become nonpoor through work live in multiple earner households.

To be successful, a state economic opportunity strategy should be reinforced by three complementary sets of federal policies. One is a bundling of incentives and disincentives in a policy that encourages family formation or at least discourages teenage pregnancy, out-of-wedlock births, lack of child support, dropping out of school, and other behavior inimical to family and work. Next, our current antipoverty policies are biased against working poor people and working near-poor people. We must support these working people in their struggle to stay out of poverty, for example, through refundable child tax credits, increases in the earned income tax credit, some form of national health insurance, and more effective unemployment insurance. If these two sets of policies are not in place, the public and popular support necessary to sustain antipoverty programs targeted to non-working poor people will never hold.

Finally, the federal government should initiate programs, especially housing programs, that permit states and others to use federal resources to address poverty in a regional or metropolitan-wide context. Federal policies need to be oriented much more to mobility and much less to concentration in place. Otherwise, the intense problems that afflict residents in areas with very high poverty rates may carry forward for decades, further eating away at our society. If funding for these three sets of policies should come in part from a more progressive tax on the wealthiest Americans, it, along with increasing the earnings and assets of poor people, will help overcome our perniciously increasing income inequality.

References

Alegria, Fernando L., Jr. 1990. "OJT: A Tradition That Works," *Labor Notes*, Washington, D.C.: National Governors' Association, June 30, p. 2.

American Public Welfare Association. 1990. *Early State Experiences and Policy Issues in the Implementation of the JOBS Program: Briefing Paper for Human Service Administrators*, Washington, D.C.: American Public Welfare Association.

Applegate, Jane. 1991. "SBA Loan Guarantees, Asset-Based Financing Help in Credit Crunch," Washington Business, *Washington Post*, September 16, p. 11.

Barringer, Felicity. 1991. "Changes in U.S. Households: Single Parents Amid Solitude," *New York Times*. June 7, p. A1.

Bartlett, Sarah. 1991. "Cooperation Treaty is Signal to Bolster Regional Economy," *New York Times*, October 8, p. A1.

Bates, Timothy. 1989. "The Changing Nature of Minority Businesses: A Comparative Analysis of Asian, Nonminority, and Black-owned Businesses," *The Review of Black Political Economy*, (Fall), pp. 26-42.

Bates, Timothy and Constance Duncan. 1991. "The Changing Nature of Business Ownership as a Route to Upward Mobility for Minorities," paper presented at the Conference on Urban Labor Markets and Labor Mobility, Urban Opportunity Program, The Urban Institute, March 7-8, Airlie House, Virginia.

Bennett, Amanda. 1989. "Aetna Schools New Hires in Basic Workplace Skills," *Wall Street Journal*, November 10, p. B1.

Bishop, John H. and Suk Kang. 1991. "Applying for Entitlements: Employers and the Targeted Jobs Tax Credit," *Journal of Policy Analysis and Management*, (April), pp. 24-45.

Book Review Forum. 1988. *Policy Studies Review*, (Summer), pp. 851-874.

Boyett, Joseph H. and Henry P. Conn. 1991. *Workplace 2000*, New York: Dutton.

Bradbury, Kathrine L. 1990. "The Changing Fortunes of American Families in the 1980s," *New England Economic Review*, (July/August), pp. 25-40.

Brown, Charles, James Hamilton and et. al. 1990. *Employers Large and Small*, Cambridge: Harvard University Press.

Burbridge, Lynn C. and Demetra Smith Nightingale. 1989. "Local Coordination of Employment and Training Services to Welfare Recipients," Washington,D.C.: The Urban Institute, (May).

Burghardt, John and Anne Gordon. 1990. *More Jobs and Higher Pay*, New York: The Rockefeller Foundation.

Burroughs, Sheree L. 1980. "Oklahoma Department of Human Services Job Opportunities and Basic Skills Program," *Labor Notes*, Washington, D.C.: National Governors' Association, July 18, pp. 6-8.

Buss, Terry F. and Roger J. Vaughn. 1987. "Organizing for Economic Development," (August).

Burtless, Gary. 1990. "The Economist's Lament: Public Assistance in America," *Journal of Economic Perspectives*," (Winter), pp. 57-78.

Butler, Stuart. 1989. "Razing the Liberal Plantation," *National Review*, November 10, pp. 27-30.

Butterfield, Fox. 1991. "Record Number in U.S. Relying on Food Stamps," *New York Times*, October 31, p. A1.

Cattan, Peter. 1991. "Child Care Problems: An Obstacle to Work," *Monthly Labor Review*, (October), pp. 3-9.

Cautley, Eleanor and Doris P. Slesinger. 1988. "Labor Force Participation and Poverty Status Among Rural and Urban Woman Who Head Families," *Policy Studies Review*, (Summer), pp. 795-801.

Citro, Jeremy F. 1991. "The Federal Role in Skill-Upgrading: Summarizing A Pelrvin Associates Report on Upgrading Training for Employed Workers," *Labor Notes*, Washington, D.C.: National Governors' Association, July 31, pp. 20-24.

Clarke, Marianne and Dobson, Eric. 1989. *Promoting Technological Excellence: The Role of the State and Federal Extension Activities*, Washington, D.C.: National Governors' Association.

Cohen, Helen S. 1990. "How Far Can Credit Travel?," *Economic Development Law Center Report*, (Spring), pp. 3-13.

Commerce News. 1991a. "Large Plants Much More Likely to Use Advanced Technologies, U.S., Canadian Survey Shows," Washington, D.C.: Department of Commerce, August 7.

_____. 1991b. "Large Companies Dominate Nation's Businesses, Census Bureau Reports," Washington, D.C.: U.S. Department of Commerce, September 12.

_____. 1991c. "1990 Median Household Income Dips, Census Bureau Reports in Annual Survey," Washington, D.C.: Department of Commerce, September 26.

_____. 1991d. "One-half of Women On Child Support Don't Get Full Amount, Census Bureau Report Shows," Washington, D.C.: Department of Commerce, October 11.

Committee on Ways and Means. 1989. Overview Entitlement Programs; Background Material and Data on Programs Within the Jurisdiction of the Committee on Ways and Means, 1989 edition (referenced as the *1989 Green Book*), March 15.

Committee on Ways and Means. 1990. Overview Entitlement Programs; Background Material and Data on Programs Within the Jurisdiction of the Committee on Ways and Means, *1990 Green Book*.

Committee on Ways and Means. 1991. Overview Entitlement Programs; Background Material and Data on Programs Within the Jurisdiction of the Committee on Ways and Means, *1991 Green Book*, May 7.

Corporation for Enterprise Development. 1988. *Sharing Opportunities*: Business Development for Low-Income People, Washington, D.C.: Council of State Community Development Agencies, (December).

Corcoran, Mary, Roger Gordon, Deborah Lauren, and Gary Solen. 1990. "Effects of Family and Community Background on Economic Status," *AEA Papers and Proceedings*, (May), pp. 363-366.

Crane, Jonathan. 1991. "Effects on Neighborhood on Dropping Out of School and Teenage Childbearing," Christopher Jencks and Paul E. Peterson, editors, *The Urban Underclass*, Washington, D.C.: The Brookings Institution.

Crenshaw, Albert B. 1991. "Rising Costs of Benefits May Hold Down Wages," *New York Times*, July 14, p. H3.

Dabney, Dan Y. 1991. "Do Enterprise Zone Incentives Affect Business Location Decisions?" *Economic Development Quarterly*, (November), pp. 325-334.

Davis, Steve J. and John Haltiwanga. 1991. "Wage Dispersion Between and Within U.S. Manufacturing Plants, 1963-1986," Martin Nell Bailey and Clifford Winson, editors. *Brookings Papers In Economic Activity: Microeconomics*, Washington, D.C.: The Brookings Institution, pp. 115-200.

Dellinger, Gwen. 1990. "Taking Care of Business," *Labor Notes*, Washington, D.C.: National Governors' Association, June 30, pp. 6-8.

DeParle, Jason. 1990. "Skills Training Policy Opening Doors to Jobs," October 25, *New York Times*, p. A16.

_____. 1991a. "Suffering in the Cities Persists as U.S. Fights Others Battles," *New York Times*, January 27, p. A1.

_____. 1991b. "Child Poverty Twice as Likely After Family Split, Study Says," *New York Times*, March 1, p. 1.

_____. 1991c. "Using Books Instead of Brooms to Escape Welfare," *New York Times*, September 9, p. A1.

Dertouzos, Michael L., Richard K. Lester, et. al., and the MIT Commission on Industrial Productivity. 1989. *Made in America: Regaining the Productive Edge*, Cambridge: MIT Press.

Downey, Kirsten. 1991a. "Ruling May Encourage Multifamily Housing," *Washington Post*, August 8, p. E1.

_____. 1991b. "Neighborhoods Block Lower-pricced Housing," *Washington Post*, November 11, p. A1.

_____. 1991c. "Suburbs Support Cheaper Housing, But in Someone Else's Back Yard," *Washington Post*, November 12, p. A1.

Duncan, Emily. 1990. "Entrepreneurial Training Program: The Snohomish County Private Industry Council," *Labor Notes*, Washington, D.C.: National Governor's Association, May 31.

Duncan, Greg J. and Saul D. Hoffman. 1991. "Teenage Underclass Behavior and Subsequent Poverty: Have the Rules Changed?," Christopher Jencks and Paul E. Peterson, editors, *The Urban Underclass*, Washington, D.C.: The Brookings Institution.

Economic Developments. 1988. "Experts Paint Changing Picture of U.S. Workforce by Year 2000," National Council for Urban Economic Development, April 30, pp. 4-5.

Eisinger, Peter K. 1988. *The Rise of the Entrepreneurial State*, Madison, Wisconsin: University of Wisconsin Press.

Ellickson, Robert. 1977. "Suburban Growth Controls: An Economic and Legal Analysis," *Yale Law Journal*, pp. 387-511.

Ellwood, David T. 1989. "Conclusions," Phoebe H. Cottingham and David T. Ellwood, editors, *Welfare Policy in the 1990s*, Cambridge: Harvard University Press.

FCB Associates. 1989. *American's Next Crisis: The Shortfall in Technical Manpower*, Arlington, Virginia: Aerospace Education Foundation, (September).

Feiock, Richard C. 1991. "The Effects of Economic Development Policy on Local Economic Growth," *American Journal of Political Science*, (August), pp. 643-655.

Fiske, Edward B. 1989. "Impending U.S. Jobs 'Disaster': Work Force Unqualified to Work," *New York Times*, September 25, p. 1.

Forrant, Bob. 1990. "The American Experience: From Training Consortia to Technology Networks," *Proceedings: Dialogue on Flexible Manufacturing Networks*, Southern Technology Conference, January 16.

Freeman, Richard B. 1991a. "Employment and Earnings of Disadvantaged Young Men in a Labor Shortage Economy," Christopher Jencks and Paul E. Peterson, editors, *The Urban Underclass*, Washington, D.C.: The Brookings Institution.

_____. 1991b. "Crime and the Economic Status of Disadvantaged Youth," Airlie.

Fuchsberg, Gilbert. 1990. "Many Businesses Responding Too Slowly to Rapid Work Force Shifts, Study Says," *Wall Street Journal*, July 2, p. B1.

Glaser, Mark A. and Joe Pisciotte. 1991. "Listening to Business Executives: Labor Concerns for Job Conservation and Business Investment," *Economic Development Quarterly*, (May), pp 168-174.

Gottschalk, Peter. 1990. "AFDC Participation Across Generations," *AEA Papers and Proceedings*, (May), pp. 367-371.

Gramlich, Edward. 1991. "Moving Into and Out of Urban Underclass Areas," Airlie.

Grubb, W. Norton, Cynthia Brown, Philip Kaufman, and John Lederer. 1989. *Innovation Versus Turf: Coordination Between Vocational Education and Job Training Partnership Act Programs*, Berkeley: National Center for Research in Vocational Education, (April).

Grubb, W. Norton and David Stern. 1989. *Separating the Wheat from the Chaff: The Role of Vocational Education in Economic Development*, Berkeley, California: National Center for Research in Vocational Education, (June).

Gueron, Judith M. 1990. "Work and Welfare: Lessons on Employment Programs," *Journal of Economic Perspectives*, (Winter), pp. 79-98.

Gueron, Judith M. and Edward Pauley. 1991. "Summary: From Welfare to Work," New York: Manpower Demonstration Research Corporation.

Guy, Cynthia A., Fred Doolittle and Barbara L. Fink. 1991. "Self-Employment for Welfare Recipients: Implementation of the SEID Program," Manpower Demonstration Research Corporation, (May).

Hagey, Ellen. 1991. *Linking Technical Assistance with Credit Assistance: A Guidebook for State CDBG Program Managers*, Washington, D.C.: Council of State Community Development Agencies, (August).

Hanson, Susan B. 1989. "Targeting in Economic Development: Comparative State Perspectives," *Publius*, (Spring), pp. 47-62.

Hargroves, Jeannette S. 1989. "The Basic Skills Crisis," *New England Economic Review*, (September/October), pp. 58-68.

Hatch, C.R. 1988. "Flexible Manufacturing Networks: Cooperation for Competitiveness in Global Economy," Washington, D.C.: Corporation for Economic Development.

_____ . 1990. "Progress of a New Networking Project in Denmark," *Proceedings: Dialogue on Manufacturing Networks*, Southern Technology Council, January 16.

Hinds, Michael deCourcy. 1990. "Doors to a Business of One's Own Can Be Good Exit From Welfare," *New York Times*, June 30, p. 1.

Hoachlander, E. Gareth. 1989. *"Performance-Based Policy Options for Postsecondary Vocational Education and Employment Training Programs*, Berkeley: National Center for Research in Vocational Education, (September).

Holushua, John. 1991. "An Industrial Policy, Piece by Piece," *New York Times*, July 30, p. D1.

Holzer, Harry and Wayne Vroman. 1991. "Mismatches and the Urban Labor Market," Airlie.

Hororwitz, Carl F. 1991. "New Life for Federal Enterprise Zones: Seven Lessons from the States," *The Heritage Foundation Backgrounder*, June 4.

Housing and Development Reporter. 1991. "New Hampshire Court Strikes Down Portions of Zoning Ordinance That Keeps Out Lower-Income Families," August 19, p. 253.

Howard, Robert. 1990. "Can Small Business Help Countries Compete?," *Harvard Business Review*, (November-December), pp. 88-103.

ICF, Incorporated. 1990. *Evaluation of the Low-Income Housing Tax Credit*, (March).

Illinois Department of Commerce and Community Affairs. nd. "Export Manufacturing Networks, Requests for Proposals," Springfield, Illinois.

Iowa Entrepreneurship Task Force. 1991. *Final Report*, February 13.

Jargowsky, Paul A. and Mary Jo Bane. 1990. "Ghetto Poverty: Basic Questions," Laurence E. Lynn, Jr. and Michael G.H. McGeary, editors, *Inner-City Poverty in the United States*, Washington, D.C.: National Academy Press.

Jencks, Christopher. 1991. "Is the American Underclass Growing?," Christopher Jencks and Paul E. Peterson, editors, *The Urban Underclass*, Washington, D.C.: The Brookings Institution.

Jencks, Christopher and Susan E, Meyer. 1990. "The Social Consequences of Growing Up in a Poor Neighborhood," Laurence E. Lynn, Jr. and Michael G.H. McGeary, editors, *Inner-City Poverty in the United States*, Washington, D.C.: National Academy Press.

Jensen, Lief. 1988. "Rural-Urban Differences in the Utilization and Ameliorative Effects of Welfare Programs," *Policy Studies Review*, (Summer), pp. 782-794.

Johnson, James H. and Melvin Oliver. 1991. "Economic Restructing and Black Male Joblessness in U.S. Metropolitan Areas," Airlie.

Johnson, Kirk. 1991. "Take Our Poor, Angry Hartford Tells Suburbs," *New York Times*, February 12, p. A1.

Judson, George. 1991a. "Bridgeport Declares It Cannot Go It Alone," *New York Times*, June 16, p. E6.

_____. 1991b. "Housing Law Challenges Power of Zoning Boards," *New York Times*, November 5, p. B5.

Kasarda, John D. 1991. "The Severely Distressed in Economically Transformed Cities," Airlie.

_____. 1989. "Urban Industrial Transition and the Underclass," William Julius Wilson, editor, *The Ghetto Underclass: Social Science Perspectives*, Annals of the American Academy of Political and Social Science, (January).

Klein, Bruce W. and Phillip L. Rones. 1989. "A Profile of the Working Poor," *Monthly Labor Review*, (October), pp. 3-13.

Knight, Jerry. 1991. "Race Factor Seen In Mortgage Lending," *Washington Post*, October 22, p. A1.

Kolbert, Elizabeth. 1991. "New York's Medicaid Costs Surge, But Health Care for the Poor Lags," *New York Times*, April 14, p. A1.

Kosters, Martin H. 1990. "Schooling Work Experience, and Wage Trends," *AEA Papers and Proceedings*, (May), pp. 308-312.

Koven, Steven G. and Mark C. Shelley, III. 1989. "Public Policy Effects on Net Urban Migration," *Policy Studies Journal*, (Summer), pp. 705-718.

Kwass, Peter and Beth Siegel. 1990. *Aiding Rural Economies: A National Survey of Business Lending with State CDBG Funds*, Washington, D.C., Council of State Community Development Agencies.

Labor Area Summaries. 1989. "The Workforce 2000," (July), pp. 5-14.

Leonard, Jonathan S. and Louis Jacobson. 1990. "Earnings Inequality and Job Turnover," *AEA Papers and Proceedings*, (May), pp. 289-302.

Lerman, Robert I. 1989. "Employment Opportunities of Young Men and Family Formation," *AEA Papers and Proceedings*, (May), pp. 62-66.

Levitan, Sar, Garth Mangum, and Marion Pines. 1989. *A Proper Inheritance: Investing in the Self-Sufficiency of Families*, Washington, D.C.: George Washington University.

Levy, Frank. 1988. "A Growing Gap Between Rich and Poor," *New York Times*, May 1.

Loveman, Gary and Werner Sengenbeger. 1990. "Introduction: Economic and Social Reorganization in the Small and Medium-sized Enterprise Sector," Werner Sengenberger, Gary W. Loveman, et. al., editors, *The Re-Emergence of Small Enterprises*, Geneva: Institute for Labor Studies.

Lueck, Thomas J., 1988. "45% of New Yorkers Are Outside Labor Force," *New York Times*, August 3, p. A1.

Lynn, Laurence and Michael G.H. McGeary. 1990. "Conclusions," Laurence Lynn and Michael G.H. McGeary, editors, *Inner-City Poverty in the United States*, Washington, D.C.: National Academy Press.

Marmor, Theodore P., Jerry L. Mashaw, and Philip L. Harvey. 1990. *America's Misunderstood Welfare State*, New York: Basic Books.

Massey, Douglas S. and Andrew B. Gross. 1991. "Explaining Trends in Racial Segregation, 1970-1980," *Urban Affairs Quarterly*, (Spring), pp. 13-35.

Mauro, Frank J. and Glenn Yago. 1989. "State Government Targeting in Economic Development: The New York Experience," *Publius*, (Spring), pp. 63-82.

Mayer, Susan E. 1991. "High School Racial and Socioeconomic Mix," Christopher Jencks and Paul E. Peterson, editors, *The Urban Underclass*, Washington, D.C.: The Brookings Institution.

McDonald, Bernard. 1990. "Alleviating vs. Eliminating Poverty: An Important Distinction," *Economic Development and Law Center Report*, (Summer/Fall), pp. 17-20.

McDonnell, Lorraine M. and W. Norton Grubb. 1991. *Education and Training for Work: The Policy Instruments and the Institutions*, National Center for Research in Vocational Education, Berkeley, California, (April).

McGeary, Michael G.H. 1990. "Ghetto Poverty and Federal Policies and Programs, " Laurence Lynn and Michael G.H. McGeary, editors, *Inner-City Poverty in the United States*, Washington, D.C.: National Academy Press.

MDC, Inc. 1988. *Building Capacity to Expand Economic Opportunities*, Washington, D.C.: Council of State Community Development Agencies, (December).

Mead, Lawrence. 1988. "The Potential for Work Enforcement: A Study of WIN," *Journal of Policy Analysis and Management*, Vol. 7, No. 2, pp. 264-268.

_____. 1991. "The New Politics of Poverty," *The Public Interest*, (Spring), pp. 3-20.

Melaville, Atelia I. and Martin J. Blank. 1991. *What It Takes: Structuring Interagency Partnerships to Connect Children and Families with Comprehensive Services*, Washington, D.C.: Education and Human Services Consortium, (January).

Michel, Richard C. 1991. "Economic Growth and Income Inequality Since the 1982 Recession," *Journal of Policy Analysis and Management*, Vol. 10, No. 2, pp. 181-203.

Mincy, Ronald B. and Susan J. Wiener. 1991. "Balancing Act," *Northeast-Midwest Economic Review*, March 4, pp. 9-11.

Molina, Frieda. 1990. "Reflections: Looking Closely at the Self-Employment Strategy," *Economic Development and Law Center Report*, (Spring), pp. 18-20.

Moore, Thomas S. and Aaron Laramore. 1990. "Industrial Change and Urban Joblessness: An Assessment of the Mismatch Hypothesis," *Urban Affairs Quarterly*, (June), pp. 640-658.

NADO News. 1991. "Whither the Business Incubator?," National Association of Development Agencies, September 27, p. 2.

National Alliance of Business (NAB) and SRI International. nd. "The Competitive Challenges " Strengthening America's Workforce."

National Center on Education and the Economy. 1990. Commission on the Skills of the American Workforce, *America's Choice: High Skills or Low Wages!* Rochester, (June).

National Commission on Children. 1991. *Beyond Rhetoric; A New American Agenda for Children and Families*, Final Report, Washington, D.C.

NCI Research. 1990. "Inner-City Entrepreneurship: Target Industry Analysis," Evanston, Illinois: Institute for Urban Economic Development.

National Association of State Development Agencies. 1991. *Directory of Incentives for Business Investment and Development in the United States*, Washington, D.C.: Urban Institute Press.

Nelson, Arthur. 1990. "Regional Patterns of Exurban Industrialization: Results of Preliminary Investigation," *Economic Development Quarterly*, (November), pp. 320-333

Nightingale, Demetra Smith, Douglas A. Wissoker, et. al. 1991. *Evaluation of the Massachusetts Employment and Training (ET) Program*, Washington, D.C.: Urban Institute, Report 91-1.

Orfield, Gary. 1991. "Schooling Outcomes and Employer Requirements," Airlie.

Ortiz, Vilma, 1991. "Latinos and Industrial Change in New York and Los Angeles," Airlie.

Osterman, Paul. 1991. "Impact of Full Employment in Boston," Christopher Jencks and Paul E. Peterson, editors, *The Urban Underclass*, Washington, D.C.: The Brookings Institution.

Papke, James A. 1990. *The Role of Market Based Public Policy in Economic Development and Urban Revitalization: A Retrospective Analysis and Appraisal of the Indiana Enterprise Zone Program*, Center for Tax Policy Studies, Purdue University, (August).

Passell, Peter. 1990 a. "Economic Scene," *New York Times*, September 5, p. D2.

_____. 1991b. "The Truth About Welfare," *New York Times*, July 24, p. D2.

_____. 1991c. "When Children Have Children," *New York Times*, September 4, p. D2.

Pear, Robert. 1991. "Rich Got Richer in 80's; Others Held Even," *New York Times*, January 11, p. A1.

Peterson, Jonathan. 1991. "Welfare Rolls Hit Record; Numbers Called Incredible," *Los Angeles Times*, June 6, p. A1.

Peterson, June. 1991. "Why Older people Are Richer Than Other Americans," *New York Times*, November 3, p. E3.

Pior, Michael J. 1990. "United States of America," Werner Sengenberger, Gary W. Loveman, et. al., editors, *The Re-Emergence of Small Enterprises*, Geneva, Switzerland: Institute for Labor Studies.

Porter, Kathyrn H. 1990. *Making JOBS Work: What the Research Say About Effective Programs for AFDC Recipients*, Washington, D.C.: Center on Budget and Policy Priorities, (March).

Public/Private Ventures. 1988. *Using Education, Employment and Training Resources to Expand Economic Opportunities*, Washington, D.C.: Council of State Community Development Agencies, (December).

Pyatt, Rudolph A., Jr. 1990. "Encouraging Minority Entrepreneurs," Washington Business, *Washington Post*, December 10, p. 5.

Quint, Michael. 1991. "Racial Gap Found in Mortgages," *New York Times*, October 22, p. D1.

Redfield, Kent D. and John F. McDonald. 1990. *Enterprise Zones in Illinois: A Legislative Issue for the 87th General Assembly*, Springfield: Illinois Tax Foundation, (December).

Redman, John M. 1991. "Metro/Nonmetro Performance Under the Job Training Partnership Act," *Economic Development Quarterly*, (November), pp. 357-368.

Reiff, Rick. 1991. "Hatching Small Companies," *Your Company*, (Winter), pp. 36-39.

Rich, Spencer. 1991a. "Welfare Mother Job Training: Don't Expect Miracles," *Washington Post*, February 17, p. A15.

_____. 1991b. "A $1 Billion Welfare Gamble that May Pay Off," *Washington Post*, July 24, p. A17.

_____. 1991c. "Chipping Away at Welfare Rolls," *Washington Post*, October 4, p. A23.

Ricketts, Erol and Isabel Sawhill. 1988. "Defining and Measuring the Underclass," *Journal of Policy Analysis and Management*, Vol. 7, No. 2, pp. 316-325.

Rifken, Glenn. 1991. "From Unemployment Into Self-Employment," *New York Times*, September 19, p. D1.

Roberts, Sam. 1991. "The Region: How Long Can New York Redistribute Wealth Before the Wealthy Leave?," *New York Times*, August 4, p. K16.

Robertson, David Brian. 1989. "Planned Incapacity to Succeed? Policy-Making Structure and Policy Failure," *Policy Studies Review*, (Winter), pp. 241-263.

Rosenbaum, James E. and Susan J. Popkin. 1990. "The Gautreaux Program: An Experiment in Racial and Economic Integration," *The Center Report: Current Policy Issues*, Center for Urban Affairs and Policy Research, Northwestern University, (Spring).

Rosenfield, Stuart. 1990. *Technology Innovation and Rural Development*, Washington, D.C.: The Aspen Institute, (December).

Rowen, Hobart. 1991. "Unemployment Benefits: Out of Sync," *Washington Post*, May 10, p. A19.

Rowland, Mary. 1991. "Why Small Businesses Are Failing," *New York Times*, August 11, p. 16.

Rubin, Marilyn and Regina Armstrong. 1989. *The New Jersey Urban Enterprise Zone Program: An Evaluation*, Wayne, New Jersey: Urbanomics.

Ryscavage, Paul and Peter Henle. 1990. "Earnings Inequality Accelerates in the 1980s," *Monthly Labor Review*, (December), pp. 3-16.

Sack, Kevin. 1991. "Plan Offered to Cut Welfare Rolls with Paychecks," *New York Times*, April 3, p. A1.

Sanger, Mary Byrna. 1990. "The Inherent Contradiction of Welfare Reform," *Policy Studies Journal*, (Spring), pp. 663-680.

SGPB Alert. 1988. "Adult Functional Literacy in the South: Program Represents A Proposal for a Regional Approach," Southern Growth Policy Board, (November).

SGPB Alert. 1990 "Creating an Entrepreneurial Culture: Microenterprises in the Southern Economy," Southern Growth Policy Board, (April).

SGPB Foresight. 1990. "Building a World Class Workforce: Southern Strategies," Southern Growth Policies Board, (April), pp. 3-4.

Shipp, E.R. 1991. "Intergration Without Violence," *New York Times*, October 20, p. E16.

Sidor, John. 1984. *Influencing Land Supply Development for Affordable Housing: Massachusetts, California, and Oregon*, Washington, D.C.: The Council of State Community Development Agencies, (February).

_____. 1990a. *Aiding Rural Economies: The Role of the State CDBG Program*, Washington, D.C.: Council of State Community Development Agencies.

_____. 1990b. *Developing Rural America: State Assistance in Rural Economic Development*, Washington, D.C.: Council of State Community Development Agencies.

Stahura, John M. 1989-1990. "Rapid Black Suburbanization of the 1970s: Some Policy Considerations," *Policy Studies Journal*, (Winter), pp. 279-291.

Stone, Nan. 1991. "Does Business Have Any Business in Education," *Harvard Business Review*, (March-April), pp. 46-62.

Suro, Robert. 1991. "Where Have All the Jobs Gone? Follow the Crab Grass," *New York Times*, March 3, p. E5.

Swagger, Ronald J., editor. 1991. *Economic Development Tomorrow: A Report from the Profession*, Rosemont, Illinois: The American Economic Development Council, (July).

Swoboda, Frank. 1991. "GAO Finds Job Training Discrimination," *Washington Post*, July 17, p. A21.

Taylor, Paul. 1991. "Family Seen As Key to Aiding Children," *Washington Post*, March 11, p. F4.

Tickameyer, Ann and Cynthia Duncan. 1990. "Poverty and Opportunity Structure in Rural America," *Annual Review of Sociology*, Vol. 16, pp. 67-86.

Tienda, Marta. 1990. "Welfare and Work in Chicago's Inner City," *AEA Papers and Proceedings*, (May), pp. 372-376.

Turner, Margery Austin, Raymond Struyk, and John Yinger. 1991. *Housing Discrimination Synthesis*, The Urban Institute and Syracuse University, (August).

Urban Institute. 1991. "Hiring Discrimination Against Young Black Men," *Policy and Research Report*, (Summer), pp. 4-5.

U.S. Bureau of the Census, 1991a. "How Much Are We Worth?," *Census and You*, (February).

_____. 1991b. "The Economics of Family Disruption", *Census and You*, (June), p. 5.

U.S. General Accounting Office. 1990a. Statement of John M. Ols, Jr., Director of the Housing and Community Development Issues before the Senate Committee on Small Business, April 18.

_____. 1990b. *The Urban Underclass*, Washington, D.C., (September).

_____. 1991. *Workers at Risk*, Washington, D.C., (March).

Vencil, Mary P., Lauren Causen, et. al. 1991. *Workplace Education Efforts in Small Business: Learning from the Field*, Oakland: Berkeley Planning Associates, (March).

Veum, Jonathon R. and Philip M. Gleason. 1991. "Child Care: Arrangements and Costs," *Monthly Labor Review*, (October), pp. 10-17.

Vinouskis, Mary A. 1988. "Teenage Pregnancy and the Underclass," *The Public Interest*, (Fall), pp. 87-96.

Virginia Department of Housing and Community Development. 1990. *The Virginia Enterprise Zone Program: An Assessment of Performance*, Richmond, Virginia, (May).

Vobejda, Barbara. 1991. "25% of Black Women May Never Marry," *Washington Post*, November 11, p. A1.

Wacquant, Lois J.D. and William Julius Wilson. 1989. "The Cost of Racial and Class Exclusion in the Inner City," William Julius Wilson, editor, *The Ghetto Underclass: Social Science Perspectives*, *Annals of the American Academy of Political and Social Science*, (January).

Wander, Stephen A. and Jon C. Messenger. 1990. "The Self-Employment Experience in the United States: Demonstration Projects in Washington State and Massachusetts," paper submitted to the Organization for Economic Cooperation and Development Evaluation Panel No. 11, October 25.

Weinberg, Daniel H. 1987. "Poverty Spending and the Poverty Gap," *Journal of Policy Analysis and Management*, Vol. 6, No. 2, pp. 230-241.

White, Sammis B. and Jeffrey D. Osterman. 1991. "Is Employment Growth Really Coming from Small Establishments," *Economic Development Quarterly*, (August), pp. 241-257.

Wiggenhorn, William. 1990. "Motorola U: When Training Becomes Education," *Harvard Business Review*, (July-August), pp. 71-83.

Wolman, Harold, Cary Lichtman, and Suzie Barnes. 1991. "The Impact of Credentials, Skills Levels, Worker Training, and Motivation on Employment Outcome: Sorting Out the Implications for Economic Development Policy," *Economic Development Quarterly*, (May), pp. 140-151.

Zipp, John F. 1991. "Quality of Jobs in Small Business," *Economic Development Quarterly*, (February), pp 9-22.